CGI Filmmaking: The Creation of GHOST WARRIOR

Timothy Albee

Wordware Publishing, Inc.

Library of Congress Cataloging-in-Publication Data

Albee, Timothy.
    CGI filmmaking : the creation of Ghost warrior / by Timothy Albee.
       p. cm.
    Includes index.
    ISBN 1-55622-227-0 (pbk.)
    1. Ghost warrior (Motion picture : 2004). 2. Animated
    films—Technique. I. Title.
    PN1997.2.G56 A43 2004
    791.43'72—dc22   2003026686
                             CIP

ISBN 1-55622-227-0

10 9 8 7 6 5 4 3 2 1
0401

All inquiries for volume purchases of this book should be addressed to Wordware Publishing, Inc., at the above address. Telephone inquiries may be made by calling:

(972) 423-0090

This book is dedicated to all who have felt the pull to "dream aloud." May it be for you what I wished had been there for me.

"For the sake of attaining enlightenment, one should try to accomplish the impossible..."

— Bukkyo Dendo Kyokai, Tokyo

The truth is simple. We often like to complicate matters to make ourselves feel better about how long we think the journey should take.

About the Author

(Photograph by Joanne Klumb)

I currently live and create in a small valley north of Fairbanks, Alaska, on the very edge of the Alaskan frontier. I share my life and adventures with my team of sled-dogs, Rascal, Peter Pan, Wolf, Toby, Mojo, and Strawberry. I owe them my life many times over (see "Brooks Range" in the "Books" section of my home page).

I have animated for Walt Disney Feature Animation, worked with "big names" in the industry, and have founded and co-founded two Los Angeles area animation studios.

And yet, to live in a place where there is stillness, where the song of wolves soars in the night air, where one can see by the light of the stars and read by the light of the moon, to exist in a place where that which I hold dear and holy surrounds me, every moment of every day — this is the magic that has shown me that all things are possible. One can achieve anything by continuing to put one foot in front of the other, and knowing in one's heart that the light shines not on us but through us.

We each have our own path; we each represent our own truths.

Only by allowing ourselves to learn as much as we can from one another can we realize our fullest potential — only by walking the path do we know that its edges do not meet at the horizon.

Your path is your choice.

Timothy Albee
http://Timothy.ArtistNation.com
http://wordware.com/ghostwarrior

Contents

Part 1

The World of K^K GHOST WARRIOR

There has always been a very real magic within cinema. Motion pictures have the ability to transport us to places and experiences beyond anything we know in daily life. They allow us to live, for brief spans of time, lives that may be beautiful counterpoints to our own struggles. They also allow us to confront "learning experiences" that could be dangerous to touch "for real." Yet, we come away from the best films with the benefits of having, on some level, lived them.

As there is magic within all cinema, that magic is multiplied tenfold within the medium of animation. Through its artistry, fantastic worlds and beings are limited solely by the imagination. No matter how unlike our own world the images may seem, a good animated film leaves in its wake a feeling that is halfway between a memory and a wish.

Over the course of the creation of *Kaze, Ghost Warrior,* a simple series of focused decisions were made each day, doing what needed to be done and learning what needed to be learned. (Where a film itself may be magic, there is nothing rarified about its creation.) Necessary skills were collected. Necessary tools were gathered. Eventually, the small archive of completed scenes grew to become the film known as *Kaze, Ghost Warrior.*

It is an honor to share these visions with you.

Whether these collections of light and shadow come from a long-forgotten past or from a future that has not yet been written, may they help to sustain in your own heart the belief in your dreams and your ability to make them real.

Chapter 1

KAZE GHOST WARRIOR Production Stills

A masterless samurai seeks to avenge his own murder… and the murder of his dearest love.

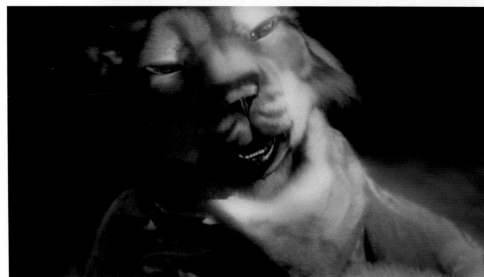

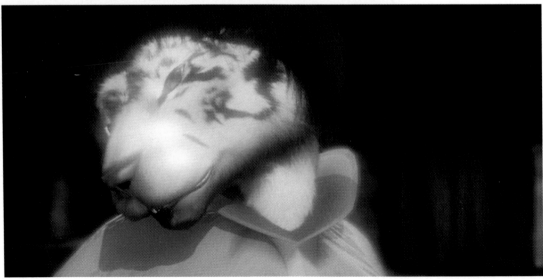

The Cast of GHOST WARRIOR

Kaze
(wind)

Primary Species: Tiger
Secondary Species: Tiger
Age: Unknown
Height: 6'9"
Weight: 260 lbs.
Eye Color: Yellow-green
Occupation: Killer
Hobbies: Unknown

Itsua
(parable)

Primary Species: Wolf

Secondary Species: Wolf

Age: 38

Height: 6'4"

Weight: 175 lbs.

Eye Color: Green-yellow

Occupation: Innkeeper

Hobbies: Music, storytelling, herbology

Naósu
(healer)

Primary Species: Rabbit

Secondary Species: Rabbit

Age: 34

Height: 5'4"

Weight: 105 lbs.

Eye Color: Brown

Occupation: House-
wife/server

Mate: Itsua

Hobbies: Healing arts, storytelling, music

Utsukushii

(beauty)

Primary Species: Tiger

Secondary Species: Tiger

Age: 27

Height: 6'4"

Weight: 145 lbs.

Eye Color: Brown

Occupation: Server

Hobbies: Dance, mathematics, ancient weapons

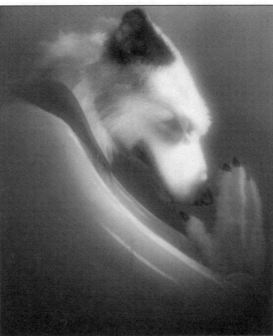

Yasashii
(gentleness)

Primary Species: Dog
Secondary Species: Wolf
Age: 15
Height: 5'7"
Weight: 125 lbs.
Eye Color: Brown
Occupation: Server
Hobbies: Meditation, spirituality, "way-seeking"

Hanekáeru
(to rebound)

Primary Species: Dog
Secondary Species: Dog
Age: 23
Height: 6'2"
Weight: 135 lbs.
Eye Color: Ice-blue
Occupation: Laborer
Hobbies: Philosophy, comedy

Yashin
(ambition)

Primary Species: Rat

Secondary Species: Ferret

Age: 35

Height: 6'0"

Weight: 140 lbs.

Eye Color: Brown

Occupation: Lead Enforcer - Dahlis Territory

Hobbies: Chemistry/alchemy

Koten
(classic)

Primary Species: Fox

Secondary Species: Fox

Age: 27

Height: 5'10"

Weight: 165 lbs.

Eye Color: Brown

Occupation: Enforcer - Dahlis Territory

Hobbies: Poetry, theatre, archery

Togé
(thorn)

Primary Species: Jackal

Secondary Species: Red Wolf

Age: 32

Height: 6'1"

Weight: 175 lbs.

Eye Color: Brown

Occupation: Enforcer - Dahlis Territory

Hobbies: History, strategy, wind instruments

Ikari

(rage)

Primary Species: Cat

Secondary Species: Cat

Age: 19

Height: 5'8"

Weight: 140 lbs.

Eye Color: Brown

Occupation: Enforcer - Dahlis Territory

Hobbies: Studies in the application of pressures

Yasei

(wildness)

Primary Species: Lynx

Secondary Species: Lynx

Age: 29

Height: 5'10"

Weight: 160 lbs.

Eye Color: Amber

Occupation: Enforcer - Dahlis Territory

Hobbies: Weapons, ancient songs and histories

Sóshi

(to impede)

Primary Species: Raccoon

Secondary Species: Raccoon

Age: 41

Height: 5'8"

Weight: 250 lbs.

Eye Color: Brown

Occupation: Feudal Lord - Dahlis Territory

Hobbies: (you don't want to know)

Chapter 3

The Set of GHOST WARRIOR KAZE

EXTERIOR - MOUNTAINS

EXTERIOR - GRASSLANDS

INTERIOR - TAVERN

INTERIOR - TAVERN'S BACK ROOM

INTERIOR - LORD SOSHI'S CHAMBERS

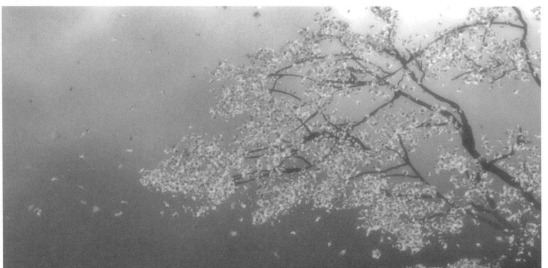

EXTERIOR - CHERRY BLOSSOMS

EXTERIOR - BAMBOO FOREST

Chapter 4

On Location with GHOST WARRIOR

A glimpse "behind the scenes" at the "windows" that were my portals into the world of *Ghost Warrior*…

These images are a collection of work-in-progress screen shots from LightWave, the 3D software package I used to create *Kaze, Ghost Warrior*.

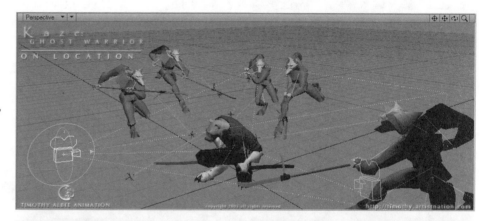

29

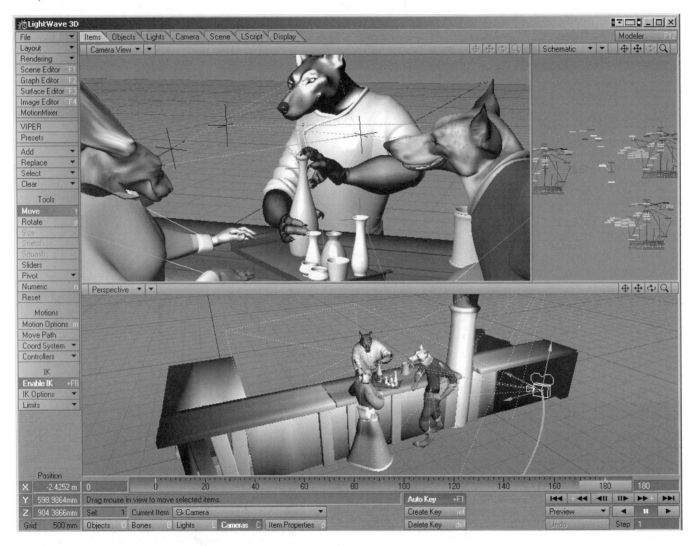

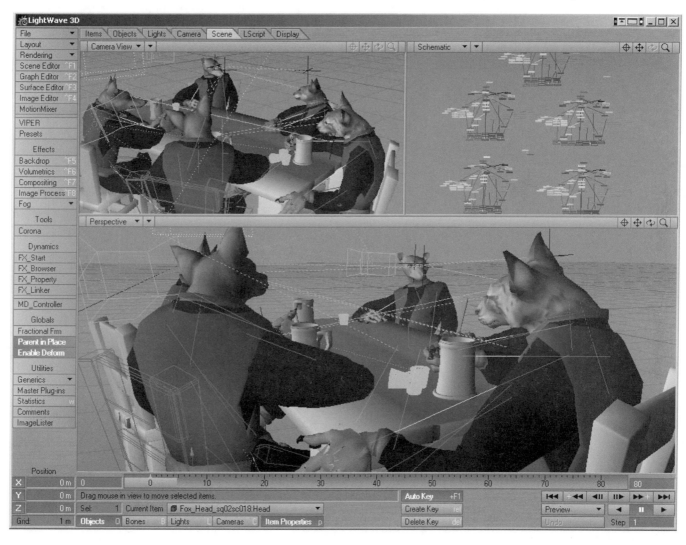

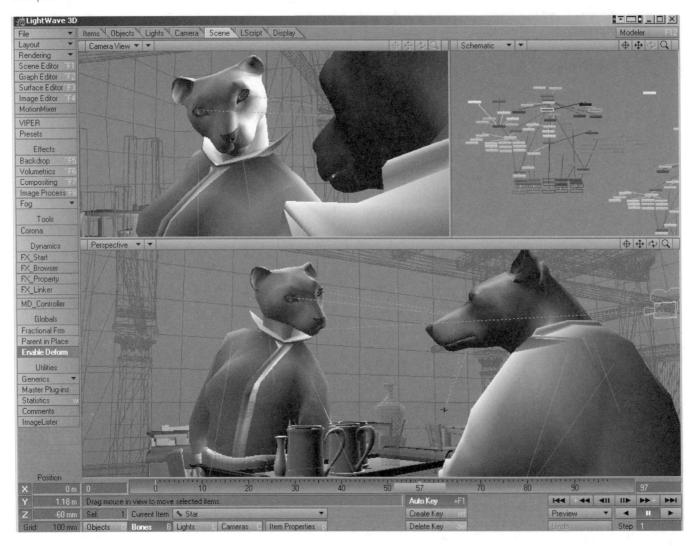

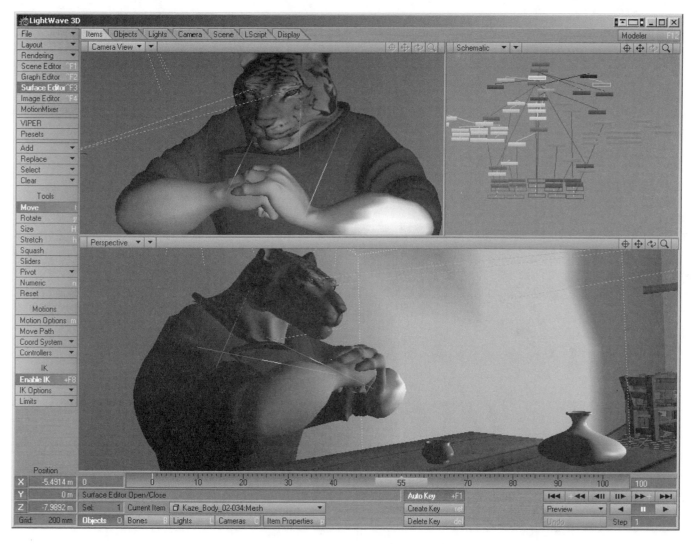

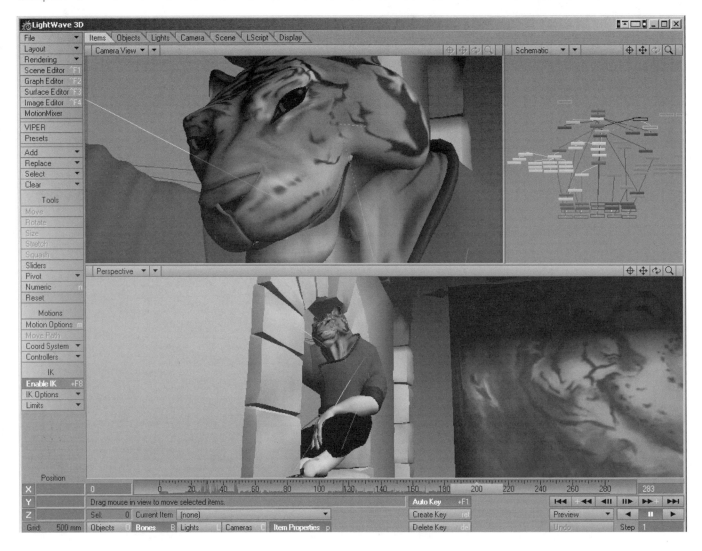

Chapter 5

The Script of KAZE: GHOST WARRIOR

FADE IN:

EXT. WOODS - EVENING

KAZE stoops to test the freshness of the tracks pressed into the damp earth. He brings some of the earth to his nose, savoring the scents within dirt as he crumbles it with his fingertips. His quarry is near.

He looks off in the direction in which the sets of footprints lead. He stands, dusting his hands, and walks in that direction as we...

                                                    DISSOLVE TO:

INT. SMALL, RAUCOUS TAVERN - NIGHT

The tavern is awash with people lost in their own small worlds, defined by their companions and their booze. "SERVERS," almost elegant (nothing of the kind of "harlot" we might expect), can be seen intimating their "wares" to interested parties. A BARTENDER watches, managing the situation as he attends to drinks. His gaze warily flirts again and again to a group of TROUBLEMAKERS working their way from group to group in his establishment.

The doors open and a lone TIGER walks to the bar. KAZE orders a small bottle and a glass and retires to a shadowed corner.

The BARTENDER catches the eye of one of his "SERVERS" and motions her to the quiet, powerful man who sits in his shadowy corner nursing his drink and quietly watching the others in the room.

KAZE politely but firmly declines the "SERVER." The BARTENDER and the "SERVER" exchange puzzled glances and shoulder shrugs as she leaves the man to his shadows. As she walks away, inadvertently, she draws the attention of the TROUBLEMAKERS.

The TROUBLEMAKERS head straight for the quiet corner where KAZE sits absorbed in his drink. The LEAD TROUBLEMAKER snags a young, pretty male, obviously another of the establishment's "SERVERS," as he makes his way toward KAZE.

> LEAD TROUBLEMAKER
> Turnin' away women, eh? Big, strong man like
> you? Someday, they may be scarce. Maybe *this*
> one's more your type?

The LEAD TROUBLEMAKER scruffs and holds the very frightened male "SERVER" out to KAZE.

KAZE, looking pointedly away, slowly finishes his small glass, sets it methodically on the rough wood of the table.

> KAZE
> (in a low growl, building from the
> back of his throat)
> Put him down.

> LEAD TROUBLEMAKER
> (happy to have gotten some kind of
> rise out of this stranger)
> Oh, so 'e *is* your type then, is 'e?

With a flash, the LEAD TROUBLEMAKER has a wicked-looking blade in his hand, pressing it to the "SERVER"'S throat.

> LEAD TROUBLEMAKER (CONT'D)
> Maybe we'll get more of a rise from you if we
> start gettin' 'im all *wet* fir ya!

The LEAD TROUBLEMAKER punctuates the word "wet" by pressing the
blade dangerously deep into the "SERVER"'S throat.

                         KAZE
               (in a soft, horrible whisper)
          I said,

With movement too quick to follow, KAZE slides his hand between the
"SERVER" and the blade, disarming the LEAD TROUBLEMAKER, and in a
spin, slams him hard against the timbers of the pub. KAZE'S hand
tightens on the other's throat.

                    KAZE (CONT'D)
          ...put ...him ...down.

KAZE lets the claws of his free hand slide from their sheaths in
front of the LEAD TROUBLEMAKER'S bulging eyes. KAZE runs his thumb
up along the other's snout, through a trail of glistening sweat.

KAZE makes a point of almost savoring the scent of the sweat on his
fingertips, much in the same way he did the dirt at the beginning
of this episode. A look of recognition comes over him, and he
smiles.

                    KAZE (CONT'D)
               (slowly, succulently)
          (I've been looking for you.) Who do you work
          for?

The LEAD TROUBLEMAKER is dazed but still belligerent. He gurgles
something incoherent through KAZE's grasp on his throat which KAZE
pinches off.

KAZE smiles a knowing smile and shakes his head.

                    KAZE (CONT'D)
          Wrong answer.

One of the other TROUBLEMAKERS swings a chair at the back of KAZE'S
head. KAZE is faster and wheels the LEAD TROUBLEMAKER into the

path of the chair, which drops him like a rock.

Weapons appear from every fold of the TROUBLEMAKERS' clothes, falling into their waiting hands. They fly at the lone KAZE.

The bar erupts as people flee and run for cover. KAZE, open-handed, eliminates two, then three of the attackers.

One of the TROUBLEMAKER'S chain weapons swings wide as its wielder goes berserk. KAZE plots the blade's trajectory as it whips around on its chain, straight at a helpless BYSTANDER.

KAZE leaps at the berserker, taking a blade to the arm as he does so. He drops the berserker, whipping his wounded arm up to ensnare the flailing chain, stopping the blade micrometers from the BYSTANDER.

KAZE whips the chain around his arms, losing his hands in the steel macrame. With a quick motion, he snaps the remaining length of chain, shooting the blade to bury itself in the mass of links webbed around his hands.

KAZE turns slowly toward the remaining TROUBLEMAKER. He snaps his hands apart again, sending the blade rocketing out toward the last standing TROUBLEMAKER. The blade pierces the staff held by the TROUBLEMAKER and stops a hair's breadth before making contact with the TROUBLEMAKER'S throat. KAZE yanks the chain back, snapping blade and staff with it to clatter noisily to the floor in the silence between them.

KAZE walks calmly toward this last TROUBLEMAKER and reaches deliberately for the other's throat, claws slowly sliding from their sheaths. The TROUBLEMAKER stares, transfixed, until the claws almost touch his throat, whereupon he faints dead away.

KAZE turns and walks over to the LEAD TROUBLEMAKER, grabbing a bottle as he passes an upright table. He forces the contents of the bottle down the throat of the LEAD TROUBLEMAKER.

Sputtering and very dazed now, the LEAD TROUBLEMAKER comes to.

                     KAZE (CONT'D)
You didn't answer me. Who do you work for?

                    LEAD TROUBLEMAKER
        (trying to still play it tough)
Fffffgh.....

KAZE shakes his head, smiling a knowing smile. His thumb is
pressed up against the other's trachea, his claw sliding out of its
sheath.

                        KAZE
        (softly)
I don't want to... but if you force me, I will
kill you.

KAZE puts his face so close to the other's that they almost touch.

                     KAZE (CONT'D)
Who...

KAZE'S claw slides a little further from its sheath.

                     KAZE (CONT'D)
Do...

The claw slides a little further.

                     KAZE (CONT'D)
You...

A scarlet droplet pools at the claw's tip.

                    LEAD TROUBLEMAKER
        (almost inaudible)
Lord Soshi... a day's ride... to... the
south... in the hills...

Satisfied, KAZE slowly draws his hand away from the other's throat, but pinning him, he wipes the blood from his thumb's claw across the other's lips.

                         KAZE
               (amused)
          Lord... Soshi?
               (satisfied)
          Good...

KAZE puts his mouth close to the other's forehead.

                    KAZE (CONT'D)
               (whispered)
          Now... Live with your shame...

KAZE stands away. BYSTANDERS, recovered from their fright, converge on the TROUBLEMAKERS, hauling them bodily outside.

KAZE watches silently through the closing door of the tavern. He turns to the BARTENDER who is seeing tenderly to the shaken "SERVER."

                    BARTENDER
          Are you sure you're alright?

The "SERVER" shakes his head "yes," though tears stream down his face.

                    BARTENDER (CONT'D)
          I'm gonna have Miuchi make sure you get safely
          home....
               (paternally)
          And I want you to take the next couple of
          nights off, OK?
               (gently reassuring)
          You'll be paid as if you'd worked them full.

The "SERVER" nods, but is still very shaken. MIUCHI drapes a heavy
cloak around the "SERVER" and helps him out into the night.

KAZE turns to the BARTENDER, when they are gone.

> KAZE
>
> That was very kind of you.

> BARTENDER
>
> No. Sir, that was very kind of *you*. Those
> "enforcers" have been coming around a lot more
> often now, demanding payment, or else they
> start breaking up the place.
> > (sighing...)
>
> Contrary to popular belief, there isn't much
> money to be made in owning a tavern
> nowadays... not with everyone up and down the
> line taking their cut and all...
> > (indicating the cut on KAZE'S arm)
>
> Why don't you come in the back. I can have my
> wife clean that up for you.

> KAZE
>
> (declining)
> No... I must be...

> BARTENDER
>
> (an almost "Crouching Tiger"
> military-respect emphasis on "Sir")
> Please, Sir?

DISSOLVE TO:

INT. TAVERN'S LIVING QUARTERS - LATER

The BARTENDER'S WIFE walks away with the bowl and rag she used for
cleaning KAZE'S now bandaged wound. The BARTENDER brings over a
service of tea for KAZE.

                         BARTENDER
          Things just haven't been the same...
               (in confidence)
          and though I know it'd be my head for even
          sayin' so, just between you and me, I wish the
          coup had never happened. It...
               (hesitating)
          ...seems like you're the kind of man who
          agrees?...

The BARTENDER goes to a locked shrine, opens it, and lights two
sticks of incense, placing them in the sand before a weathered,
shadowed painting.

                      BARTENDER (CONT'D)
          Why... if... you don't mind my asking...

                           KAZE
          I don't mind.... But I have my own reasons.

                         BARTENDER
          What brings you to these parts?

                           KAZE
          Again... I have my reasons.

                         BARTENDER
          I'm sorry... I didn't mean to pry. I am very
          grateful to you and...
               (searching for the right words)
          many stories come through here. This is a
          tavern after all...

As the BARTENDER stands back from the shrine, KAZE sees the faded,
parchment painting of Princess Bay at the shrine's center.

                           KAZE
               (whispered)
          'Kumbay...

KAZE stares as if in a trance, teeth clenched, jaw muscles tensing, pain reflected in his eyes.

> BARTENDER
> (backtracking a little)
> Look... I know it's death for me and my
> family to have an image of... But... Y-you
> are "him"... aren't you?...

> KAZE
> (snapping out of his trance)
> Yes...
> (looking away)
> Yes, I am.

> BARTENDER
> (noticeably relieved)
> Oh... thank the Gods.

In the background, the BARTENDER motions for his wife, suddenly with a strung and loaded crossbow in hand, to leave them. KAZE does not notice.

The BARTENDER walks to the table, to lean heavily on a chair. He looks between KAZE's fixed gaze on the painting of Bay and the painting itself.

> BARTENDER (CONT'D)
> The rumors are true then...

KAZE remains motionless.

> BARTENDER (CONT'D)
> Don't worry. Your secret is safe with me.
> I'm only an innkeeper, and I hear many
> things...

KAZE stands, facing away.

                              KAZE
              (I... I...) Thank you for kindness...

KAZE turns to leave. The BARTENDER reaches out gently to touch his
arm.

                            BARTENDER
              Sir? I just want to say that it is an honor
              to have met you. I'm on your side... for what
              it's worth. I hope you get those bastards who
              killed the royal family. And if there's any
              way I can be of help...

KAZE turns, a tear beginning to make its way down his face.

                              KAZE
              Kind sir... the honor is mine.

                                                        FADE OUT.

FADE IN:

EXT. WOODS - LATER

KAZE sits by a small, moonlit stream, head buried in his arms, the
faded parchment painting of Bay clenched in his hand.

                              KAZE
              (whispered, full of mourning)
              Bay... I am so sorry... S-s-so sorry...

Soft footfalls and rustling begin to fan out around KAZE.

                        LEAD TROUBLEMAKER
              Well, look 'oo we have 'ere.

KAZE raises his head slightly. Tears can be seen staining his
cheeks.

                              KAZE
              Go away. I'm busy.

>   LEAD TROUBLEMAKER
>   A big strong man like you, crying? Why that
>   ain't manly, ain't it? Unless... of course,
>   unless we give you something to cry about.

From the shadows, many forms materialize, each silhouetting
strange, evil-looking weapons.

>   KAZE
>   I said go away. I don't want to have to
>   kill.... Not tonight.

>   LEAD TROUBLEMAKER
>   It ain't you who'll be doin' the killin'!

Those on the edges of the clearing fly at KAZE, the LEAD
TROUBLEMAKER staying well out of the fray.

>   KAZE
>   (whispered in resigned disbelief)
>   Why?...

KAZE waits until the last possible moment to move; when he does, it
is with lightning speed. He unsheaths his sword, and in a clean,
practiced motion, cuts through the attackers.

One of the foes, now disarmed, gawks in amazement some distance
from this killing machine.

>   KAZE (CONT'D)
>   You've lost your weapon...

With pantherine grace, KAZE removes a wicked-looking blade from one
of the fallen assailants, steps aside as another rushes at him, and
buries it in the attacker's chest. Having done so, he spins the
dying man around and propels him at his disarmed comrade at the
edge of the clearing.

                         KAZE (CONT'D)
              Here's one. Your friend isn't going to be
              using it anymore.

The dying attacker collapses in the arms of the disarmed man, the
blade sliding wetly into the other's hands as he falls heavily to
the ground.

KAZE and the remaining two face off, the LEAD TROUBLEMAKER still
staying well out of the fray.

                         KAZE (CONT'D)
              I really, **really** didn't want to kill tonight.

KAZE walks up to one of the attackers, who stands his ground. The
attacker feints, parries, and is felled.

                         KAZE (CONT'D)
              I **hate** doing this.

KAZE walks toward the attacker he passed the blade to earlier. The
man throws the weapon feebly at KAZE and runs into the dark.

KAZE sighs heavily, wiping the blood from his sword.

                         KAZE (CONT'D)
              I've always hated it.

KAZE inspects the edge of his blade.

                         KAZE (CONT'D)
              It's just so hard to get away from... once you
              get good at it.

KAZE turns to the LEAD TROUBLEMAKER as he sheaths his sword.

                         KAZE (CONT'D)
              People like you come to me... *asking* me for
              it, *begging* me for it. But you never ask for
              yourselves....

KAZE advances slowly on the LEAD TROUBLEMAKER, who stands his
ground uncertainly. KAZE gestures to the fallen men who litter the
clearing.

> KAZE (CONT'D)
> Do you see how many deaths you've asked for
> tonight?

The LEAD TROUBLEMAKER, taking advantage of what he thinks is KAZE
lowering his guard, brings his sword down in a quick arc. KAZE
steps into him, and with a quick twist of his hands, frees the
sword from the other's grasp.

> KAZE (CONT'D)
> How many more are there?

KAZE throws the blade to the edge of the clearing. The LEAD
TROUBLEMAKER stands uncertainly.

> KAZE (CONT'D)
> How many, that your fear and insecurity about
> *yourself* have caused the severance from this
> *gift* of life?

> KAZE (CONT'D)
> What is it? Are you *jealous*? Does another's
> contentment somehow detract from your own
> feelings of self-worth?

> KAZE (CONT'D)
> (sadly)
> You are going to die tonight. You are going
> to die the special death.

The LEAD TROUBLEMAKER takes a step backward, but KAZE'S hand is
around his throat, lifting him from the ground.

                    KAZE (CONT'D)
It never used to be this way. But people like
you *ask* me to do this. And you keep *forcing*
me back into this! *Why don't you just leave
other people alone?*
          (regaining composure)
It's OK, though. I don't mind so much
anymore. Everyone's got their job... and as
it turns out... I'm good at it.

KAZE forces the LEAD TROUBLEMAKER onto the ground, kneeling over
him, whispering a prayer.

                    KAZE (CONT'D)
          (practiced)
May your next life be filled with beauty. May
the hatred and fear you have chosen to
perpetuate end here, with the ending of this
life. May those you have caused pain be able
to forgive you. May those you have sent
"beyond" be able to live in peace with you in
your future lives, free from any anger that
would lead you to this path again. May your
future lives bring peace, safety, and love to
those around you. This is your duty... this
is your penance.

The LEAD TROUBLEMAKER convulses and his mouth works without sound.

                    KAZE (CONT'D)
Easy... Easy... You're safe. You're not
alone. I won't leave you ('till you're
there...)

The LEAD TROUBLEMAKER'S eyes begin to glaze over.

                    KAZE (CONT'D)
May your next life be a life of beauty.

Having said this, KAZE kisses the LEAD TROUBLEMAKER gently on the forehead.

KAZE stands slowly, the camera booms higher and higher as we...

                                        FADE OUT.

FADE IN:

INT LORD SOSHI'S PRIVATE CHAMBERS - NIGHT

LORD SOSHI stands with a tray of food, talking to a chained captive. We can hear her movements, but the CAMERA always seems to just miss her.

                    LORD SOSHI
              (distracted)
         Mm-hmmm...
              (focused)
         Oh, that's good, that's very good.

SOSHI tosses a morsel of food OS.

                    LORD SOSHI (CONT'D)
         What a good girl you are!
              (Baron Harkkonan-ish)
         Now...

SOSHI moves toward the OS captive.

                    LORD SOSHI (CONT'D)
              (instantly furious)
         No! No!
              (roar-scream)
         NO!!!
              (rage)
         Don't you **flinch**! Don't you *ever* pull away
         from me!

SOSHI reaches for a blunt stick, polished from use. He raises
ominously.

LORD SOSHI (CONT'D)

> (building)

Don't... You... Ever...

KAZE (O.S.)

Lieutenant!

SOSHI freezes, only his eyes are capable of movement.

KAZE (O.S.) (CONT'D)

I remember you being a lot thinner.

LORD SOSHI

> (panicked, like opening "bad guy"
> from "The Professional")

Guards... Guards!!!

KAZE (O.S.)

I'm afraid... they can't hear you... "*Lord*..."
Soshi.

LORD SOSHI

I know that voice... I know your voice!

KAZE (O.S.)

You've made me kill again...

LORD SOSHI

But you can't be you...

KAZE (O.S.)

And you know how I hate that.

LORD SOSHI

I saw you die...

KAZE (O.S.)

You know how precious life is to me.

> LORD SOSHI
>
> But you're dead...

> KAZE (O.S.)
>
> Life is a gift...

> LORD SOSHI
>
> You're dead...

> KAZE (O.S.)
>
> A blessing.

> LORD SOSHI
>
> I watched you die.

> KAZE
>
> Yes. You did, didn't you.

LORD SOSHI turns to find KAZE rising from the shadows barely a
meter from him. SOSHI jerks backward, hitting his head against the
rock outer-wall.

> LORD SOSHI
> (the wincing "Mmmmmngh... Nnnngh..."
> of having hit one's head on
> something hard)

KAZE walks slowly toward the other end of the room.

> KAZE
> (ignoring Soshi)
> The coup has been good to you I see.

> LORD SOSHI
>
> I don't know nuthin' about it. I just take
> orders and do what they say.

> KAZE
> ("gentling," to the captive)
> But you're still up to your old games...

> (sadly, almost to himself)
> ...aren't you... "Lieutenant."

KAZE sadly regards the silhouette, chained to the desk. The CAMERA moves from the silhouette back to where KAZE was standing at the other end of the room, but he is no longer there.

KAZE seems to coalesce from the shadows immediately around SOSHI.

> KAZE (CONT'D)
> People are not playthings, Lieutenant. They are not your toys.

KAZE smashes the heavy desk to which the woman is chained. The heavy links fall to the floor, tugging at the silhouette.

> KAZE (CONT'D)
> Keys?

> LORD SOSHI
> (swallowing hard and sweating)
> Th....
> (2 beats)
> There aren't any.

> KAZE
> (narrowing his eyes)
> Why am I not surprised?

KAZE bends close to the silhouette.

> KAZE (CONT'D)
> (whispered, "gentling")
> You won't have any trouble leaving... though I'm sorry for the mess you'll see on your way out. There is an innkeeper not far from here, about two days walk, in the valley along the north road. Can you make it?

The silhouette nods timidly.

                         KAZE (CONT'D)
                    (still whispered)
             Tell him I sent you.... He'll help.

KAZE rises, turning slowly to face SOSHI.

                         KAZE (CONT'D)
             My name... is KAZE.

OS, the women can be heard running through the door and down the
hall.

                         LORD SOSHI
                    (stammering)
             Y-y-you killed *everyone*?

                         KAZE
             Only those who needed it.

                         KAZE (CONT'D)
             You *know* me, Lieutenant. You were under my
             command for how many years? You know how much
             I hate killing. I'm just good at it... You,
             on the other hand...

                         LORD SOSHI
             What're ya gonna do?

                         KAZE
             I think you know the answer to that.

                         LORD SOSHI
                    (swallowing hard)
             You gonna kill me too, then, is that it?

                         KAZE
                    (drawing out the pause)
             No.... Not just yet.... I need you to let
             the others know I'm coming.

LORD SOSHI

> Like I say, I don't know anything about it. I
> just get orders and I follow them. That's
> all!

KAZE

> That is enough.

KAZE walks to the window.

LORD SOSHI

> I ain't afraid of you! I ain't afraid of you
> at all! Come back and fight... you *coward*!

KAZE pauses on the windowsill.

SOSHI has found a sword. Its tip trembles noticeably in his
fighting stance.

KAZE

> I was better than you before I "died."
>> (cocking his head)
> What makes you think you stand a chance now?

"Crow"-like, KAZE drops from sight.

SOSHI slams the sword into the remains of the desk, roaring in
fury.

LORD SOSHI

> Damn you, Kaze!!!

SOSHI heaves the desk, upending it and all its contents, candles
and all.

LORD SOSHI (CONT'D)

>> (filled with frustration and anger)
> Damn you to *Hell*!

EXT WOODS - CONTINUOUS

KAZE is rimmed by moonlight.

                              KAZE
                    (whispered)
              You already have.

                         THE END

Chapter 6

The Shot List of KAZE GHOST WARRIOR

sq01 sc01: Low-angle, trees and bamboo overhanging stream (HD Instance for leaves and much use of "Mononoke" multiplaning to increase what we can do visually) with water "diamonding" in the moonlight.
...Foot comes into view and settles.
...Rack focus to foot and see footprint near to foot on ground (HD Instance dirt? Multiplane for levels so not so much needs to be rendered, and things like sparkles and leaf movement can be on separate loops)

sq01 sc02: Full shot, silhouetting Kaze as he drops to his haunches.

sq01 sc03: Med. shot as he traces the outline of the footprint, moves to pick up some dirt.

sq01 sc04: CU, tracking shot as hand moves to nose. He breathes, rubbing index and thumb together. Rack focus on eyes (after FX compound-blur with animated levels for depth map) as they open.
...Camera pulls back and Dutches slightly as Kaze smiles a predatorial smile.

sq01 sc05: Tracking med. shot as Kaze rises, dusts his hands, and begins to walk OS.

FADE TO BLACK

TITLE: "Kaze, Ghost Warrior"

(Panning shots inspired from Kev's ex-father-in-law's book of photography)

TITLING: "Timothy Albee (and others who do voices). Executive Producer, Timothy Albee. Written and Directed by Timothy Albee"

UP FROM BLACK:

sq02 sc01: EXT. Tavern. Full, long shot (similar lighting to opener). Crane, push-in from high (no Dutching).

DISSOLVE TO:

sq02 sc02: INT. Tavern. High wide shot, continuing camera movement from previous shot. (Make sure Bartender is clearly visible and in a "pool of light.")

sq02 sc03: Dolly shot past tables, tracking Bartender. Stuff in Fore, Mid., and BG... (multiplane for depth-of-field). Troublemakers come into frame heckling couple. One whips out a knife (the tiger-blade, used later), holding it to someone's throat. Bartender snaps his attention to the fracas.

sq02 sc04: Med. CU of Troublemakers hassling couple. The Troublemakers toast with the couple's drinks (one is holding one of the couple from behind, knife still at his throat), downing them.

sq02 sc05: Med. of Bartender pulling (uncocked, unloaded) crossbow from shadows.

sq02 sc06: CU quick-cut to Troublemaker's face, couple's faces cut off in each frame.

sq02 sc07: CU quick-cut to other Troublemaker's face, couple's faces cut off in each frame. Things are getting really dangerous-tense!

sq02 sc08: XCU quick-cut of knife against patron's throat, his eyes read fear (weird, Dutched framing cuts top of his head off).

sq02 sc09: CU of crossbow bolt being knocked, held between two fingers as hand pulls string tight to cock bow.

sq02 sc10: CU on furious but helpless other harassed Patron's reaction, held back by other Troublemaker.

sq02 sc11: XCU on Patron with knife to his throat, beyond terrified.

sq02 sc12: XCU on Troublemaker looking OSR, head turns quickly to look OSL, camera "whip"-zooms out.

sq02 sc13: XCU (slow-mo) on hand pushing knife-Patron's head SL.

sq02 sc14: Med. (slow-mo) shot of knife-Troublemaker shoving patron SL and spinning around.

sq02 sc15: Med. table-high shot, Troublemaker holding other Patron in FG, Patron slightly behind him, then table and tipped drink glass (other is still upright). Patron still moving toward table and knife. Troublemaker coming to sharp rest, knife spinning to "safe" position, flourished high against wrist.

sq02 sc16: Med. (slow-mo) shot of knife-Patron sitting back, hand coming from throat, dry (no blood), and looking up at Troublemaker.

sq02 sc17: Med. (slow-mo) shot of Troublemakers, one lets go of other patron, crosses to knife-Troublemaker, "bo-ba" saluting. Knife-Troublemaker palms head of still-rising knife-Patron and shoves back down toward table as he turns toward camera to walk toward SR with other Troublemaker. Bartender, slightly out-of-focus in BG can be seen lowering crossbow from firing-height, back toward being hidden under bar.

sq02 sc18: Med. shot of swarthy three, the two other Troublemakers join them, sitting and bo-ba saluting all around.

sq02 sc19:   Med. of Bartender, frontal, restrained fury. Kaze enters frame from OSL, slightly out of focus, his shoulder coming to BT's head. Rack-focus to Kaze as BT looks up at Kaze.

sq02 sc20:   CU, side-shot, Kaze leans close to BT's ear, whispers something we can't hear. BT nods.

sq02 sc21:   CU of Kaze's finger leaving a coin he has placed on the countertop, implying Kaze's leaving.

sq02 sc22:   OTS, Bartender of Kaze heading toward dark corner of tavern.

sq02 sc23:   Med. shot, side, of Bartender watching Kaze go. One of his Servers walks around tables in BG, sets empties down on far side of BT absently as she passes. BT reaches out to snag her almost as she is beyond his reach (toward camera).

sq02 sc24:   OTS, BT's POV. Kaze, visible in BG, Server turns to look.

sq02 sc25:   OTS, Server's POV. Bartender puts small bottle of sake and glass on tray, gestures toward Kaze.

sq02 sc26:   Mid-CU of Server as she turns to look. She likes what she sees, smiles, turns a bit back toward BT (eyes doing most of work) and nods.

sq02 sc27:   Kaze's POV of Server. Turning from bar with tray and walking a few steps toward camera. BT is visible in BG, watching, hands folded respectfully in front of him (and nods in recognition?).

sq02 sc28:   Med. side-shot as Server sits with Kaze. Kaze goes to reach for bottle, her hand goes too.

sq02 sc29:   CU of her fingers covering his as they close on the bottle.

sq02 sc30:   CU of Kaze raising his gaze, hard.

sq02 sc31: CU of her gaze, smile, inviting, offering...

sq02 sc32: Mid-CU of Kaze as he shakes his head firmly, "No."

sq02 sc33: Mid-CU, ("A" cam) reaction shot of Server. A little surprised, a little hurt, a little disappointed.

sq02 sc34: Med. ("B" cam) side-shot of Kaze bowing respectfully to Server.

sq02 sc34a: Med. ("A" cam) side-shot of Server. Respectfully and admirably accepting Kaze's declination and moving to get up and out of frame.

sq02 sc35: CU of hand back-slapping someone else's chest (and beginning to fold into a pointing gesture).

sq02 sc36: Med. shot of two Troublemakers, the one who was slapped glaring angrily at the other, holding an almost spilled drink. The other gestures his point again, toward Kaze.

sq02 sc37: Deep shot, "hitter" in FG, "Hittee" in mid-ground and Server. Leaving Kaze's corner in BG.

sq02 sc38: Mid-shot of two Troublemakers looking back at one another, nodding, slamming their drinks.

sq02 sc39: CU of empty shot glass being laid on its side on the table. Fingers pressing down on it, snapping it loose to sail OSL.

sq02 sc40: CU on shot glass as it begins to spin and right itself, like a top.

sq02 sc41: Low-angle as all five TMs rise in slow-mo, some fist-saluting each other.

sq02 sc42: CU, empty wall with Kaze far SL, looking SL, raising a drink to his lips (which doesn't quite make it there in this shot)... Beat... A fist slams sidelong into it.

sq02 sc42a: Low-angle, camera near to where Kaze's glass might go, see Kaze, and 5 TMs. Kaze completing raise of drink to his lips.

sq02 sc43: OTS Lead TM's fist/arm/shoulder/head framing Kaze on three sides as he finishes his sip, then lowers his glass.

sq02 sc44: Low-angle, camera near to where Kaze's glass might go, see Kaze, and 5 TMs. LEAD TROUBLEMAKER: "Turnin' away women, eh?"

sq02 sc45: CU, side-shot of LEAD TM: "Big, strong man like you?" (He gestures coolly with hand he rests on wall with.)

sq02 sc46: CU of Kaze raising his glass again, LEAD TM: "...someday they may be scarce."

sq02 sc47: (establisher) Down-shot of Kaze ringed by TMs. Lead TM laughs and looks left and right to his guys. A Male Server can be seen entering OSL with a tray of drinks bound for somewhere.

sq02 sc48: Low, mid-CU of LEAD TM: "Maybe..." (starts his move).

sq02 sc49: Down-shot (near-repeat of sq02sc47) as Lead Troublemaker lashes out for Male Server.

sq02 sc50: CU of hand closing on scruff of Male Server.

sq02 sc51: CU blur-shot of arm being twisted.

sq02 sc52: CU blur-shot of knees being kicked from behind.

sq02 sc53: CU blur-shot of Male Server being forced down into a mid-shot.

sq02 sc54: Mid-shot of Lead TM holding Male Server on his knees, in a painful looking Aikido arm-twist-neck-scruff. Truck in on Server's frightened face looking up at Kaze. LEAD TM: "This one's more your type?"

sq02 sc55: Mid-CU, side-shot, Kaze not looking at action, sips another bit from his glass, setting it methodically on the table (crowd preparing for fight to break out in BG audio). KAZE: "Put him down."

sq02 sc56: Mid-CU of Lead TM, scruffed Server possible in FG. LEAD TM: "Oh, so 'e is your type then, is 'e?"

sq02 sc57: CU of cloth, with glint of metal shooting from it.

sq02 sc58: CU of hand with blade twirling around it as it arcs.

sq02 sc59: CU of Server's neck as blade comes to rest there, Lead TM pulling Server's head back.

sq02 sc60: Mid-shot of Lead TM, holding Server to him with knife. He begins to gyrate his hips lasciviously as he speaks. LEAD TM: "Maybe we'll get more of a rise from you if we start gettin' 'im all *wet* fir ya!"

sq02 sc61: CU of knife's point getting dangerously close to Server's throat as Lead TM's hips gyrate.

sq02 sc62: CU Kaze's eyes, closed. KAZE: "I said," Kaze's eyes open.

sq02 sc63: CU blur of Kaze's hand sliding between fabrics of Server and Lead TM.

sq02 sc64: CU blur of hand twisting knife away with 2 fingers.

sq02 sc65: CU low-angle of knife falling, spinning slightly toward camera as Kaze slides his body between Lead TM and Server. (Server isn't pushed by Kaze at all... stays relatively motionless.)

sq02 sc66: Blur whip-pan with bit of TM in frame as reference.

sq02 sc67: CU of empty wall. Lead TM's head, propelled by Kaze's grip around his mouth/throat, the back of the head hits first (body still out at 45 degrees from wall).

sq02 sc67a: Med. shot of sq02sc67.

sq02 sc68:   CU of knife, last revolution and embedding itself (by gravity) into table (floor or whatever).

sq02 sc69:   Mid-slo-mo of body of Lead TM rag-dolling to hang limply from TM's head/neck, held against the wall by Kaze.

sq02 sc70:   XCU of Kaze's bared teeth. KAZE: "Put... him..."

sq02 sc71:   (Dial. continuing from prev. shot) KAZE: "...down." MCU of Kaze's face and Lead TM's squinched face. Kaze's free hand in FG. Claws slowly rising from the fingertips as he twists his hand menacingly. Start hand move to TM's snout.

sq02 sc72:   CU of TM's snout as Kaze's thumb traces pattern along its fur.

sq02 sc73:   XCU tracking shot as fingers are drawn sensually over the Lead TM's head, down to Kaze's nose.

sq02 sc74:   CU on Kaze's making a production of sensuously smelling his fingers as he rubs them together in front of his nose. He opens his eyes slowly, smiling as recognition plays lusciously across his face. KAZE: (I've been looking for you...) "Who do you work for?"

sq02 sc75:   CU on Lead TM, face still mashed by Kaze's hand, eyes open different amounts and pupils at slightly different dilations. He gurgles something incoherent, which Kaze pinches off.

sq02 sc76:   CU, Kaze. Smiles and shakes his head. KAZE: "Wrong answer."

sq02 sc77:   Med. of one Troublemaker swinging a chair up from its resting point on the floor.

sq02 sc78:   OTS (slow-mo) (LTM) as Kaze whips lead TM away from wall and camera.

sq02 sc78a: OTS (Kaze) (Reverse of sc78.) Kaze whips LTM away from wall, directly at camera. Chair pieces crash down around Lead TM who begins to drop.

sq02 sc79: (SM) Med. wide bar is visibly empty, as the few remaining Patrons can be seen scramble-stumbling into the shadows. Chairs and drinks overturned in haste to leave -- they must be used to this -- as chair crashes into Lead TM and he drops with the chair.

sq02 sc80: Wide shot (real time) of Kaze holding up limp Troublemaker for a moment by his clothes. Kaze shove-drops the guy to the ground.

sq02 sc81: Med. side as Kaze raises his eyes in a "you really want to do this?" kind of look.

sq02 sc82: CU of weapon (tiger-blade) spinning from cloth, coming to a stop in a TM's hand.

sq02 sc83: CU of hands coming out of folds with double-moon weapons.

sq02 sc84: Med. CU of hand stretching chain from folds, wicked-looking-edged "morning-star" pendulating from one end.

sq02 sc85: XCU of sword being drawn.

sq02 sc86: Wide (establisher-ish) of TMs settling into their ready poses.

sq02 sc87: CU of Kaze shaking his head and sighing ("stupid morons always think they're hot stuff... Why do they always have to make it this way? They could back down... Just once they could not feel the need to keep going on this stupid path... Just once!!!") (Perhaps a hint of Grommit)

sq02 sc88: Full side-shot of Kaze, standing, "unready," close to wall. Troublemakers at "show-off-ready" around him. Bartender, crossbow at low "ready-safe" and few tougher Patrons reclining, back up to bar to watch the "show."

FIGHT SCENE (Tiger/Dragon reference... Kaze is like Lee MuBai
fighting girl with stick when she comes at him with "green dragon,"
totally in control and all about business.)

sq02 sc90:   Med. (mod. low, OTS) shot past Kaze's (relaxed, claws
in) side. Double-moon guy winds up into heaven and launches
attack.

sq02 sc91:   CU of double-moon weapons in "Heaven."

sq02 sc92:   Top-down wide shot establishing positions of players,
Double-moon guy moving into Kaze's range.

sq02 sc93:   XCU of double-moon weapons gathering speed.

sq02 sc94:   (slo-mo) (different angle) XCU of double-moon weapons.

sq02 sc95:   (slo-mo) Med. wide of Kaze stepping into "Heaven,"
still extremely relaxed (but other guy a little less so).

sq02 sc96:   (slo-mo) XCU of Kaze's L hand as he gently twists one
of the double-moons out of the TM's hand.

~~**sq02 sc97:**   Med. of Kaze blocking other "double-moon"
(sticky-hands) as he turns to set first "double-moon" down on
nearby table.~~

sq02 sc98:   CU of Kaze doing "sticky-hands" (blocking) with other
weapon.

sq02 sc99:   Med. CU Kaze sets first "double-moon" down on nearby
table.

sq02 sc100:   Med. CU Kaze returns attention toward guy he's
fighting.

sq02 sc101:   (slo-mo) Med. (start frontal-near-3/4, dolly CW around
action) of Kaze's left arm wrapping around double-moon's left arm
(and remaining weapon). (Kaze now has his back right up against
front of other guy.)

(quick-cuts)

sq02 sc102: Med. of Kaze's right arm reaching down below other guy's legs.

sq02 sc102a: CU of guy being lifted off ground by arm pressing against inner thigh.

sq02 sc103: Med. of Kaze picking guy up, starting to spin him like a "crystal stick."

sq02 sc104: Med. long of Kaze spinning guy around his arm, holding other double-moon in his left hand.

sq02 sc105: CU of guy spinning around Kaze's arm.

sq02 sc106: (cut to different angle) CU of guy spinning around Kaze's arm, hand opens up and claps over bad guy's pelvis.

sq02 sc107: Med. of Kaze throwing guy down, out of frame to floor like crystal stick (table in mid-ground topples in response -- drinks/service spill, etc.).

sq02 sc107a: (Kaze on SL facing SR) Med. low-angle of Kaze frowning at weapon in hand.

sq02 sc108: (Kaze on SR, facing SL) Med. waist-high (booming up slightly, tracking weapon) of Kaze frowning at weapon in hand. Puts weapon on top of other on nearby table.

sq02 sc109: Med. CU (reverse-angle, chest-high, Kaze on SL, facing SR) of Kaze drawing hand back from weapons on table. 1/2 Beat... quick-turn from hips, as camera whip-pans L.

sq02 sc110: Whip-pan R which settles into med. CU of Kaze grabbing wrists (one-handed) of guy coming at him with extremely fine inlaid hand-swords. Beat...

sq02 sc111: OTS of hand-sword guy. 1/2 beat... Kaze looks around at gold inlay on bejeweled blades (strange days).

sq02 sc112: XCU of inlaid blades showing tiger motif.

sq02 sc113: CU of Kaze turning toward cam (1/2 beat) raising eyebrow.

sq02 sc114: Med. Kaze snakes hands up, between guy's hands, pushing them upward.

sq02 sc115: CU Kaze rotating guy's hands out and downward.

sq02 sc116: Med. CU Kaze pushing guy's hands downward, his fingers opening.

sq02 sc117: Med. CU of feet as far-blade, then near-blade "k-thunk" into the floor (slow-mo).

sq02 sc118: (slightly slowed) Med. waist-high, camera craning up with action. Kaze (remember to get hip-twist leading the action), open-palm, hits guy right to solar-plexus, left to chest (just leading, not meant to do real damage), right to head, which pushes guy's head back, arcing away from camera.

sq02 sc119: (Slow-mo) Steady-cam on a fast-track, circling combatants CCW, showing bystanders and chain-guy (and sword-guy) in BG swinging and releasing. Med. of Kaze stepping into (leading with left leg), reaching behind guy, bringing his head forward to smash against his right knee. Guy arcs back up as Kaze's right leg comes back down behind him, leading a twist of the waist that he uses to catch (crystal-stick-style -- less damaging to Kaze's ligaments?) the guy's chest with an "inverted shudo," which pivots him around Kaze's arm and throws guy to the floor, over chain which has been released by chain-guy (Kaze's movements having carried him out of its intended path).

sq02 sc120: (slow-mo) Med. side-shot as chain shoots, arcing up from underneath falling guy. Kaze begins to react, pulling back.

sq02 sc121: (slow-mo) CU Kaze pulls back as morning-star races up past him on its chain. He tracks it with his eyes and head.

sq02 sc122: (slightly slow-mo) Kaze's POV, chain weapon arcs, near rafters, arcing back (toward bystanders).

sq02 sc123: CU (slightly slow-mo) Kaze leads motion with eyes, turning head back toward bystanders.

sq02 sc124: Med. whip-zoom to CU of startled patrons.

sq02 sc125: (slow-mo) Wide side-shot as Kaze bolts toward two remaining attackers, all semblance of "Mr. Cool" fading.

sq02 sc126: (slow-mo) "Whip-tracking pan" of edged blade moving SL.

sq02 sc127: (slow-mo, dollying left to right, tracking Kaze) Med. back-shot as Kaze pushes past first "chain-guy" (thrown down to left) and pushes past sword-guy (thrown down to right) whose sword, loose in bad guy's grip, slides its blade along Kaze's arm.

sq02 sc128: (slo-mo) CU of blade cutting through Kaze's arm.

sq02 sc129: (slo-mo) Side-shot of Kaze having pushed past sword guy, having shoved him out of the way and down.

sq02 sc130: (slo-mo) Blurred tracking shot of chained morning-star flying through the air.

sq02 sc131: CU-push-in of patrons, zooming in on guy to be hit.

sq02 sc132: (slo-mo) (guy about to be hit POV) As chain arcs morning-star toward him, Kaze running toward him, coiling and leaping... TMs still falling to the floor behind and on either side of Kaze.

sq02 sc133: (Xtreme slo-mo) CU blur-pan tracking shot (like 1000% vector-motion blur) of morning-star moving from SR to SL. ...Kaze's hand enters frame, fingers reaching... It folds around the chain. Hand, chain, and morning-star stop. Camera continues its motion to settle on side-shot, CU of bystander about to be hit. The morning-star is only inches away from the bystander.

sq02 sc134: CU/XCU bystander's POV. Kaze holds weapon, chain still taught. (BG and characters in BG blurry.) Chain and weapon begin to slowly be pulled by gravity.

sq02 sc135: X-low-angle, up, between Kaze and Bystander as chain and weapon fall slowly toward camera.

sq02 sc136: Kaze, back toward camera, slowly turns, fury and rage boiling to surface.

sq02 sc137: Kaze stomps toward chain-guy who is rising in BG.

sq02 sc137a: Med. CU of morning-star securely in Kaze's hand, being raised.

sq02 sc138: Kaze slams morning-star into/through table to "disable" it.

sq02 sc139: Kaze reaches chain-guy who is now quite frightened, holding up his hands feebly to ward him off.

sq02 sc140: Kaze "steam-rolls" past, palming the guy's face.

sq02 sc141: Kaze lifts the guy off the ground by his face.

sq02 sc142: Kaze arcs the guy and smashes his head through a table that splinters.

sq02 sc143: Reverse angle "under the table as it splinters," holding until TM's head contacts the floor, then craning up and tracking Kaze's hand as it pushes the guy on through to the floor. Kaze's back comes into frame so we don't see if the guy's head goes through the floor as well. Hold a beat.

sq02 sc144: CU side-shot of Kaze's eyes nearly anger-squinted shut, shoulders heaving as snarl forcibly fades.

sq02 sc145: Med. CU OTS, Kaze's shoulders settle, heaving. He turns his head SL.

sq02 sc146: Sword-guy's POV. Kaze over (dead?) chain-guy. Kaze's eyes are locked on camera. He rises slowly (eyes reflecting brighter than "should" be).

sq02 sc147: Med. of sword-guy as he drop-throws his sword down, spreading his hands in a "I give up" kind of way, palm-down fingers splayed.

sq02 sc148: Med. of Kaze which he walks into CU. Eyes hard, face set.

sq02 sc149: Med. of Sword-guy who backs himself up to a pillar. Kaze walks into frame, pressing hand to other's chest, pinning TM's back against pillar.

sq02 sc150: OTS of pinned TM (Kaze's left arm across TM's chest). Down-shot of Kaze's hand coming up, turning as claws slowly start to come out of sheaths.

sq02 sc151: XCU of claws coming out of sheaths.

sq02 sc152: CU of TM as eyes get bigger and mouth opens in fascination, watching claws.

sq02 sc153: CU of claws reaching for TM's throat.

sq02 sc154: CU of TM's eyes and mouth as they get really big, craning neck down, trying to track hand. Pupils get huge, then roll back, head tilts up ever so slightly.

sq02 sc155: CU of claws not quite at TM's throat. TM's head slides down past fingers. (Make obvious that Kaze didn't claw this guy.)

sq02 sc156: Med. long down-Dutch of Kaze standing over collapsed TM. TM should almost be in a sensual pose, collapsed on the floor.

sq02 sc157: Rear med. CU shot as Kaze's head leads turn to SR.

sq02 sc158:   Table-level dolly shot behind Kaze as he walks past the wreckage. He snags an upright, corked, small bottle from a table he passes.

sq02 sc159:   Med. side-shot of collapsed Lead TM. Kaze stops and kneels into frame, reaching for Lead TM's scruff. He picks him up slightly off the ground.

sq02 sc160:   Med. CU of wall onto which Lead TM's head bounce-lolls as he is thrown into a sitting position (still unconscious).

sq02 sc161:   CU of Kaze's thumb flipping out cork from bottle.

sq02 sc162:   Med. shot of Kaze raising bottle toward knocked-out Lead TM, who he is holding up against wall.

sq02 sc163:   (Med.) XCU of Lead TM's eyes. Bottle end tips up into frame. Eyes snap blearily open. He coughs and leans forward out of frame.

sq02 sc164:   Med. side-shot of Kaze holding Lead TM forward so he can cough out the rest of the liquid from his lungs (almost tenderly).

sq02 sc165:   A little closer cut as Kaze whip-forces the guy back up.

sq02 sc166:   CU of wall as Lead TM re-enters frame, head bouncing off wall.

sq02 sc167:   Med. CU of Kaze and Lead TM. TM's head lolls slightly (á là Rodrigo from "Ladyhawke") as Kaze patiently says, "You didn't answer me. Who do you work for?" ...Troublemaker has to be shaken to regain focus (á là Rodrigo). He then says, "Fggghhh..." ...Kaze begins "no" head shake.

sq02 sc168:   CU of Kaze, smiling a knowing smile and shaking his head almost laughingly.

sq02 sc169: Med. CU of Kaze and Lead TM (same as two shots ago) Kaze's hand supporting TM slides up toward TM's throat.

sq02 sc170: XCU of thumb reaching TM's throat. The tip of the claw slides out of its sheath and stops. The thumb bends down from the tip-knuckle, and the tip of the claw disappears below fur. (Bone deformation or morph to get fur to indent slightly as skin responds to pressure of claw.)

sq02 sc171: CU of Kaze. KAZE: "I don't want to... but if you force me, I will kill you."

sq02 sc172: XCU of Lead TM's eyes, a little more focused and widening. Kaze's muzzle comes into frame, right by TM's eyes. KAZE: "Who..."

sq02 sc173: XCU of claw at throat (same as two shots before). Fur indention makes pronounced increase as Kaze says, "Do..."

sq02 sc174: XCU (same as two shots before). Kaze's muzzle and Lead TM's eyes, wider, KAZE: "You..." TM's eyes get really big to punctuate Kaze's line.

sq02 sc175: XCU of Lead TM's lips, LEAD TM (whispered) "...Lord Soshi..."

sq02 sc176: XCU (same as two shots before). LEAD TM: "...a day's ride... to... the south..."

sq02 sc177: XCU of throat and claw. Lead TM: "...in the hills..." Thumb pull back, indention in fur reverts to normal. Claw is way out of its sheath. A drop of blood glistens on its tip.

sq02 sc178: Kaze's POV (CU on Lead TM) as claw comes up into frame and wipes the droplet of blood across Lead TM's lips.

sq02 sc179: CU of Kaze, KAZE: "'Lord' Soshi?"

sq02 sc180: Med. of Kaze and Lead TM, side-shot. Lead TM nods silently, notably still afraid yet relived. KAZE: "Good... Now..."

Kaze leans closer, TM's eyes grow instantly wide again.

sq02 sc181: XCU of Kaze's muzzle close to TM's eyes. KAZE: "...live with your shame." Kaze kisses the TM on the forehead.

sq02 sc182: Med. side-shot of Kaze standing up and backing away, arms spread wide (like Jenner leaving Brisby).

sq02 sc183: Med. of people surrounding Bartender (who is noticeably deep in thought, probably with arms folded across chest, one finger, bent, over frown). After a beat, they look to him.

sq02 sc183a: CU of BT, head bowed, frowning over finger. He looks OSL (beat), then nods, and returns eye to scene (farther out, SL).

sq02 sc184: Low full-shot of Kaze still backing away, arms spread, crucifix-like. Pool of light on Bartender in BG. Patrons rush in under Kaze's arms on both sides past camera.

sq02 sc185: Med. shot: hauling up Lead TM.

sq02 sc186: Med. shot: hauling up other Troublemaker.

sq02 sc186a: Med. shot of hauling up another KO'd TM.

sq02 sc187: EXT. Continuous. Med. dolly and pan left, shot of ground, low-angle, outside of Tavern, still peaceful and silver-moon-lit. Out of frame, door opens (we see light cast and shadows) and TM gets thrown up and out, who lands, rolls, and settles with head/hand in CU (moves to show not dead). Second Troublemaker lands close behind first. (Camera continues moving throughout shot.)

sq02 sc188: INT. Continuous. Wide, high-ish as the last two are dragged, unconscious, out the door (3 (pairs of?) patrons stepping back, because they've already thrown their dudes back). Kaze watches from lower SL, while mid-low SR, Bartender is kneeling before, seeing to Male Server (and Miuchi who is kneeling, holding hands of Male Server). Other Patrons and staff can be seen righting tables and stuff. Kaze looks at BT.

sq02 sc189: Med. BT and Male Server. Another helper or two is standing nearby. BT: "Are you sure you're alright?"

sq02 sc190: Med. of Male Server. He shakes his head "yes," though tears stream down his face. (Miuchi, kneeling by him, holding his hands in hers.) Miuchi looks at BT.

sq02 sc191: OTS Miuchi. BT, looking from Male Server, to Miuchi, then back to Male Server as he says: "I'm gonna have Miuchi take you home."

sq02 sc192: Med. CU of Miuchi and Male Server and BT. BT putting his hands on top of Miuchi's holding Server's. BT (paternally): "And I want you to take the next couple of nights off, OK?"

sq02 sc193: ("A" cam) Male Server, showing a little bit of gratitude mixed with apprehension.

sq02 sc194: ("B" cam) Male Server. BT, smiles gently: "You'll be paid as if you'd worked them full."

sq02 sc195: Med. shot Male Server, Miuhchi, and BT. BT pats hands. Male Server nods.

sq02 sc196: Med. wide Male Server, Miuchi, and BT. BT stands up and back while Miuchi helps Male Server up. Kaze walks into frame, obscuring Miuchi and Male Server. BT looks back over his shoulder at Kaze.

sq02 sc197: ("A" cam) KAZE: "That was very kind of you."

sq02 sc198: ("B" cam) Kaze. BT: "No. Sir, that was very kind of *you*."
... Camera moves back and away, framing two, and dollying CW as BT talks. BT: "Those 'enforcers' have been coming around more regularly now, demanding payment, or else they start breaking up the place." BT sighs and stoops to right a table. "Contrary to popular belief, there isn't much money to be made in owning a tavern nowadays... Not with everyone up and down the line taking

their cut and all." ...BT has stooped again, picking up bits of food and trash (people move out of focus in BG). BT has been looking at the cut on Kaze's arm as he finished his line. Gesturing to the arm, then rising as he speaks, "Why don't you come in the back. I can have my wife clean that up for you."

sq02 sc199: ("A" cam) Kaze shaking his head, KAZE: "No... I must be..."

sq02 sc200: Wide shot of BT and Kaze as Kaze is finishing above line. BT throws trash on righted table as he stands, then performs "Crouching Tiger" sincere bow. BT: "Please, Sir?" (military way of saying "Sir").

DISSOLVE TO:

sq03 sc01: Multi-level. Wife putting wet, bloody rag into bowl and walking OSL in X-FG. Mid-ground shows Kaze with *clean* bandaged arm resting on table that seeps slightly red with blood as scene progresses. (Kaze, on SR, facing SL, BT farther toward BG, on SL, facing SR.) BT: "Things just haven't been the same..."

sq03 sc02: Kaze, OTS (camera push in slowly over dialogue). BT leaning forward slightly so as to not have to speak so loud. BT: "...and though I know it'd be my head for even sayin' so, just between you and me, I wish the coup had never happened. It..." beat... (BT looks up from table) "...seems like you're the kind of man who agrees?"

sq03 sc03: Med. table-high of Kaze, completely impassive (slight push-in). Kaze makes no sign. Beat... Beat...

sq03 sc04: Wide shot with both BT and Kaze. Beat... BT rises and walks to little shrine on near back wall between himself and Kaze (hand going into fold of fabric).

sq03 sc05: CU of key going into keyhole.

sq03 sc06: CU, side-shot, BT in thought about what he's doing. BT: "Why..."

sq03 sc07: CU BT, getting two incense sticks. BT: "If..." (line at utter tail of shot, after incense sticks have already left frame).

sq03 sc08: CU of incense sticks brought into candle flame. BT: "...you don't mind..." (dialogue is slow, but continuous, just broken up here to show shot pacing).

sq03 sc09: Med. shot of Kaze looking tired, in chair. BT: "my asking..." KAZE, not moving a bit, not looking at BT, cuts him off: "I don't mind..."

sq03 sc10: CU of smoking sticks going into sand in front of shrine before a faded, cracked painting of a beautiful, elegant woman. KAZE: "...But I have my own reasons."

sq03 sc11: Med. of BT, still facing away from camera, toward shrine. Beat. BT turns toward cam (which is dollying slightly CW). Perhaps leaning back with hands on table edges on which shrine sits. BT: "What brings you to these parts?" KAZE: "Again..."

sq03 sc12: Med. CU. Kaze opens his eyes and turns toward BT. "...I have my own reasons."

sq03 sc13: Med. wide of BT, tracking dolly shot, pushing in, dollying past Kaze in FG. BT always stays between cam and shrine's picture, until end. BT: "I'm sorry... I didn't mean to pry. I am very grateful to you and... (searching) many stories come through here... This is a tavern, after all... " BT moves to step away from shrine.

sq03 sc14: CU of shrine, push-in, BT moving in slow-mo out of the way. Painting of Bay clearly at center with two incense sticks before it.

sq03 sc15: XCU of Kaze's mouth. KAZE: "Bay..."

sq03 sc16: CU push-in to painting. BT: "Look... I know it's death for me and my family to have an image of..."

sq03 sc17: CU Kaze, looking in a lot of pain, teeth clenching, SCMs flexing... BT: "...but... Y-you are...him... Aren't you?"

sq03 sc18: (another angle) CU Kaze blinks and snaps out of his trance. Looking from shrine, up to (standing) BT. KAZE: "Yes." He breaks the glance and looks away (camera dollying slightly now toward BT (SL)). KAZE: "Yes, I am."

sq03 sc19: Wide shot of Kaze looking away, BT collapses on hands/arms on table. His movement exposes his wife in BG, clearly with crossbow, ready and paused in the process of raising to firing height. BT: "Oh... Thank the gods."

sq03 sc20: Med. of BT with wife in BG. He looks back and motions for his wife to withdraw, and she disappears into the shadows. He looks back toward Kaze. BT: "The rumors are true then..."

sq03 sc21: Med. wide of BT and Kaze. Kaze still in same pose, turned away, now left fist clenched and bandage showing some blood. (Perhaps break continuity with bandaged arm for sake of shot composition?)

sq03 sc22: Closer shot, as BT pulls up chair as he sits. BT: "Don't worry. Your secret is safe with me."
...Camera begins to dolly left, for an OTS of the BT. BT: "I'm only an innkeeper, and I hear many things..." Kaze stands (turning as he does so).

sq03 sc23: Wide of Kaze facing OSR, back to BT on SL. KAZE: "I apologize for taking so much of your time..."

sq03 sc24: CU on Kaze, still looking OSR, very pained... KAZE: "(I...I...)...Thank you for your kindness..." Kaze turns away from cam.

sq03 sc25: Med. of Kaze's back. BT's hand lightly reaching to touch him on the shoulder. BT: "Sir?"

sq03 sc26: Med. CU, Kaze's face caught in shadow, raises from bowed.

sq03 sc27: Med. CU of BT looking up at the back of Kaze's head. Camera dollies (orbiting) around Kaze to a "reverse OTS of Kaze" as dialogue progresses. BT: "I just want to say that it is an honor to have met you." Camera continues orbiting around Kaze, Kaze's face completely obscuring BT, registering Kaze's pain through his eyes. BT: "I'm on your side... for what it's worth. I hope you get those bastards who killed the royal family..." The camera is now on Kaze's left, continuing around, and lowering to mirror the starting position, but low on the BT, and now with Kaze in frame. BT: "And if there's any way I can be of help..."

sq03 sc28: CU back of Kaze's head. He turns slowly 3/4 view, a tear can be clearly seen dampening his fur. Very crow-like and very un-tough-guy-like, "Kind sir..."

sq03 sc29: OTS of BT. Kaze puts his hand over the other's shoulder... KAZE (whispered, on the verge of completely crying): "The honor is mine."

FADE OUT.

FADE IN:

EXT. WOODS -- LATER

(Use multi-plane layers, just like in Mononoke to make BG... ("panorama" plug-in to generate plates).)

sq04 sc01: Long shot, clearing by river, very similar to opener... Perhaps with cherry blossoms in moonlight, maybe a few of them floating through the scene on updrafts. Push in, crane down.

sq04 sc02:   DISSOLVE TO: Med. long shot, dollying around Kaze who sits, head on knees, arms folded over to hide face. In one hand is the same faded, cracked painting of Bay.

sq04 sc03:   DISSOLVE TO: Med. shot, still dollying around Kaze. KAZE: "Bay... I am so sorry... "

sq04 sc04:   DISSOLVE TO: Med. CU, still dollying around Kaze. The sounds of night slowly fill with the cracklings of people moving closer and fanning out. KAZE: "...s-so s-sorry..."

sq04 sc05:   DISSOLVE TO: CU, still dollying, but coming to rest on Kaze's hidden eyes. KAZE (still crying) "...Bay..." Painting can be seen in corner of frame. Shadow of Lead TM falls over Kaze. LEAD TM: (line may be cut) "Well, look 'oo we 'ave 'ere." Beat... Half-beat... ...Kaze raises head just enough to show eyes and tears on cheeks from crying. KAZE: "Go away. I'm busy."

sq04 sc06:   Kaze's POV. Lead TM (who is now standing directly in front of Kaze, about 2.5' away) silhouetted and rimmed by moonlight (eating in at silhouette just a little) LEAD TM: "A big strong man like you... Crying? Why, that ain't manly, ain't it?"

sq04 sc07:   Med. CU side-shot of LEAD TM: "Unless... Of course" ...Camera pulls back, turning, briefly framing Kaze and TM as it turns to include the twelve or so new TMs that materialize out of the shadows to ring Kaze, as LEAD TM continues: "we give you something to cry about." (Camera does a 180, stepping between Kaze and LTM coming back to (reversed) frame Kaze and LTM in med. wide, extra TMs now out of focus in BG.)

sq04 sc08:   CU, Kaze, side-shot (can still see painting in hand somewhere in frame). KAZE: "I said go away. I don't want to have to kill... Not tonight.

sq04 sc09:   Med. X-up-shot (very anime, in pose and in angle). LEAD TM takes a step backward, gesturing comic-bookishly: "It ain't you who'll be doin' the killin'!"

sq04 sc10: Down-shot, establishing positions as TMs directly behind Kaze (5 of them) rush at him, still seated on the ground. Lead TM backed a safe distance away.

sq04 sc11: Med. CU that begins to pull back (KAZE: "Why?..."("are you doing this?")), leaving Kaze on SR, looking SR, to show the 5 TMs coming up from behind. ...Camera begins to over-crank as TMs reach Kaze. ...Kaze waits until the last possible moment to move. He jams a hand down onto his sword, thumb-propelling it right into his open, waiting other hand (painting has already been safely stowed). He leaps upward, arcing up and back, over the attackers in a "crucifix" kind of pose.

sq04 sc11a: (inter-cut with sq04 sc11) CU of Kaze's RH thumbing sword out of frame.

sq04 sc11b: (inter-cut with sq04 sc11) CU of Kaze's LH receiving sword hilt from OS.

sq04 sc12: X-slow-mo. Down-shot of Kaze, cruciform over the attackers flying by beneath him. He brings his hands together on the hilt (sheath has been left on ground), raises the sword over his head, all with a peaceful, almost "sad Jesus" kind of look on his face.

(all heavy slow-mo and VECTOR motion-blur)

sq04 sc13: CU of black clothing, a sword cuts through it.

sq04 sc14: CU of sword sliding one way over black.

sq04 sc15: CU sword sliding another way over black, through something.

sq04 sc16: CU of sword slicing against weapon.

sq04 sc17: CU of sword slicing against weapon.

sq04 sc18: CU of sword slicing against weapon.

sq04 sc19: CU of sword slicing through garment one way "(X)."

sq04 sc20: CU of sword slicing through garment the other way "(X)."

sq04 sc21: Med. CU of sword cutting horizontally low, through 2 pairs of legs.

sq04 sc22: Med. CU (slightly farther back than prev. shot) of sword cutting horizontally mid-way, just above pelvis of 2 bodies.

sq04 sc23: Med. wide (dollying CW) of Kaze spinning to a stop, sword out in "backhand" as the pair of TMs fall apart behind him (Kaze ends facing SR). ...Camera pulls back throughout shot to reveal a TM's silhouette on SL. ...Kaze looks directly at camera: "You've lost your weapon..."

sq04 sc24: Med. of TM who was silhouetted, showing broken hilt of something in his hand, looking very dumbstruck.

sq04 sc25: Med. of Kaze kneeling by fallen lump of clothing, sword tucked along his arm, holding strange weapon in hand. KAZE: "Here's one. Your friend..."

sq04 sc26: Long "Army of Darkness" shot "running" at Kaze's back, TM with broken weapon still visible on far side of clearing. KAZE: "isn't going to be using..."

sq04 sc27: CU of feet running SL, leap, and camera still whipping along ground at same speed. KAZE: "it anymore."

sq04 sc28: Med. of Kaze rising. Flying attacker in BG. At last possible moment, without even looking, Kaze reaches up with free hand, closing over guy's crotch.

sq04 sc29: Slight-slo-mo CU of hand closing over fabric. Camera slight whip-pans to:

sq04 sc30: Slight-slo-mo CU wicked blade buried into fabric. Camera slight whip-pans to:

sq04 sc31: Slow-mo: CU of flying attacker's blade falling from his hand.

sq04 sc32: Med. down-shot (looking over Kaze's right shoulder) as he lands the guy, spins him once, then open-hand-slaps him SR.

sq04 sc33: Waist-high "OTS" of "weaponless" TM as guy slams-collapses into him. Kaze is seen in mid-ground SL.

sq04 sc34: CU of faces of dying TM and "weaponless" TM... Dying TM *looking as if* saying "I can't believe I'm dying... I'm scared... Don't make the same mistake I made..." Dying TM slides down, out of frame (SL).

sq04 sc34a: CU, reaction shot, of horror and disgust, looking down at weapon in hand... (this guy may be a paid fighter, but he isn't a killer).

sq04 sc35: Med. Kaze Beat (taking in guy's reaction)... Then turns away from cam.

sq04 sc36: Med. OTS (Kaze) as he steps up to group of 5 to 6 guys who take a collective step back.

sq04 sc37: Low-angle dolly around Kaze: "I really, *really* didn't want to kill tonight."

sq04 sc38: Med. Kaze steps forward. All but one of the group step back (who raises to strike).

sq04 sc39: CU of Kaze's pained face as his arms slice.

sq04 sc40: Dollying side-shot, Kaze SL, there is now a noticeable gap in the line of TMs on SR. As camera reaches line of TMs, one closest to camera "peels off" and runs OSR, followed by the rest, in turn, as cam. continues its curve around Kaze.

sq04 sc41: Long shot Kaze, facing empty SR on SR, last hired TM (weapon-pass-guy) on SL, looking SR. Kaze: "I *hate* doing this."

sq04 sc42: Waist-high OTS of last paid TM, which pushes in toward Kaze who turns slowly (CCW) to face cam.

sq04 sc43: Med. of LPTM, who starts shot looking aghast at Kaze... he looks down at the weapon in his hand.

sq04 sc44: X-low-angle, slow-mo as LPTM just opens his hands and lets the weapon drop toward camera (remember to have hand lift limply as weight of weapon leaves it). He has turned and run out of frame before the blade reaches camera.

sq04 sc45: CU of Kaze, facing SL. KAZE: "I've always hated it."

sq04 sc46: Med. of Kaze who drops to squatting in frame, reaching down with free hand, preparing to wipe sword clean.

sq04 sc47: Kaze OTS, wiping blood from sword.

sq04 sc48: XCU of wiping blood from sword. KAZE: "It's just so hard to get away from..."

sq04 sc49: Upshot of Kaze still squatting, opening his eyes: "once you get good at it."

sq04 sc50: CU of sword tip finding its hold in sheath.

sq04 sc51: CU of hand sliding sword back into sheath.

sq04 sc52: Shot of Kaze still kneeling (over fallen foe), sword sheathed. He stands and turns toward camera. KAZE: "People like you come to me..." Kaze begins to walk toward camera. Camera continues with Kaze who gets closer and closer to the lens. KAZE: "*asking* me for it, *begging* me for it. But you never ask for yourselves..."

sq04 sc53: Med. side-shot of Lead TM, sword still ready in a very white-knuckled stance. Kaze stops easily into frame, right at TM's perfect striking-distance. KAZE: "Do you see..."

sq04 sc54: High, establisher, showing ground of little clearing littered with bodies and detritus. Kaze spreads his arms, "...how many deaths you've asked for tonight?"

sq04 sc55: Back to 2 shots ago... Med. side-shot, Lead TM raises and snaps blade down. Kaze casually takes the weapon away from him.

sq04 sc56: OTS as Kaze brings his hand to a stop, then opens it to reveal a beautiful, gold and jewel-inlaid sword.

sq04 sc57: CU of sword in Kaze's hand.

sq04 sc58: X-up-shot, jewel-sword in hand visible in lower SR, Kaze looking sadly at sword, then looks up at TM. KAZE: "How many more are there?"

sq04 sc59: Reverse-shot, Kaze now on SR, LTM on SL. Kaze throw-flicks sword at cam (edge of clearing). KAZE: "How many,"

sq04 sc60: Med. Kaze in 3/4, dollying around so back of LTM's head crosses frame in middle of Kaze's speech, camera resolving into an OTS reaction-shot, Kaze looking at LTM. KAZE: "...that your fear and insecurity about *yourself* have caused the severance from this *gift* of life? What is it? Are you *jealous?* Does another's contentment somehow detract from your own feelings of self-worth? (2 beats, looking away and down) You are going to die tonight. (LTM takes a bit of a step backward, 2.5 beats, then looks up, eyes leading) You are going to die the special death." Lead TM takes a step back, beginning to leave frame.

sq04 sc61: CU of Kaze's hand reaching and closing around LTM's throat.

sq04 sc62: Med. Kaze and TM being lifted off ground. KAZE: "It never used to be this way. But people like you *ask* me to do this!"

sq04 sc63: CU of LTM's face as he's being shaken as Kaze emphasizes his words. KAZE: "And you keep *forcing* me back into this!"

sq04 sc64: CU of Kaze, *"Why don't you just leave other people alone!?!!"*

sq04 sc65: Same med. Kaze and TM from 3 shots ago. KAZE: "It's OK, though. I don't mind so much anymore." ...cam begins to dolly to a Kaze OTS. KAZE: "Everyone's got their job... And as it turns out... I'm good at it." LTM begins to sink from view, followed quickly by Kaze.

sq04 sc66: Med. of LTM being forced to his knees. Kaze kneels on one leg (almost like proposing?).

sq04 sc67: CU of Kaze, muzzle close to LTM's eyes. KAZE: "May your next life be filled with beauty." LTM's eyes suddenly bulge wide and head jerks a little, mouth opens slightly...

sq04 sc68: ~~CU of Kaze's fingers around LTM's throat. Blood wells up from where finger presses into the other's throat.~~

sq04 sc69: CU, cam dollies around behind LTM as Kaze speaks. KAZE: "May the hatred and fear you have chosen to perpetuate end here, with the ending of this life. May those you have caused pain be able to forgive you. May those you have sent 'beyond' be able to live in peace with you in your future lives, free from any anger that would lead you to this path again. May your future lives bring peace, safety, and love to those around you. This is your duty... This is your penance." ...LTM begins to convulse/spasm. ...Kaze reaches up to caress the back of other's head gently, "Easy... Easy... You're safe. You're not alone. I won't leave you." ...Cam pushes in over dialogue to XCU on TM's eyes, wide and staring, making little darting movements to see things only he can see.

sq04 sc70: DISSOLVE TO: Slightly dollying wide shot of Kaze, curved, holding LTM.

sq04 sc71: DISSOLVE TO: High angle *(Enya-like feel to music)* Dutching of same.

sq04 sc72: DISSOLVE TO: CU, behind LTM, slight dolly, Kaze's arm around his head.

sq04 sc73: DISSOLVE TO: Slight dolly, Kaze OTS.

sq04 sc74: DISSOLVE TO: CU, up-shot, Kaze, tears fully on his face. KAZE: "May your next life be a life of beauty." ...Cam tracks Kaze as he leans forward and kisses dead LTM on forehead. LTM's mouth is slightly open, eyes dull. Cam pulls back slowly as LTM is begun to be lowered slowly out of frame.

sq04 sc75: Long shot of Kaze laying LTM back on ground.

sq04 sc76: DISSOLVE TO: Camera booming higher and higher, out of clearing...

FADE OUT

FADE IN:

INT. LORD SOSHI'S PRIVATE CHAMBERS -- NIGHT

sq05 sc01: Dolly shot, table-high. Fire burning in fireplace somewhere... Candles in elaborate holders on polished, dark-wood table. Soshi, back to us, moves slightly... "Mmm-hmmm..."

sq05 sc02: Med. front, 3/4, low-ish-angle, dollying slightly CW, Soshi holds tray of leftovers in RH, in LH, he has gilt serving knife, he uses to flip scraps to captive. SOSHI: "Oh, that's good!" He flips a morsel OSL. He reacts with oily pleasure and surprise, "That's very good!" Another morsel...

sq05 sc03: CU on SOSHI (Baron Harkkonan-ish), "What a good girl you are... " lascivious, Harkkonan beat... 5... "now..." He leans forward.

sq05 sc04: CU on Soshi's eyes as he still moves... that go from half-lidded to wide-ish, then back. Then start to snarl...

sq05 sc05: Low-angle med. (like Darkness when taunted by Lilly) on SOSHI: "No, no..."

sq05 sc06: CU on Soshi's extra-wide scream, "No!!!"

sq05 sc07: Med. shot of mahogany wall, firelight flickering, perhaps shadow of two somewhere... SOSHI: "Don't you flinch!" On flinch, the tray flies in from OSR, hits the wall, dents/cracks it, folds the tray in half, and the camera very quickly over-cranks to super-slo-mo to show tray and contents reacting to impact as SOSHI continues (in surreal, real time): "Don't you ever pull away from me!"

sq05 sc08: CU on Soshi's robes as he slowly pulls a worn and dented "caning" stick. SOSHI: "Don't.... You..."

sq05 sc09: Low-angle med. on Soshi as he raises the cane with extreme threatening over his head, "Ever..."

sq05 sc10: (Kaze's line starts in prev. shot, reverberating and wrapping in this one.) Wide, almost repeat of establisher (Kaze's POV). KAZE: "Lieutenant!"

sq05 sc11: CU Soshi... frozen but eyes darting (like first "client" in "The Professional").

sq05 sc12: Med. wide, dollying over table, as if Kaze is moving as he speaks. KAZE: "I remember you being thinner."

sq05 sc13: Med. Soshi, still frozen with cane raised, looking around without moving body. SOSHI: "Guards, Guards!"

sq05 sc14: Wide, dolly and light pan around the room ("looking" for Kaze). "I'm afraid they can't hear you..."

sq05 sc15: (Kaze's word continues from prev. shot.) Med. CU of Soshi, still frozen but head getting more animated, body/arm shaking a little. KAZE: "...'*Lord*'... Soshi."
...SOSHI: "I know that voice... I know your voice!"

...KAZE (audio panning around surround channels): "You've made me kill again...

...Cam begins slow (but increasing in speed) dolly around Soshi. He finally begins to lower the stick... SOSHI: "But you can't be you..."

...Cam pulls back a bit to show Soshi frightened, brandishing stick like a sword with both hands in front of him. He spins around, making a complete revolution, backing himself up against a wall as first, "You're dead." KAZE: "And you know how I hate that."

...SOSHI: "I saw you die..."

...KAZE: "You know how precious life is to me."

...SOSHI: "But you're dead..."

...KAZE: "Life is a gift..."

...SOSHI: "You're dead..."

...KAZE: "A blessing."

sq05 sc16: Wide shot of Soshi backed up against wall, alone in the firelight. SOSHI: "I watched you die."

sq05 sc17: Med. close (pull-back), CU of Soshi (SR, looking SR). Kaze starts out of frame, starts entering frame just before "you" and is fully in Soshi's face just after "did." (Surround sound of Kaze's line moving to settle SR.) KAZE: "Yes. You did... Didn't you."

...Soshi jerks his head backward, cracking it on the stone of the outer wall. Kaze pulls back, smiling slightly.

sq05 sc18: Med. wide of Kaze walking away from Soshi, completely ignoring the fool grasping his head in pain. Camera follows Kaze, leaving Soshi out-of-frame. KAZE: "The coup has been good to you I see."

sq05 sc19: Med. low-angle of Kaze stopping, looking sadly down OSL. He kneels and camera tracks hand as it gently strokes the silhouette as Kaze begins to deliver his lines.

...SOSHI: "I don't know nuthin' about it. I just take orders and do what they say."
...KAZE: "But you're still up to your old games..."

sq05 sc20: Low-ish angle med. CU on KAZE (sadly, almost to himself): "aren't you... 'Lieutenant.'"

sq05 sc21: Med. CU, side-shot on Soshi who has moved slightly toward girl/Kaze. Shot turns and pulls back slightly to reveal that Kaze is no longer kneeling before the silhouetted girl.
...KAZE (OS): "People are not your playthings, Lieutenant..."
...Kaze's silhouette seems to coalesce out of the shadows behind Soshi but very close to OSR. Kaze: "They are not your toys."

sq05 sc22: Med. CU of Soshi whip-turning SR to find empty air.

sq05 sc23: Kaze opens eyes as he delivers, "Why am I not surprised..." Before then, there is a med. shot that pulls back to a med. wide, Kaze's silhouette blending perfectly with the BG (Iron Giant-like). Soshi rotates toward (and past) cam (CW, away from Kaze), eyes locking on points as he searches for Kaze.
...KAZE: "Keys?"
...SOSHI: "Th... There aren't any"
...KAZE: "Why am I not surprised?"

sq05 sc24: Med. of Kaze stepping forward, out of shadows that silhouette woman. He picks up chain that leads to her with his right hand and winds up to smash it with his left.

sq05 sc25: CU of hand smashing desk to which chain was attached.

sq05 sc26: Med. dollying CU of silhouetted woman (firelight almost romantic), who comes partly into the light as shot progresses. Kaze kneels (gentling, holding out chain end to her): "You won't have any trouble leaving... Though I'm sorry for the mess you'll have to see on your way out. There is an innkeeper not too far from here, about two days walk, in the valley along the north road. Can you make it?"

...Woman nods timidly. She closes her hand over Kaze's and the chain.

sq05 sc27: CU light dolly side-shot on KAZE: "Tell him I sent you... He'll help."

sq05 sc28: Med. of Kaze's back as he rises to full height and turns to Soshi (silhouette woman leaves BG frame). KAZE: "My name... is KAZE."
...2 beats as woman can be heard bare-footing it down the hall.

sq05 sc29: Wide of Kaze on SL (near fireplace) and Soshi on SR, between table and outer wall. SOSHI: "Y-y-y-you killed *everyone?*"
...KAZE: "Only those who needed it."

sq05 sc30: Med. Kaze and Soshi. Kaze turns away, playing his fingers on the polished wood of the table as he speaks. KAZE: "You *know* me, Lieutenant. You were under my command for how many years?"

sq05 sc31: Reverse shot of Kaze, silhouette, walking around table toward SR as cam. dollies SL. Soshi is in full light in mid-BG. KAZE: "You know how much I despise killing." Kaze stops. KAZE: "I'm just good at it."

sq05 sc32: Reverse angle, CU on Kaze. Kaze's face raising from looking at table to look at Soshi and coming into chiaroscuro as he delivers line. KAZE: "You... on the other hand..."
...SOSHI (OS): "What're you gonna do?

sq05 sc33: Med. close-CU on Soshi for his reaction. KAZE: "I think you know the answer to that."
...Beat...
...SOSHI (swallowing hard): "You gonna kill me too, then, is that it?"

sq05 sc34: Med. CU, up-shot on Kaze. 2.5 beats... KAZE: "No." Beat... "Not just yet..." Beat... "I need you to let the others know I'm coming."   (Focus on getting "Harrison Ford" acting into this.)

sq05 sc35:   Med. wide. Kaze silhouetted in FG, walks past cam, Soshi tracks him in and out of frame. Cam. dollies slightly SL. SOSHI: "Like I say, I don't know anything about it! I just get orders and I follow them. That's all!

sq05 sc36:   Med. CU of Kaze, side-shot, chiaroscuro silhouette. Kaze opens eyes and looks slightly toward just off OSL as he finishes his line. KAZE: "That is enough."

sq05 sc37:   Med. of Soshi beginning to gesture boldly as he sees he's going to live. SOSHI: "I ain't afraid of you!"

sq05 sc38:   Med. of Kaze climbing with graceful deliberation onto windowsill. SOSHI: "I ain't afraid of you at all! Come back and fight..."

sq05 sc39:   Med. of Soshi swinging from retrieving sword from somewhere OSL into wobbly "ready," tip of sword trembling noticeably. SOSHI: "...you *coward*!"

sq05 sc40:   Med. side-shot (along wall). Kaze leans back in. KAZE: "I was better than you before I 'died.'"

sq05 sc41:   CU of Kaze, cocking head, "What makes you think you stand a chance now?"

sq05 sc42:   Med. shot along wall, as "Crow-like" (when Crow disappears from fun-boy's window) he gracefully "pours" through window.

sq05 sc43:   Wide, empty room, Soshi near "perfect" 1/3 SL, "ready" facing nothing but empty, open window. SOSHI (roaring) and lowering sword slightly (still shaking): "Damn you, KAZE!!!"

sq05 sc44:   Med. CU as Soshi raises sword, roaring with fury.

sq05 sc45: CU of polished table as sword impacts in, but only goes a *very* short distance into the wood.

sq05 sc46: Med. Soshi leaning shoulder into picking up table. (Second, more violent roar starts.)

sq05 sc47: Med. wide as (with effort) Soshi upends table, candles and all. (Roaring with full fury.)

sq05 sc48: Tracking shot as Soshi screams line (like Soshi is moving with so much fury, camera-operator is trying to track moving target). SOSHI: "Damn you to Hell!"

EXT. WOODS -- CONTINUOUS

sq05 sc49: Kaze, rimmed by moonlight, bamboo in BG, pauses and looks upward. KAZE: "You already have."

FADE OUT.

END: EPISODE 1

Part 2

From Concept to Presentation

"And as water has no constant form, there are in war no constant conditions. Thus, one able to gain the victory by modifying his tactics in accordance with the enemy situation may be said to be divine."

— Sun Tzu, *The Art of War*

There are four kinds of people I can imagine being interested in this "travelogue" section of the book: accomplished filmmakers, specialized artists already within the industry, people who are not yet in the industry, and people who simply enjoy learning as a hobby.

For the accomplished filmmakers, I imagine you are looking for new angles, new takes on "age-old" problems and solutions. Since my own tradition is that of non-tradition, I hope this section is an "idea farm" for moving from live action into CGI. This is also a gallery of my own ways of finding the most expeditious and enjoyable path between the points of filmmaking.

For those artists already specializing in certain areas of the industry, it is a common thread to be very, very good at that one thing you do. While you have some experience in other aspects outside your area(s) of expertise, they tend to seem mysterious (or at least not as "comfortable" as the area you know you can work

wonders within). This section of the book will hopefully serve as a map for you to see how all the pieces and parts connect with one another. Hopefully, it will lift the shroud of mystery so you can say to yourself, "Hey! I can do that too!"

For those dreaming of making their own films, but without practical industry experience, this section is like a trail map, letting you know about the terrain you will likely experience. However, as with any challenging undertaking, if the map shows that you'll be climbing the side of a mountain and you don't *already* know how to correctly use pitons, crampons, and other climbing gear, you should *learn these things first before setting out!* (I point out what I feel to be the best resources, but *the responsibility of learning these skills lies exactly where it needs to — with you!*)

For those with a fascination for finding out, it is my aim that this section is conversational, with enough explanation of industry terms for you to enjoy following the journey.

So, if I've done my job well, for the experienced this will be a resource of the unique and different ways of fitting the jobs of hundreds of people into an "itty-bitty living space." For those simply interested in seeing the path that brought Kaze to the screen, I hope this is an interesting and enjoyable travelogue of a journey that, on so many levels, was totally out of this world!

Chapter 7

Filmmaking: The Union of All Arts

We succeed not in spite of the risks we take, but because of them.

All forms of filmmaking represent the union of nearly every practice and field of study on the face of this planet. From astrophysics to animal husbandry, films have incorporated knowledge and experience from every facet of human existence.

All arts — music, dance, painting, poetry, writing, spirituality, martial (and all the rest) — find themselves integral to the filmmaking process. All crafts and skills that have survived to this day (and even some that haven't) are also called upon to participate in the creation of cinema.

Putting these elements together in a way that captivates audiences is very much an art in and of itself. Even managing the mind-boggling sums of money dedicated to today's "blockbuster" productions is an art!

But let me let you in on a little secret. Let me break apart the myth and mystery surrounding "art." For all the fantastic things that all arts are capable of, at its core, art is but one thing — something of which we all are capable. *The essence of art is problem solving.*

The Essence of Art

What is art? Well, there are many angles to this debate that have lasted for thousands of years and will most likely last for thousands more. Art is emotion, passion, spirit. But these are all ethereal concepts, which are hard to pin down and put into words to which others can really relate. Is art the material upon which it takes its form, or is it the connection between the symbol and the viewer? (Like the number of licks it takes to get to the Tootsie Roll center of a Tootsie Pop, the world may never know.)

However, there is most definitely one clear-cut thing about art that can be proven. That is that the creation of art, no matter the form, is an act of problem solving.

A painter approaches a canvas, knowing the image he would like to produce; the path from empty gesso to that last coat of Damar varnish is a connected series of one-step-at-a-time problems to be solved.

A musician sits to play a Mendelssohn concerto; each note she plays is a combination of solved problems as to note frequency, length, volume, pressure, etc.

What "scares" most people away from thinking they are artists (and it has been my experience that *we are all artists* when given the chance to explore) is that the act of creating something "artistic" is the practice of *approaching situations where there are no "clear-cut" answers*. Unless art is for a client or a class, the artist alone must take responsibility for knowing what is "right" and how to achieve that result.

The artist must stride confidently into this sea of uncertainty. Even a single timid or uncertain stroke, note, or movement will weaken the overall strength of the finished piece.

NOTE

> A *craftsman's* strength is within his *skills*. An *artist's* strength is within his *faith*.

I once heard it said that in the average work of art, the artist confronts about 10,000 situations that could completely alter the preconceived notion he has for the work. (I hesitate to say "ruin" because an artwork is usually only "ruined" when the artist stops working on it before it is complete. Quite often, an unexpected mark or note leads to more powerful results than originally envisioned when the unexpected is worked *with* and not against.)

Art is learning to approach those kinds of "odds" with excitement and expectation! It is saying, "I'm not 100 percent sure how I'll do this…" and loving every moment of the journey (well, most of the moments, anyway). It is the same spirit at the core of every adventure story ever told. It happens in every single work of art, from the simplest sketch to the most tightly rendered masterpiece.

Art teaches one to think for one's self. It is the actual practice of being confident that one is capable of finding one's own answers. It is the essence of adaptability. It is the life focus of knowing through experience that *the unknown* is but a path to something far more amazing than any human can imagine.

Because of this, it is such a tragedy that art is among the first to go when schools need to cut corners. This results in countless people who are more comfortable with someone else thinking for them than they are with thinking for themselves. It creates multitudes of people who become rigid, frightened, and lost when they find that two plus two doesn't *always* equal four.

The greatest leaps in every single field are achieved by individuals whose art is that field of study itself! Max Planck, Albert Einstein, and Nikola Tesla were all *artists*, and their media was that of mathematics, physics, and the building blocks of understanding the very nature of "reality" itself!

Like science, art requires that a base of understanding and technique be achieved before the artist can really cut loose and turn his fantastic explorations of the theoretical into exhilarating masterpieces. Through the same rigors of empiricism, problem solving, and exploration, the artist's theory becomes his completed proof.

When almost any kind of artist really gets going, they lose all sense of time, often with hours passing without their even noticing. (Ask any programmer you know if this has ever happened to him — for the best programmers, the answer will invariably be yes.)

When an artist practices his art, he becomes almost an outside observer to the creation process, as amazed as anyone else at the work being created *through* him. An artist's basic training lets him go on autopilot, his subconscious solving the constant string of "simpler" problems while his conscious mind guides the process, swept away in the exhilaration of solving even greater problems!

Filmmaking, an art form itself, touches and employs nearly every other form of art and science and craft known to man — music, painting, dance, writing, logistics, physics, chemistry, programming, carpentry, architecture, management, anthropology. The list goes on and on. All of these play crucial roles in the incredible amalgamation that is cinema.

3D CGI: Infinite Resources "In a Can"

3D CGI is a double-edged sword. On the good side, you have the ability for a single person to do the work that would normally require hundreds or thousands of highly skilled, highly trained individuals to do the same within the parameters of a "practical" ("real-world") production. On the bad side, you have the ability for a single person to do the work that would normally require hundreds or thousands of highly skilled, highly trained individuals to do the same within the parameters of a "practical" ("real-world") production.

The effect this will have on filmmaking as we know it cannot help but be profound. There will always be practical filmmaking, with live actors and sets, but as CGI enables smaller and smaller groups of people to achieve higher and higher levels of quality for less and less money, I can see the majority of filmmaking being done increasingly through CGI.

With 3D software, you don't need the teams of carpenters, electricians, makeup artists, etc., that are needed on even the most meager of live-action feature films (to say nothing of the veritable armies it takes to produce masterworks like *Blade Runner, Gladiator,* or *Lord of the Rings*). Through CGI, one single person can build all the sets, without the need for extensive sound-stage rental, scouting, or location permits. One person can create all the costumes, even if that person has never sewn a stitch in his life. One person can even deliver all the performances!

With the resources available and within reach of most people, there are no sets too vast, no armies too numerous, no detail too fine for CG to reproduce. All it takes is time, knowledge, and dedication.

But even though one person *can* do all this (and did, as in the case of *Ghost Warrior*) using CGI, a one-man show is quite an undertaking. One must be proficient at a vastly diverse set of skills

(or at least know how and where to study to gain the needed proficiency).

Doing a one-man show also requires that you be your own "creative fire." Creating in a vacuum can often be like burning a candle in a sealed container. All people, artists especially, *need* a constant influx of outside ideas and interpersonal contact.

When artists who just "click" with one another get together, the sum total of what they can produce is exponentially greater than what they could do individually. Ideas bounce around from artist to artist, refining themselves at the speed of thought. Even simply drawing with another artist present and working in close proximity can result in creative insights that would never have appeared while working alone.

But regardless of whether you are part of a small, tightly knit team or the only one that you can depend on, *Ghost Warrior* is living proof that no matter how small the team, feature-quality filmmaking is within the reach of every dedicated individual, regardless of geographic location!

If you wish to create a film, regardless of where you are, you have the ability to do so! Filmmaking, like all art, can be reduced to a simple matter of problem solving. Problem solving itself can be reduced to two even simpler issues: knowing what it is that needs doing, and knowing how to get done what you need to get done.

If you know what needs to be done, know how to get that done, and *follow through* on getting it done, you can accomplish anything, no matter how grand or idealistic the goal! It may take a while, but if you do at least something toward your goal each and every day, it will eventually become a reality (barring, of course, the catastrophic or simple *choice* to no longer pursue that goal).

Even if your resources are limited, you have antiquated equipment, and can only afford freeware or shareware programs, CGI filmmaking is still 100 percent within your reach. You don't have to start out with a "cast of thousands." You can start very simply, focusing on *storytelling*, leaving *spectacle* for later when your films have begun to pay for themselves. (Everyone knows what a success *South Park* is, relying entirely upon the prowess of its writing!)

"You can unlock any door if you only have the key."
— Mrs. Brisby, *The Secret of NIMH*

A $700 "best-buy special" desktop PC system today is astronomically more powerful than the SGI that I used on *Dinosaur*! The code optimizations in both hardware and software, the "shortcuts" that intimate things that are too complex to be reasonably rendered, have left me absolutely in awe. The quality of an hour's worth of doodling with LightWave and Digital Fusion yields renders the likes of which I never would have thought possible even from a Cray array a few short years ago. Yet, the beauty of today's renders are what I had dreamed of when I was a child!

Advancements in both hardware and software algorithms have made industry-state-of-the-art feature film quality possible from a single, consumer-end desktop workstation. This encompasses *both* the ability to do the work and the ability to have the work rendered and finaled (all the extra stuff that needs doing in order to get the look to *exactly* match what the artist has in mind — more on this later) in a "production-friendly" amount of time (about six months for a short film, between 18 months and three years for a feature film).

NOTE

I've heard it said that the sum total of scientific knowledge has *doubled* over the last *two years*.

Here is where the excitement begins to build; almost any skilled 3D artist reading this book is probably saying to themselves, "Well, if I had that much time, you bet I could do that!" The trick is to be able to have the six dedicated months to do your short film or the dedicated 18 months to three years to make your feature film a reality.

* * *

The first really "workable" 3D software I personally owned was Imagine, which was included with the $7 purchase of a European Amiga magazine. (My actual first 3D software was manually typed-in hex code from *Rainbow Magazine* for the old TRS-80 color computer back in 1982, but I'm not counting that.) I slowly worked a few gigs, saving money until a friend and I could go in "halfsies" on LightWave when it was first released for the PC.

Together, my friend and I worked gigs on his PC until we could afford a newer, faster "company" PC. Gig led to gig, allowing for the purchase of more software and hardware, never going into debt while growing our little enterprise.

Thinking that in order to work production you need the "biggest," "best," and "fastest" in hardware and software is an outright falsehood. The freeware and shareware software for all applications is phenomenally better than what professionals were doing high-end production on back in the early days. You may not be able to do *Lord of the Rings* on POV Ray — but then again, with the right force of creativity, maybe you could! However, if you know what you *can* do and do that well, you can still do great-*looking* work (and also find clients and jobs that can pay for your upgrades).

As far as machinery goes, even the slowest in-use laptop would mop the floor with the screaming 40 Mhz, Motorola 040 (with the cavernous 8 MB of RAM on an insanely huge 1 GB HD) that I used to render my first fully CG short film on! (It took a month just to render those seven minutes, but back then, that was what was expected, so I didn't complain.) My old 366 Pentium II laptop was about five times faster (doing high-poly, full-character animation using LightWave) than the R10K running Maya and Softimage that I was using to animate on *Dinosaur*. (I wrote *LightWave 3D Character Animation* to have *all* characters, practice scenes, and lessons yield 24 frames-per-second real-time updates on that little ol' 366 laptop.)

Knowing the capabilities of your hardware and software, working comfortably within those "limitations," and *having the skills required to "fake" excursions beyond those bounds* is the key to feature quality work on a microscopic budget!

Changing the Face of Filmmaking

Most of the people I have worked with, including myself, over the course of various other productions, were working to save up enough money to go off on their own with a small team and work on their own film ideas. The problem is that no matter how hard one worked and how much one seemed to make, the money just didn't seem to accumulate.

Our own world is very much like *The Matrix* in the sense that for the dedicated mind/body, almost anything is possible. *If you truly want to make something happen, you can simply make it happen*. You can rewrite the rules of your own "Kobayshi Maru." When you do, when you can influence the system itself, you can make it easier for those who also wish to free their minds.

My own "system rewrite" was in the form of packing up my skills and experience and moving to Alaska. I have pared the sum total of my monthly expenses down to less than $1,000 so I can focus entirely on what I feel to be my truly important work. This is in part exploring ways to pass on what I have learned so the creation and sharing of similar dreams can be done by everyone who dreams of doing so.

Once this path has been proven, once it has become a commonly accepted fact that small teams of filmmakers are a *viable* way to produce CGI films, the establishing of a network of funding and distribution for similarly made films can enable any dedicated artist or group to also have the ability to focus on making their own films a reality.

Without the traditionally accepted overhead of filmmaking, films could begin turning a profit their first weekend out! (This is great news for people who have the ability to fund such filmmaking.) Even a film directed at a highly selective audience could easily be immensely profitable when produced by a small core of people whose focus is doing what is best for the film itself. (This is great news for the people who have the ability to make such films!)

This simple, quiet, pragmatic shift has the possibility of being one of the most profound changes in filmmaking since the evolution of the studio.

Because traditional filmmaking is so costly, studios *need* to turn a profit on what they make. In short, this has the same result of a person trying to be liked by everyone. It's like someone trying too hard to be funny.

Films that should have been great, such as *Dark City*, were garroted by producers who (due to feedback at screenings with audiences far below the intellectual level of the film's actual target audience) have *destroyed* works of art. ("Like… I don't get it," the living Barbie-doll from the screening audience said.) So, pabulumatic narration is inserted, spilling the film's punch line before it has even begun. ("Like… I was totally bored.") So the original, hypnotic, elegant, graceful pacing and rhythm were mangled into MTV quick-cuts. The result is the utter destruction of a film in the vain hopes of reaching an audience *for which the film was never intended!*

> NOTE
>
> Even the smallest falsehood or affectation within a work of art will lodge like a splinter within the soul of the viewer.

"Dumbing down" a story in any way will always be unsuccessful because the story will *still* be over the heads of those for whom it was never intended! Even worse, in the lobotomic process, the film will then have become too imbecilic for its intended audience and will have lost *them* as well!

The truly successful films are the ones that were made because the makers have always wanted to see that specific film (and often, like in the case of Peter Jackson's *Lord of the Rings*, got tired of waiting for someone else to make it). When a work of art is *exactly* as the artist wishes it to be, it will *always* connect deeply and powerfully with some and glide right over the heads of others. *This is the natural way of art!*

My goal throughout this book (and through the creation of *Ghost Warrior*) is not only to show pathways for making your own film but, in so doing, *proving* the viability of this new model of filmmaking.

An investor with $4 million in a $200 million film loses money unless that film makes $200 million. That same $4 million funding a CGI film of this nature returns a profit after the film makes $4 million!

> NOTE
>
> *Ghost Warrior* was made for $5,000. Just think what could be done with $5 million.

> NOTE
>
> Even short films can be viable at the local cineplex! Packaging short films of similar genre and quality can give audiences two hours of great storytelling from several completely different perspectives. (Imagine paying your eight bucks and knowing you've got four or five great stories ahead of you in a genre you love!)

The possibilities are limitless when taking a step outside of mainstream thought and looking at what potential *already exists* all around us! The wish of seeing your own dreams come to life is a valid one, one that is within your grasp. Even if you're hundreds or thousands of miles into the middle of "nowhere," you can take heart in the fact that *Kaze, Ghost Warrior* was made by one person in a small, one-room cabin without running water or indoor plumbing on the very edge of the Alaskan frontier.

> NOTE
>
> Everything is possible when you know where you would like to be and what you can do to get there from where you are now.

This book is a journal. It is a recounting of the actual process that resulted in the film *Ghost Warrior*. This book details my current practices of the *ever-evolving* processes that have worked for me in productions I have overseen.

This book represents only one way of working. It is a documentation of what worked for me during *Ghost Warrior*'s creation. Keep only what connects with your sensibilities, and let the rest filter to the winds.

In my pursuit of getting done what I need to get done quickly and correctly so I can go do other things, I have sought the clearest, most successful way within everything I do. I am not interested in "style points." I am only interested in the tools and techniques that *successfully* bring me closer to my goal in as quick and enjoyable a way as possible (so long as they fit within my own personal code of honor).

I may be using a tool in a way in which it was never intended to be used, but if it gives me the result I need, that's all that matters. In not simply accepting the "answers" I have been given (from software or plug-ins), I have found optimizations that have cut render times by a factor of *ten* for rendering characters' fur! By bringing together seemingly unrelated plug-ins and manually creating the functionality I thought should exist, proofs-of-concept were provided to the software's creators, hopefully to be included in future releases!

The end result of this kind of mind-set is *simplicity*, *speed*, and a way of working that is *focused toward producing a completed product* (working with the intent of success). Even people who have never thought of themselves as filmmakers have said, "Well, heck! If you put it that way, even I could do that!"

NOTE

> Learn as much as you can about as many things as you can. When you do, your world becomes an infinite playground of possibilities. Don't worry about knowing *everything*. Just know how and where to look for the answers!

I believe that there are hundreds, if not *thousands*, of Walt Disneys, Hayao Miyazakis, and Peter Jacksons out there. You may be one of them! But how can you grow to your full potential unless you believe that you can?

It is my hope that through this and the other books I've written (and will write) you'll be able to see that your dreams *can* come true. CGI filmmaking *is* a possibility that is entirely within reason for you to pursue!

* * *

There are people born every minute who can change this world for the better in ways we can't even imagine. Because of well-meaning friends, parents, and teachers urging them to "be realistic," many people with genius potential end up slipping through the cracks. (It has been my observation that genius is more a matter of *choice* than it is a matter of *chance*.)

I grew up in a small Michigan farming community of less than 1,200 people. The town was a mile square and had one traffic light that was a "blinker" most of the time. I am thankful that I had a family that supported my "way-out" dreams of one day animating a Disney feature. They helped me stay strong in my vision while "friends" derided me for thinking I could actually make those dreams come true.

I made it happen. Through little more than what could easily be called stubbornness, I learned the skills and eventually found myself animating within the mighty structure that was Walt Disney Feature Animation. What I've done since then has been even more rewarding.

I have accomplished much of what I have done because of adherence to the belief that while we are all uniquely individual, all humans have essentially the same biomechanical makeup. What differentiates us as individuals is what we choose to allow into our heads. Any set of skills can be imprinted within the physical synaptic memory structures of the human mind. The hands, feet, and whatever else that is driven by these imprinted skills are for the most part physically the same.

> "The ability to draw is not born into an artist. The desire to draw is."
>
> — Richard Schmid, *Alla Prima, Everything I Know About Painting*

NOTE

Among artists of similar technical skill, the most precious thing is the artist's own personal point of view.

NOTE

All it took was the chance happening of Peter Jackson recognizing the potential within a young film student, Orlando Bloom. His performance in both *Lord of the Rings* and *The Pirates of the Caribbean* has clearly shown him to be one of the world's most promising young actors.

A lot of "threads of probability" need to come together correctly in order for someone else to recognize what you are capable of and honorably make mutual beneficial use of it. The chances of your dreams coming true are increased dramatically when *one takes things into one's own hands.*

> "I got tired of waiting, so I saved myself."
>
> — Anna Baragli, *Hudson Hawk*

If you feel the *dream* of filmmaking burning within you, *you can make it happen!* You know what I'm talking about — that exhilaration, that, "Oh my God! I've *got* to do that some day," when you see a movie that really touches you. You can make it happen! A little secret I'll share with you is that from the *beginning* of the path, there is no way anyone can imagine the incredible vistas that exist when you're actually *on* the *path itself!* (You think you get turned on by a good film now? The more you learn, the more powerful and positive the impact of experiencing another's resounding success is upon your own inner fire!)

NOTE

Jealousy is the domain of the weak. Those who are comfortable within their own abilities are not threatened by others' successes.

Whether you're just now beginning your journey or you're already an accomplished artist working on another's dreams of filmmaking, the power to make your own films is within your hands. It is but a simple decision to claim that power as your own, begin the journey, and focus whatever time and abilities you can into the making of your own films — the fulfillment of your own dreams.

The Journey

This book is a journal, a travelogue, a documentary of the process of making *Ghost Warrior*. It is a *trail guide* that you can use to think ahead in the planning of your own film, plotting paths around pitfalls, flagging trouble areas, and, in general, making educated decisions about how to solve the problems you may encounter on your own path.

In making your own film, you need certain things, like the preparations you'd make for taking a long road trip. You or your trustworthy companion(s) need, at the very least, skills in the 3D and compositing programs that you have selected to use for the course of your production, animation skills, an understanding of acting and performance, and a solid grasp of good ol' project management.

> ## NOTE
>
> The *specifics* of CGI filmmaking will change with every project. The *underlying thought processes* will largely remain the same.

If your chosen 3D program is LightWave, my two previous books can prove invaluable to your path. I wrote them in part because there was no single source available to attain the skills required for producing feature-quality work when I was learning LightWave. I also wrote them because even today, I still feel the existing resources are inadequate for truly explaining the actual practice of achieving the results we see in the finest feature films of today. Lastly, I wrote these books because I need textbooks to teach those who work for me how to do what I do (plain and simple, they are the way I achieve what I do — quickly, easily, and with a heck of a lot of fun along the way).

Essential LightWave 3D (from Wordware Publishing) takes you from square one and teaches you techniques that are commonly associated with the skill sets of people with five to eight years of actual studio production experience. (From comments I've heard from other experienced LightWave artists, quite possibly more.) From understanding and customizing the interface itself and facial modeling to multilayer procedural surfacing, lighting, animation basics, and simulations, this book has illustrations for almost every step, so success in even the most complex LightWave techniques is almost a no-brainer!

LightWave 3D Character Animation (also from Wordware Publishing) gives you the tools and training that you need to actually become a feature-quality animator. (It's quite simple: Do the exercises to the best of your ability, and you will see yourself producing feature-quality animations by the time you've finished all the lessons.) *LightWave 3D Character Animation* is a proven combination of techniques that I developed while running two animation studios (and had to have new hires capable of feature-quality animation in very short order). Even if you're working on another platform, the book will still be of immeasurable use. (I've had other animators from Disney Feature Animation comment that it is the best book on animation — CG, traditional, or otherwise.) The techniques of feature-quality character animation are the same *regardless of medium or software package*.

You also need a clear vision of what it is you are wanting to create. We'll get into story and storytelling in the next chapter, but know that almost every *successful* artistic endeavor begins with a clear vision of what it is going to be before the project starts. Even if the vision evolves as the project is nurtured, clarity in vision will increase the confidence in yourself and the "brush strokes" your audience will eventually see on-screen.

Problem-solving ability will forever be one of your greatest assets along this path. You may not know exactly how to get to that point over the horizon, but if you can get to Point B from where you are and then to Point C using what you've learned in the process, the horizon gets a little closer. All you need to do is continue this process to achieve any goal that you set for yourself.

Above all else, you need to believe that you are right in your belief that *you can, you should*, and *you have every right* to be a CGI filmmaker. There is a subtle shift that happens when you give yourself permission to do what has always been within your ability.

Through the pages of this book, you should be able to realize that there is nothing within this process of filmmaking that alone is not within your ability to *learn, understand*, and *do*. You should be able to see that the stringing together of each one of these pieces into the creation of your own film is also a goal that exists completely within your reach.

Armed with the ability, dedication, and knowledge of how to find the answers you seek, every *goal*, every *dream*, every *wish* is yours to transform into reality!

$$Self = (Thoughts + Dreams)^{Actions}$$

Chapter 8

Ideation

A great film begins very simply. It begins with an idea.

What you do at the start of a film determines the entire course of the production of the film. As mentioned in the previous chapter, the journey before the *average* short film is one of about six months. If you are planning an animated *feature film*, you can expect to spend between eighteen months and three years working on bringing it to reality. It's a significant journey that begins simply with the thought, "Hey, I've always wanted to see a movie like that!"

That's a lot of time to focus on any one thing. Why spend that amount of your *life* focusing on something that you are not absolutely in love with?

The Idea

Maybe you're driving along, listening to some good tunes and — wham! — something from out of the blue hits you, and you think to yourself, "Hey, that'd make a great movie!" Maybe you're hiking in the mountains, or standing in the shower, or melting pleasantly in a hot tub; wherever you are when it strikes, you know for certain when those great ideas do hit.

We all have them — those "power ideas" that are at the core of all genius. One of the differences between people labeled as "genius" and the "normal" crowd is that the genius folks *remember* these ideas. When they come, jot them down *right away!* ("Oh, I'll get to it later..." and "later" never comes. Or, when you do get around to jotting them down, they've become diffused, like trying to remember a dream you had from several nights ago.)

With the practice of remembering to write these ideas down the moment they come to you, like remembering your dreams by writing them down first thing upon waking, they will begin to stick with you longer and longer. Wherever you go, you have got to be prepared to put these ideas into some form that can jog your memory later when you have time to more fully explore them. Maybe it's in the form of a sketch, a few words, or the way you touch two of your fingers together (the only way I could remember things for school). Whatever it is, you've got to do it the moment the idea comes to you so that when you come back to it, so does the flood of ideas around the "main idea" that you may not have noticed at the time. The little details are preserved when the synaptic connections were made very near to the moment of ideation itself.

You know when a good idea comes to you. You also know the places and times when you get your very best ideas.

Many get their best ideas while driving. Some get them while doing housework or cooking. Usually the best ideas stop in for a visit when your mind and body are occupied with something repetitive, like driving, gardening, hiking, or mushing. The best ideas usually come at the times when our "presentation self" is fully engaged in the act of doing something "mindful."

Me? I get my best ideas when I'm out and about. It doesn't matter if I'm driving, mushing, hiking, or just walking to get the mail. If I'm outside and my body is engaged in something repetitive and my mind can wander, I know I can expect to be presented with several good ideas that I should pay attention to.

I've got an old (in computer age) Compaq iPAQ that I use to record voice notes when I'm out and an idea appears. I just flip open the case, press a button, and start talking, never having to take my eyes off where they need to be.

Later on, when I can type, I pick up a foldable keyboard for the iPAQ and transcribe the audio notes into readable notes that I can print and tack around my workspace. More often than not, the recorded voice notes themselves serve as "pointers" for me to get back into the same mindspace that I was in when the original idea hit. Once I'm able to access that same mindspace, I let my fingers fly over the keyboard with the things that pointer brings to mind.

As you're gathering ideas, don't worry about judging them. This isn't the time for that. The ideation phase is simply for *collecting* ideas! Store everything that comes to mind about your story. You never know when an idea that you let slip by could be a pivotal point that you will be looking for when you settle into the actual process of writing!

NOTE

My practice of writing comes in two distinct parts. I apply this technique to everything from rough notes to the real writing of manuscripts and screenplays.

The first phase is known as "free-write." I just type everything that comes into my head. No thought slips by untyped (even if that thought is "I can't think of anything to type"). I just let everything pour out of me, the good and the bad alike, not judging or stopping to correct or annotate.

Later, once all the ideas are there on the page, I go back and make sure things make sense. I clean up whatever needs cleaning up, expound on what needs explanation, and remove anything that does not forward the main point of the story or script. These two parts together give me my first draft.

I like working this way because the writing I do is much more conversational, more *accessible* than if I were to try to get things right, right from the start. It also opens the floodgates to my creativity; things just pour out onto the page at times like that — things I might not have thought of otherwise. This is where the real magic happens.

NOTE

While ideas come to us, don't make the mistake of believing that they come *only* to us. Like the idea for the radio, the internal combustion engine, or the lightbulb, good ideas make themselves known to all who will listen and *remember*. There's *always* enough to go around!

If your plate is full of cool things you're working on and an idea comes your way, don't hesitate to pass it on to someone who might be looking for something good on which to work. The great thing about us all having unique ways of looking at and experiencing this world is that no two people's take on the same idea will ever be alike! Even if you do decide years down the road to take up that idea you had previously passed along, you will still have a unique and viable point of view that will be just as important to share with viewers (perhaps even more so because of the life experience you've stored up between the ideation and creation).

Because ideas come to so many people at the same "local" time, don't get all pouty if you hear that someone else may have an idea that's close to yours! Don't spend a moment's worry that your ex-best friend's second cousin may have mentioned "your" idea to someone who knows "Mr. Big." That kind of thinking just puts a lid on the candle in the jar that is creativity itself.

However, that being said, it is usually a grand idea to register your drafts with the Writer's Guild of America and your finished product with the Library of Congress, just in case.

The ideas for Kaze and *Ghost Warrior* came, for me, through a series of almost spiritual experiences spread over nearly a ten-year span. From dreams and visions I still remember as vividly as if I had lived them myself to inexplicable experiences in daily life, I slowly got the hint that my own work lay along that story's path.

I began writing ideas down whenever they came. I started fiddling in 3D with models and technical issues. Before I knew it, the stories for Kaze were beginning to gather real strength.

The script for the film practically wrote itself, the characters telling me what they were doing and me racing like a court stenographer trying to keep up with them.

During the just over 3,000-mile drive from Los Angeles to Fairbanks, as the roads wound unendingly ahead of me and my dog Jo, the story for *Ghost Warrior* began to play itself out before my eyes. The final script for *Ghost Warrior* sticks very closely to what I *saw* as I wove northward through the Yukon.

Good Idea/Bad Idea

How do you tell if an idea is a good one or a bad one?

Figure out how much time it would take to make that idea happen. If you're willing to spend that amount of your life and feel it would be well spent, that's a good sign that you're dealing with a good idea.

If you have an idea that you can live intimately with for six months, you know you can make a short film with it. If you feel you can be in close quarters with the idea for 18 months to three years and still feel good about it, you know you've got something worthy of being a feature. (If you feel you could still respect both the idea and yourself through nine or more years of dedicating your life to it, you've either got an epic idea or you need to get out more often.)

Another fantastic test of an idea's validity is to record yourself talking about it. (I know it sounds campy, but try it.) When you hear your own voice talking in depth about something, if you still feel good about being associated with it afterward, you know the idea is probably a good one.

The ultimate test that I use to ascertain whether an idea is good or not is to *imagine* the honest reaction I'd get in telling it to a trusted friend (one who will "tell it like it is"). If you wouldn't feel the least bit self-conscious or embarrassed (these are the flags of bad ideas) in telling them, a coworker, or an industry icon, you know you've got something worth dedicating yourself to.

"Hollywooding"

Now, the reason in the above litmus tests that I say *imagine* telling one of the aforementioned people is that, sadly, a lot of stealing does actually go on in the industry. I call this "Hollywooding."

Stealing a concept, changing it just enough to make it past the Writer's Guild's lawyers if a suit is brought, and running like hell to get the story to the screen before the originator can is common-place in "the city of a million lies." It is a simple fact of the current state of the industry's lack of confidence in itself.

You can do what you can to protect yourself. You can do a "poor-man's copyright" by mailing a copy of your concept or script to yourself via registered mail and leaving it unopened in a file cabi-net (which I've heard doesn't hold up in court). You can register with the Writer's Guild of America or even get a full-fledged copy-right from the Library of Congress. But the best way to protect yourself is abstinence, or basically keeping your mouth shut until you're far enough along that no one could possibly "catch up."

NOTE

> I look at things this way: You are allocated a certain amount of energy to any concept. You may expend that energy either by *doing* it or by talking about it.

However, if you find your idea has indeed been ripped off by some-one else (not simply the result of an idea manifesting to multiple people at the same relative time), after the initial 30 seconds of ranting, *don't worry about it!* Why? Because *the idea came to you*, not them! Anyone working from a stolen idea is making a cheap knockoff of something they've only had a glimpse of. There is no way anyone can possibly make *your* story to the degree of richness, truth, and quality that you can!

Which means, if you ever feel the urge to rip off someone else's idea, don't even bother. There is no way that you can take someone else's idea, duplicate it, and come out on top. (This is similar to almost every film from a book or book from a film being substan-dard to the story in its original medium; the original medium is where the original idea "lives.")

Now, this isn't to say that someone else's film won't strike a chord within you so strongly that you feel compelled to "exist" for a production within a similar but unique world. If you find this hap-pening, do everything you can to remove yourself from any influence of the other work. *Find your own truths about your own existence within a world of that kind.*

Be honest with yourself; don't do something if the reason for wanting to do it is a "me too" or "Sword movies are big — I've got to do a sword movie to be cool too" kind of thing.

This is the other aspect of what I call "Hollywooding" — doing something that you think will sell.

Audiences are far more intelligent, far more perceptive than Hollywood gives them credit for. They know when they're being pandered to. They know when director was not in love with a film's idea, story, characters, and production.

The phrase "give the people what they want" has resulted in a downward spiral in story, writing, and filmmaking quality in general of proportions almost beyond imagination. Yes, we must be wary of becoming so rarified that we are "entertainers entertaining enter-tainers," but to do something you don't believe in simply because you think it will make you successful is a mistake that will be seen almost instantly by every audience!

There have been many animated films, especially recently, that died horrible deaths from audience nonchalance because the mantra of the filmmakers in charge was, "Oh, the kids are going to love this," not, "Oh, *I* am going to love this!"

This goes back to the whole idea of having a good idea to start with. Your idea must be something that you are *in love with*. This is a *marriage* between yourself and this idea, and the child that results from that union is the film itself.

So don't bother about what other people are making or what seems popular, hip, or "now." Don't follow the crowd. Don't follow any impetus other than the strongest desire within you to watch a particular story that you have always wanted to see.

Idea Tips

Write about what you know and be bleedingly specific. The things that we try most to keep hidden are often the things that are the most common to us all. As artists, we lay our souls bare — secretly, our audiences nod their heads and say, "yeah, I've been there."

The most powerful stories are the ones where the audience can say, "God yes, I've felt like that, but I've never told anyone about feeling that way!"

"The secret to the creative life is to feel at ease with your own embarrassment."

— Paul Schroder

Now this doesn't mean that you simply write about *exactly* what has happened in your life. You write about specific emotions and events but within a framework of an interesting string of events that supports them.

In many ways, Kaze's journey is connected with his feelings of responsibility for Bay's death. Through a series of foolish decisions, I was not there for my soulmate when he needed me most. Though I know I am not responsible for his death, I feel that had I been there, I could have helped to prevent his leaving this world.

Is Kaze's story an act of atonement? Is it therapy? In the end, the whys and wherefores don't matter. All that matters is that it is a story that is deeply engrossing, highly emotional, and something that I believe in to the core of my being. I know how Kaze feels in a way that words can never describe (but perhaps animation can). His story is, in a way, my story. All it took was a decision to transfer those very personal feelings and experiences into a form that can be shared with others.

"Every great book is about a choice."

— Azar Nafisi

Wondering if we've made the right decision is a great part of the human condition. When we have no choice in a matter, we can easily stride boldly forward. *It is when we are presented with choices that the deepest struggles exist within u*s. When characters that an audience connects with are presented with choices that they, themselves, can relate to (on any number of levels), the audience develops an emotional investment in both the characters and the outcome. The audience begins to *care*. When the audience *cares* about the characters and what happens to them, they too are *inside* the story.

As filmmakers, we've got to find believable ways of *showing* the struggle within the characters as they try to make the *right* choices. Kaze, seeing the image of his lost love within Itsua's shrine, struggles for balance of the overwhelming emotions welling up within him and the maintaining of his "public," outward calm. Each and every one of us has known times like this.

Kaze has his "hot spots" and "push buttons," as we all do. He knows what should be done, and he knows that sometimes his rage gets the better of him (like when the irresponsibility of the chain weapon troublemaker almost kills a bystander).

Kaze is no two-dimensional hero. Kaze battles with decisions and the repercussions of those decisions on a constant basis. His world extends far beyond the boundaries of the screen. His life *before* what is shown in *Ghost Warrior* has brought him to the place where the audience first finds him, tracking his quarry. It is easy to see that he continues on, doing the best he can, long after the end credits roll.

Through the believable portrayal of common struggles, within an environment that clearly extends "off the page," the audience is able to completely forget that it is watching what is, in strictly mechanical terms, a digital marionette. Kaze becomes *real* for them. Through story, acting, and animation, he becomes as real to the audience as he is real to me.

NOTE

> The tellers of successful tales find that their role is one of *biographer* more than of *creator*.

Left Field

Connection with the audience and their experiences is important but *never* be afraid to have elements that go over the heads of your audience.

Not every line needs to be clearly heard (see Chapter 10, "Screenwriting"). Not every concept needs to be completely accessible. Not everything in life is clearly heard (or *meant* to be clearly heard). Not everything in life is understood (or *meant* to be understood). This helps the work expand *beyond the edges of the screen*.

The relationship between Kaze and Bay is never explained in the film. The audience only knows that there must be something very deep between them and that Kaze feels sad and responsible for something relating to Bay's death. This, in part, says to the audience that I trust their ability to figure things out for themselves. (In short, I don't consider them to be imbeciles.) It also draws viewers deeper into the story, letting them put together the hints gleaned from Itsua's response to Kaze's reactions. Through the "detective work" that plays an important role in almost every daily interaction with other human beings, the audience begins to piece together their own impressions of Kaze and Bay's past.

Humor

As you begin to shape your story, you should also consider the inclusion of humor. This episode of the *Ghost Warrior* storyline, as intense as its overall impression, has flashes of humor within it; from the ironic (Kaze: "You've lost your weapon") to the physical (when Soshi is startled and bangs his head on the wall — á là Mel Brooks).

The more serious the story, the more necessary congruous "breathers" of comedy are. These breathers help the audience reset their stress/tension levels so they don't fatigue emotionally while watching the story. (When an audience fatigues emotionally, they lose the ability to care about what they're shown.) We all have limits as to how much stress we can take before we get fatalistic. This is important to note for both our potential audience and our characters.

No matter how bad the situation, as long as an individual hasn't been "broken," he or she tries to make the best of things. Usually, this coping mechanism expresses itself by trying to find some humor in what's going on. In *Gladiator*, the food-tasting gag after Maximus' identity is revealed is brilliant; here are these *slaves*, facing the possibility of horrible deaths on a daily basis (the tension of the movie was high at that point), and here is this completely believable, *in-character* way of making each other laugh. The gag was not for the benefit of the audience; it was for the characters themselves!

Every story has a tone, and everything that happens must fit within that tone. The humor that you use must be congruent with that tone. Something too broad in a serious film like *Gladiator* will break the suspension of disbelief. It is a delicate balance but one that is usually well solved by putting yourself in your character's place and seeing what you, yourself, would do — living the life they lead, being in the situation they are in, with the hopes, dreams, and expectations of what will happen after the last reel; what would you do? This keeps things in character.

Humor is also a powerful tool in that it can be used to get the audience to lower their emotional guards before you hit them with something extremely powerful. Using humor in this way lets you reach beyond the skepticism that audiences often build when preparing for something they fear might be coming.

However, one way in which humor should *never* be used is to dissipate the effect of a strong emotional scene. Let time heal the blow of a strongly emotional impact — using humor utterly destroys the integrity of the impact that preceded it. If you find yourself using humor to "soften the blow," you're far better off not having the "blow" in there to begin with.

Playing It "Close to the Vest"

Something else to remember in storycrafting for your characters is that we, as "real" people, don't try to show what's going on inside of us; we try to hide our motivations and feelings. For a character to give away a bit of himself, it must slip from him in a way that reads as *unintentional* or *unaware*.

> "It's important not to indicate. People don't try to show their feelings; they try to hide them."
>
> — Robert DeNiro

NOTE

> At a party, it would go over much better to have *someone else* mention that you are an animator working on your own film than it would to waltz in and declare the same.

When Kaze is struck by the flood of emotion that seeing an image of Bay brings, he first tries to "play it cool." Realizing that he is losing the battle to conceal the painting's impact on him from Itsua, he turns away to leave.

You could almost see this as a set of balancing scales. On the one side there is Kaze's desire to maintain a public image of strength and control. On the other side is the respect and honor he feels toward Itsua. Each event puts more weight on one side or the other.

As Kaze turns to leave, the scales are heavily tipping toward preserving his public image. When Itsua tells Kaze how much he respects him, his fight, and his strength in light of what has happened to him, it overwhelmingly tips the scales the other direction. Turning to Itsua, revealing the deepness of the impact of his words as tears stream down his face and he struggles to maintain his composure, reveals the enormity of the struggle and the weight Kaze places on the importance of Itsua's caring.

Viewers may not fully register the subtext that is conveyed by these subtle and complex bits of interplay and acting, but they *feel* that something more is going on than is being portrayed on the surface.

Layering

Inside jokes, throw-away lines, and implied meanings are all things that exist within our own daily lives. Used well, they add the layering that echoes the reality we know from our own everyday experiences, making the story even more real to the audience. This layering also gives the audience reasons to watch your work a second (or forty-second) time.

The comic book *The Watchmen* is still one of the most brilliant examples of this kind of "multilayered" storycrafting. There are so many things buried within the panels that there is no way that a reader can grasp them all — from headlines on newspapers and magazines to what the "extras" are doing in the panels' backgrounds. You're still catching things even after your *tenth* read-through!

One of the best inside jokes I've seen is in the movie *True Lies*. It references the book *Schrodinger's Cat Trilogy* by Robert Anton Wilson.

In the book, Wilson, slowly over the course of the novel, begins replacing certain words with other words, requiring the reader to assign new meanings to semi-common words (like the last names of justices in the United States Supreme Court). Once Wilson substitutes a word, he adheres to it religiously for the remainder of the book. (Everything and every character must adhere to the "rules" of the world that the author is defining.)

Wilson replaces the vulgar term for the male sexual organ with the word "Rhenquist." So, when Arnold Schwarzenegger comes front and center and says, "Hello, my name is Harry Rhenquist," anyone in the theatre who has read *Schrodinger's Cat Trilogy* busts up laughing. The rest of the theatre remains silent, completely missing the joke.

Another, more accessible, inside joke is in the movie *The Matrix*.

When Neo is "learning" kung fu, the computer monitor displaying the list of styles of martial arts being dumped into his brain shows "drunken boxing" for all of about one second before the editor cuts to another shot. I was surprised at the number of people who either didn't notice that line of text or were unfamiliar with martial arts master Jackie Chan's films *Drunken Master* and *Drunken Master II* (which at the time *The Matrix* was released, hadn't yet made it to American cinema).

Leaving incidental things here and there for your audience to figure out or notice on their second, third, or fourth viewing strengthens your film! (Just because some guy in a suit with a checkbook doesn't get something doesn't mean your *intended audience* won't. It doesn't mean that you should strike it or 'splain it to death.)

The Human Condition

Even though we're talking here about making completely CGI films, our stories aren't about the CGI; they are about the characters and how they deal with and feel about the situations in which they find themselves. No matter what the medium, the best stories are always about *the human condition*.

The events and situations that happen to the characters over the course of a film may be hyperbole, but the audience must also be able to connect the allegory to situations and events within their own lives. This is one of the primary reasons why *Star Wars: A New Hope* and *Star Wars: The Empire Strikes Back* were so successful! Their success was a combination of believable, likable characters making the best of experiences that were an allegory for things we have all known, wished for, and feared. (The visual effects and production design just made the films all that much more enjoyable to watch.)

> **NOTE**
>
> It is no coincidence that within the Celtic Cross tarot card spread one card placement represents *both* hopes *and* fears.

Luke Skywalker is the proverbial Everyman. *Everyone* wants to feel that they are special in some way and that those around them just haven't noticed it yet. Many people have had secret thoughts that they were adopted and that their "real" family would somehow find them and they would be swept up into a life much more exciting and rewarding than their own. The events in *Star Wars* were fantastical, but the character's *reactions* within them were very much the way we, or people we know, would indeed react in similar situations.

The tools we use are computer graphics. The stories we tell are about the human condition. The medium we use to convey these things to our audience is emotion itself.

Even the "Bad Guys" Need to Be Likable

Above all else, the audience must *care* about the characters *and what happens to them*. This made writing the death scene for Yashin (the lead troublemaker) a challenge. (In the vernacular, the guy's a "prick!")

Kaze let Yashin live once. Then Yashin went out of his way to antagonize Kaze again. Yashin, however, isn't just "evil-in-a-can"; his actions reflect the things within ourselves that we battle secretly on a daily basis.

The challenge with Yashin's death scene is that Kaze has just killed *six other people*! Why should we, the audience, *care* if one more person dies? Does it matter more to the audience that Yashin has had speaking lines and the other "sword fodder" have not? (This is the big trouble with war movies where you see *thousands* of people die. Why should we care that one more person dies just because he has his name on the poster?)

The key pointers to the audience that this death is important are gleaned by watching Kaze's own reaction. Kaze's care, attention, and compassion for this character (who represents aspects of us all) direct our own focus into a state of "sympathetic vibration." Yashin has *earned* this attention. The sensitivity and tenderness of the scene makes it a most disturbing death scene. (And with the layering aspects of storytelling, it leaves in its wake many open-ended questions as to *why* Kaze has killed Yashin in this manner and how he can respect and care so deeply for those who have so clearly *earned* death.)

Trail Markers

Right now, in this ideation phase, *the sky's the limit!* You shouldn't fixate on what you can or can't do with your resources and/or abilities. (Within reason, of course. I mean, it's not wise to think of animating something of the scope of Herbert's *Dune* series by yourself, but don't overly limit yourself by thinking some things are too tough before you've had a chance to see how necessary they might be to your story!)

In the industry, this is known as the "blue sky" phase. (Shoot for the stars, and you'll at least hit the Moon!) This is the phase where you let your creative juices run wild and, by doing so, go deep into territory that you might otherwise never see!

So, go all the way with what you love to do! Keep a notepad, audio recorder, or Post-it Notes on hand at all times for your ideas. (Post-its factor heavily in the next chapter where we begin to cultivate our "idea farm.")

At every step of the way, imagine seeing the work you've done play out before you as if you're watching someone else's film. Use this simple visualization test to find the bits of brilliance within your work. ("Dude! I wish I'd thought of that!") Use this as a test to see what strikes you as things that shouldn't be in your film. ("Man, I'd have done something different if it were *my* film.")

Envision seeing your work play at a double-feature next to your favorite works in your film's genre! (For me, I picture a double-feature of *Kaze* and *The Crow* at the Mann's Chinese Theatre with the lobby filled with original works by Rembrandt, Parrish, Richard Schmid, and Craig Mullins.) If you can stand tall with your work being shown amid the best-of-the-best, you know you did okay! (Conversely, if you feel even the slightest bit self-conscious, you know something needs fixing.)

Aaah, but always remember *humility!* Remember that old saying of pride going before a fall? From personal experience, this seems to be the case. Whenever you feel that you're really hot stuff, *stop!* Like Indiana Jones in a booby-trapped ruin, freeze! Don't take another step! Think about what you're doing, what you've done, and what you're about to do. You can *use* your feelings as warning signs and figure out what they might be warning against! If you really take an honest look at things when you get those kinds of warnings, you can usually spot trouble *before* you step in it!

The making of a film — short or feature — is a long journey. It requires you to hold onto this initial idea, this core focus throughout the length of production. In order to do this, you need to take time away from your project. Take at least one day off per week, no matter how tempting it may be to work straight through. Like a marathon runner, you have to *pace yourself*. When you come back to work, you'll be able to see things that you wouldn't have seen before because you were "standing too close." When you come back to a work in progress that you've been having some issues with, the answers will usually be so obvious that you'll wonder why you didn't see them before. (It's that age-old forest-for-the-trees thing.) You can usually tell when you need to step back from your work; it's when you feel that you absolutely can't take a break (usually when you're struggling with something refusing to settle into place).

Also bear in mind that *momentum* applies to cognitive and emotional states every bit as much as it does to *physical* things. When you have a big project, it often takes an amount of focused energy to get it rolling. Once it is moving, it is very hard to redirect it (which is one of the reasons it is so important to know from the *start* that you've got an idea/story worth dedicating yourself to). So, if you ever feel at a loss over what to do, just pick what you can do at the moment; the momentum you generate will quickly roll you into doing what needs to be done.

As you work your idea, remember to focus on story, not "hot-shot" visuals. The neatest, newest techno-tricks will be out of date in two to three years. If you base your film on techno-tricks, it too will be out of date in two or three years. Remember that the media in which we are working may be only a few years old, but the art of storytelling that we are practicing extends well beyond the dawn of recorded human history. Study its successes, use its time-honored tools and methods, and know that any story worth telling is a story worth telling regardless of whatever medium through which you are telling it!

> **NOTE**
>
> It is refreshing to have heard more "buzz" about the student films in the SIGGRAPH Electronic Theatre than about the corporate works. What the student works may lack in polish, they more than make up for in *story!*

> **NOTE**
>
> Think of filmmaking like doing dishes. It's far easier to make sure things are done correctly to begin with than it is to have to go through the cupboards later, looking for and trying to clean dishes with gunk dried and fused onto them.

Yes, I know, it can be so hard to sit still and work out all these details (and the details in the coming chapters), but remember, *what you do right now will dictate the entire path of your production*. If you create a solid foundation, start with a good idea (an idea to which you can commit yourself, like your "one, true love"), "channel" believable characters, and really get to know and respect them as beings (just because someone isn't "real" in our world's definition doesn't mean they are not worthy of respect), the film will almost begin creating itself. All you need to do is keep the momentum directed toward completing your goal!

The path of filmmaking isn't like a novel where you can turn to the last page to see if the hero gets the girl. If you try to jump to the juicier parts, you'll find yourself quickly overwhelmed by the morass that always forms around poor planning.

Give yourself all the time you need to craft an idea in which you can believe, an idea that you can find yourself falling in love with as you get to know it ever more intimately over the course of production. This is a marriage of souls, real and imagined. This is a union of trust and commitment. The kind of environment that is created when you spend every "working" moment within a story and with a cast that you have fallen deeply, intimately in love with is a joy beyond measure.

Never before in my adult life have I been so excited to wake up in the morning and breathe another day's air than I have while working on *Kaze, Ghost Warrior*.

Chapter 9

Pre-Pre-Production

A director takes upon himself a great responsibility. As director, you are the filter through which everyone else's work on the film is seen.

A great director can coax, suggest, and showcase stellar performances from average actors. Conversely, the performances of premier actors have been mangled through the misjudgment of poor directors.

The director is the "vision keeper" of a production. Every dedicated, hard-working, talented individual working to make that vision a reality is counting on him to do his job to the best of his ability. To do this, the director must implicitly know his vision, and even more importantly, the director must adhere implicitly to the strength of that vision!

This means that every step you, the director of your film, takes is a step toward the constant fulfillment and improvement of your vision. As director, you eliminate everything that does not further your story toward that goal (no matter how "pretty" any individual part may be). This also means that you let no one and nothing deviate you from the fulfillment of your vision!

This *does not*, however, mean that you hold so tightly to the original conception of your vision that it suffocates, unable to grow and mature as the production progresses. As director, yours is a balance of knowing the truth of your own artistic centers and standing strong amid a wash of creative currents while still retaining the flexibility to know a good thing (and act upon it) when you see it.

> "There is nothing so perfect that it cannot be improved upon."
>
> — Winston Hudson

For most people, it is easier to work with something that already exists than to try to pull perfection from thin air. So in the process that I use, I sculpt with broad, easily changeable brushstrokes first. As the production progresses, the details and refinements work on these strong foundations, shaping them into the polish of the finished film.

At every step of production, the measuring stick I use for evaluation is to imagine experiencing the work *as if I were watching someone else's film*. I do this while walking along my wall-o'-Post-its that represents my film even before storyboarding begins (more on this later in this chapter). I do this with my storyboards, my animatic (storyboards edited onto videotape), and with every other step of the filmmaking process.

What I look for when evaluating in this manner is the slightest hint of, "Oh, I know how I would do that if this were *my* film." The wonderful thing about working in this way is: This *is* my film!

"The best way to criticize a film is to make another film."

— Godard

So with each and every step toward the finished product going per-petually forward from a solid, strong beginning, the artwork that some say already exists is freed from its "stone" by carving away all that is not integral to the representation of the core vision/idea of the film. Work and step back. Polish and step back. Always look-ing at the film as if seeing it for the very first time, with no prior emotional connections or reasons to cut it slack, gives me a no-nonsense assessment of where it is and where it needs to go.

This is the process that I follow. The result is a work that is an honest, true representation of the idea and vision initially held in one's heart and head. With this process, as with everything that represents the truth of its creator, one must always know that one's own individual truth will reach some and will completely pass by others. This is exactly as it should be!

Concept Farm (The Power of the Post-it®)

Up until now, the process has been about jotting down ideas, little bits of ideas that may or may not work. Up until now, it wasn't our place to judge whether or not these ideas would come together well or not. Up until now, our job has been to keep the ideas safe, keep them fresh and alive, and keep them from fading into the rush of our daily lives.

Up to now, we have been nurturing these ideas, letting them grow to the point where we are ready to start "harvesting" the ideas into a story.

The time for harvesting those ideas is now.

Gather up all the notes for your story; the ones you've written down on napkins, transcribed into your PDA, and that still remain as audio recordings, yet to be transcribed. Go through them all and write down the most concise, as-close-to-one-sentence-as-possible blurb about each idea on a single Post-it Note.

When you have all your ideas in that magical, movable medium that Post-its enable, tack them up to a (Post-it safe) wall, arranging and rearranging them as you go.

This is the first workable format for your film.

My own wall-o'-notes is shown in Figure 9-1. While they aren't great literature, the notes allow me to see my story in a format I can reorder almost instantly. I can see holes that need to be filled and bridges that need to be created between main story points. Walking along this wall, I can also picture each scene in my mind — in so doing, creating the first "screening" of my film.

Figure 9-1: Tacking ideas on a wall using Post-its allows you to rearrange your storyline.

Ideas that don't fit or further the single, main vision of the story are removed and perhaps stored away for a future story. Idea notes that I like but can't quite find a place for get tacked up along the margins, helping me to remember to find ways of working them in — if possible.

Sometimes it seems that the good ideas rather hide behind a mass of not-quite-so-good ones, and the only way to get at those good ones is to start getting the not-quite-so-good ones out of the way. So let ideas fly out of you through the inexpensive medium of Post-its! Once those not-quite-so-good ones have worked their way through your system, you have free access to the ones with which you'd really want to work!

As you work your story, take time out from your wall-o'-notes frequently to give things time to digest. It is amazing how just a little time away from a creative endeavor will often make things obvious that were hidden before.

You will find places where you need to add more notes here and there to connect the bits of story that you have already worked out. Shift both small pieces and large chunks of notes around to get a real "read" as to how different things are *implied* simply by the order in which your story's ideas are told.

As you go through your notes, picture each scene in your mind as if you were watching it in a theatre (yes, in a theatre filled with people, watching your film — friends, peers, mentors, heroes — the people whose opinions of your work matter to you). You'll find this to be a great help in spotting things that need adjusting. If you feel nervous or uncomfortable about having friends and colleagues see a sequence you have committed to a Post-it, you might want to think about replanning that sequence (unless, of course, that scene is *intended* to make both you and the audience feel uncomfortable).

Watching the film play out in your mind is one of the most powerful tools you have to make something really good. As you "watch" your work, letting the visuals come from each note on your wall, compare what you're seeing with the films that you've really found powerful.

Having seen the successful results of other filmmakers (your favorite movies), you have already become an expert in knowing what you feel is successful visual storytelling. Why is your opinion important? Because the most successful film you can make is a film for *you*. In making a film for you, making it everything you want to see, you are making it real. Audiences will feel this and be moved by it. Those who feel the same way you do will find their own truths within the truths of your story's vision.

NOTE

Regardless of the medium, when you make a work of art that *you* connect with, that work of art will also connect with others who experience their lives similarly to the way you experience yours. These are the people with whom you would hang out if you knew each other, the people who would connect with your work of art — if you make it *true* to the vision within your heart. (People who wouldn't connect with you may not connect with your work of art no matter what you do, and that's okay!)

Remember the Æsop fable of the father, son, and donkey? You can't please everyone, and trying to do so pleases no one in the end!

Being true to your own ideas and *ideals* will go further than anything else in ensuring your film's completion. Making what you personally want to make helps keep momentum going when you're knee-deep in the nuts and bolts of filmmaking, with the film's completion a distant point along the horizon. Making your film something that you can stand proudly next to your all-time favorite movies imbues your work with an honesty that will draw like-minded individuals to what you are saying through your work. As such, it will be a success!

Style

In what *style* will your piece be?

Style? Yes, style is all about how your story is told. There is no other more singularly important aspect of filmmaking that determines more about every nuance of each and every frame of a film.

Style is about the framing choices that you will use to compose your shots. It is about how quickly you will cut between them. It is about how you will have your characters perform. It is about how they will look, how they will sound, how they will be lit, and how the sets that envelop them will be constructed. Style is about more than just the design of a production, though production design itself is a part of the overall style of a film. From the moment the opening credits roll and the first notes of the score are played until the last frame of your work plays itself out, your choice of style is with and within every part and aspect of your work.

Just as every factor of every aspect of a film is affected by your stylistic choices, the stylistic choices themselves are affected by every experience you have encountered and stored as you have lived your life.

Personal Style

Whether or not any of us likes to admit it, we each have our own personal style. This is represented in our own individual choices, big and small, through *everything* in our lives. From the way we feng shui our homes to the camera angles from which we shoot a scene, every mark we make upon this world is done so through the "filter" of our own unique style.

So, love it or hate it, it is always best to know the shape of the creative decisions you tend to lean toward. In this matter, you have but two options: Beat yourself up about your personal style (something that is notoriously difficult to change — though through

focused training it *can* be changed) or learn to appreciate the unique points of view that you and you alone have to offer!

It is very common for "beginning" artists to dislike their own style. They compare their works with ones they see coming from artists with as many years of professional experience as some beginning artists have had on this planet. While it is important to compare oneself with the masters (the only way to eventually become a master yourself), what many beginning artists don't see is the people that are drawn to their unique, individual styles.

"But I can't do anything else," one very gifted high school sophomore complained to me. Why fight it then? Explore all the choices that your subconscious is making evident through your work. These are the doorways to the deepest parts of your soul.

Once you have a toehold on what you *can* do, it is far easier to explore what you would *like* to do.

Each and every one of us is at a particular stage on our own artistic path. Yes, we are always striving to achieve more, learn more, and have a more broad-reaching selection of techniques, styles, and abilities from which to paint our dreams. But do not begrudge yourself for being where you are on your path right now!

The secret to much of life is like the secret to learning how to ski: Learn to enjoy wiping out! Once you no longer fear *imperfection* (and if you can appreciate the humor of what being imperfect must look like from the outside) you will find your skills evolving at a far more rapid pace!

So, first and foremost the style of your film must be shaped by what you would want to see. Don't worry about pleasing anyone's opinion but your own. Don't worry about being "right." This is not about academia. This is about finding the *truth* about the kind of movie that would hold you enraptured — nothing more.

The combined abilities and skills you have within you (or your team) will also determine the style of your piece. You may dream of doing *The Lion King*, but *at the moment*, you have the skills for doing *South Park*. (All things change — and thank goodness, no? With focused, continual progression, you can attain any level of ability that you wish!)

Always be honest with yourself and others about your level of ability. Knowing where you *are* is key to being able to get to where you *want to be!*

Once you know, honestly, where your skill level is, target the complexity of what is required to make your film match that level. Then "bump up" the complexity level of your film so you end up being about 70 percent sure you can manage the work required.

Why work a project you aren't 100 percent sure you can attain? Because all artists need challenges if they are going to finish what they've started. Setting your sights so you are about 70 percent sure you can do what you set out to do generally offers enough challenge while still remaining within the artist's ability, based upon what is learned over the course of production.

NOTE

When I made my first CGI animated short film, my production team and I realized that we lacked the skills to do the "Milt Kahl" swash-buckling epic we really wanted to do.

Following the "next logical step" motif (explained in depth in *LightWave 3D Character Animation*), we knew what we were technically capable of doing. So I planned our first CG short film so that I was about 70 percent sure we could pull it off. From that first short film, I planned a second that would build on the skills we would learn from doing the first. From the experiences we would gain from doing that second short film, I estimated that we could then be about 70 percent sure we could handle our original dream of daring sword fights and passionate performances.

The first short film we planned would be reminiscent of the Chuck Jones *Marvin the Martian* Warner shorts. The second would push our limits as we tried to work in Tex Avery style action and acting. The third was set to recreate the classic Disney films we grew up loving.

So before even pre-pre-production began on our first short film, I outlined a series of three short films for us, each more complex and challenging than the previous one. Each film would teach us what we needed to know to do the next. Each film was stylistically something all those on the production team would go out of their way to watch.

It was a good plan. But, after we completed the first short film (before pre-production on the second began in earnest), everyone in our little group was snatched up by other companies (part of the hazards of success if the ultimate goal of the production team is not in the making of films but to be bought by other companies).

I don't know what would have happened had we stayed together to finish our films. I like to think that we all would be further along in our own careers as filmmakers, more skilled as artists, rather than learning quite well how to be someone else's tool.

Set the style of your piece so that it offers you and your team enough challenge and excitement to hold your interest for however long the film needs to be in production. (Also make sure that it isn't too ambitious, requiring the dreaded cutbacks in order to just get the piece completed at all — not fun!)

Three popular styles that can be the *beginning* of your stylistic explorations are:

- Paper cutout
- Animé
- Americana big-budget

Paper Cutout

If, years ago, someone had told me that one of the most successful animated series on television would look like paper cutout animation, I wouldn't have believed it. But, today, no one can deny the success of *South Park*.

South Park's strength is in its ideas and storytelling. The wonderful thing is that its animation is easily within the ability of almost everyone.

So, if you've got a great story idea but are uncertain of your skills as an animator, a style like this has already proven itself as being a totally viable medium for successful storytelling.

Animé

Animé is the general term for *Japanese animation*, though it can be applied to all forms of Asian animation.

I've heard one Disney "star animator" pick it apart for it not having enough in-betweens, being more like *animatics* than animation. But what those critics fail to realize is that with fewer frames, animé producers are able to stretch their budgets far beyond what is capable in a Disney film.

Animé relies heavily on close-ups focusing in on only what absolutely needs to be drawn, modeled, or animated. It also relies heavily on *tableaux* — detailed, single frames that describe a story point, which is held for several seconds.

Of course, animé is known for its cultural-based stylization in the way characters are designed and animated. *Modified timings* are discussed in more depth in *LightWave 3D Character Animation*, but in short they are altering the way things really happen in order to bring about a more *symbolic* dreamscape feeling to the action that takes place. (Some characters hover in mid-leap before crashing down to Earth with much more force than one would normally expect.) Modified timings give *visual cues* about the physical/emotional/spiritual sensations acting upon the characters and/or environment.

The dream-like nature created through these stylistic choices actually seems to allow for a greater suspension of disbelief within the audience. If it is obvious that the characters aren't acting within the same world rules as our own (but *do* have a set of rules), the audience will grant a lot of leeway as to what you can do.

The overall result of these animé stylizations appears to me to be a more emotionally powerful product, created with much less busywork than in an American film done entirely on "ones" (a new drawing for every single frame). Animé seems to reflect a savvy knowledge of where and how to best spend money — of which shots will give the most bang for their buck.

For a production by skilled artists limited by either time or money, animé style is the perfect solution to deliver an immensely powerful product for a fraction of the investment required by an Americana big-budget film.

Americana Big-Budget

You know the kinds of films that I'm talking about here. These are the films that come out of DreamWorks, Pixar, and PDI — the kind that used to come out of Walt Disney Feature Animation (before the "dark times," before "the Empire"). These are the kinds of films where perfection within all aspects of filmmaking is the name of the game (and artists are allowed to do their work without micromanaging by superiors whose creative vision is questionable).

These are the kinds of films where an animator has a week to rough-in a scene that will then be handed over to an assistant to be cleaned up. It is a luxury to be able to work in this manner. (We can all attain the levels of skills required to produce this level of quality, given the right teaching blended with the right desire within the student. After teaching many people to attain this level, I truly believe this.)

This is the style that results when you have the highest level of training, which blends with taking the time that is needed to do each job right — every job. In this style, everything that is done is done for the betterment of the film as a whole.

There are things that could be considered "traps" in this style of filmmaking. That trap is the same trap that exists within every blank page. It is far easier to approach a specific assignment than it is to approach the freedom of being able to do whatever you like.

In painting terms, an illustrator must get his brush strokes down and move on to the next in order to finish the piece on time. A "fine artist" can wonder if the stroke he made is correct and fiddle endlessly with it. Illustrators' works usually read with boldness and certainty simply because they don't have the budget or time to doubt themselves.

Another "trap" within this style is something akin to boredom. When you have the time and budget to do everything you need, when you are 100 percent sure you can do everything that is laid out before you, the artist within you has very little impetus to perform. (All artists need to be challenged; otherwise, there is no reason to be an artist!)

One more trap within this style that can come from a company that has enough resources to throw at any problem in hopes that it will go away is a kind of nonchalance. (It's that "pride going before a fall" thing.) A mega-monolithic company can feel overly self-confident that it doesn't need to follow the time-honored rules of starting with a story worth dreaming about *before* production begins.

(I mention no names here, but when a film is completely animated and then reworked almost from scratch because the story has changed, that's an example of the trap of decadence that this style comes with. This is why I recommend so strongly that you have a good concept/story *first*, a story you can believe in, a story worth telling, a concept/story you aren't going to need to change mid-production. Animated filmmaking is *not* like "workshopping" a play, if the director is worthy of directing.)

Unique Styles

Due to constraints of skill, budget, resources, or whatnot, you may be forced into exploring a unique style. You may not have the resources or ability to do voice work.

If a film's idea and story are tailored to create a film that has no *need* for dialogue, the audience will never know that its original intent may have been to have dialogue! (This is working within what I like to call "easy power.")

Knowing that there was only going to be one animator on the project, knowing how much work there was going to be, I opted for something more along the lines of an animé style for Kaze. There are many close-ups, many shots where the background is out of focus, and many held shots. All of this is reminiscent of traditional animé, because like in animé, I had a powerful story to tell and a limited budget to tell it with, and I had to spend my budget of time where it counted most!

With everything in *Ghost Warrior* being done entirely by me, I knew I couldn't have female speaking roles (I can barely do the Monty Python old-woman voice, let alone something believably female). So, even though there are several women that take center stage throughout the production, their entire performances are through *pantomime!* This is just another *stylistic choice* made at the beginning of production based upon the known parameters of the production itself.

Production Design

Everything that factors into how your production will look falls under the general heading of *production design*. Production design covers the design of costuming and characters, the colors used within the production (or lack thereof), the set design and construction, the way everything and everyone is lit, right down to the smallest smudge or smear on an "aged" prop.

Story style and production design go hand in hand (with production design being the "hand" that fits within the "hand" that is story style). Once you know *how* your piece will be told (story style), you can begin to explore the way it will *look* (production design) that will support the telling of your story in that particular style.

When beginning your exploration into the production design for your film, you start first within the existing works that you would like your own film to be most like. Through clipping, printing, and pasting reference material from those inspirational sources, you assemble a *collage* much like your story wall of Post-its. You begin to assemble a collection of images that, together, have the combined *feel* of what you would like your own work to evoke.

Expand your search to include magazines, books, and Internet finds — everything and everywhere that has something visually inspirational to the direction of your film. You are gathering things

that *inspire*, not things that exactly replicate. You're filling a creative stockpile for you to pull from as your film is created, something that can jog memory and jar complacency. You're looking for things that add fuel to the fires of passion within you about the direction and focus of your film. In addition to helping guide the choices that will shape the look and feel of your film, it is a battery bank from which you can draw creative energy when your own reserves are running low.

> "An artist is only as good as his scrap (reference material)."
> — Kevin Cunningham

NOTE

An interesting theory about creative energy is that it operates in much the same way as every other form of energy. It can neither be created nor destroyed. What we, as artists, do is charge ourselves up with inspiration, the creative energy we receive from exposure to artworks with which we connect, and then let that loose in the direction of a new creative work.

In line with this theory, when you are in the actual act of creating art, it would seem logical that the more powerful energy sources that you have around you (inspirational artworks), the more energy you can focus and redirect (Aikido-like) into your own artwork. In this theory, the artist needn't even be looking at the inspirational artworks but simply surrounded by them.

My own explorations within the framework of this theory were surprising. If you feel so inclined, I'd highly recommend your own explorations with this as well.

These "found images," "scrap material," "photo morgue," etc., will remind you of the direction your story is going whenever you need a little extra jolt. They will remind you how your film should *look* and *feel*. Bear in mind that in these early stages of development, your story and style are evolving, "finding their feet." Story and style will mature over the course of this early stage of creation, and things that once fit may no longer be the direction that you wish to go. If you notice anything from your collection of found images no longer fitting, take it down and store it away. Your film may cycle back through to where it once was, or then again, it may not. *Cohesiveness* within all your reference material and production direction is vital to creating a work that reads like a single, unified, core idea.

Production design creates an overall harmony throughout your film, making it feel like one single, solid work of art and not a collection of separate thoughts held together solely by their proximity to one another. As you design your sets, props, and costumes, design your characters, animate them, and record your dialogue, you should constantly come back to your collection of reference images to see how they compare to this anchor point for your entire film. (Even as you proceed through the final stages of editing or marketing, your production design images will help you to remember and convey the core feelings that inspired you to make your film!)

Color Theory

Color plays a huge part in the production design process and the *sculpting* of the audience's emotional states within the final film. Colors, like music, subliminally influence the audience's reaction to what is going on before them. Different colors symbolize different emotional states. Science has even shown certain colors to actually stimulate behavioral responses.

NOTE

> The general rules for color symbolism are: Reds symbolize passion and strong emotion; greens symbolize sickliness or sterility; blues symbolize coldness; yellows and oranges symbolize warmth and can also be used to hint at the "sepia" tones of old daguerreotype photography.

A scene may start out within the cool, "antiseptic" hues that elicit feelings of calmness. Then, as tensions heat up, the hues may tend toward reds and oranges, adding yet another bit of *layering* to the complex palette of emotion with which you are painting.

Or, as in the movie *Stigmata* (with the exception of Frankie Paige), all characters and sets were dressed in more neutral or cool colors (blues and greens). Amid the cool tones of her surroundings, the red of her stigmatic wounds leapt out at the audience. As she became more and more "afflicted" with the stigmata, the color of the clothing she wore became brighter and warmer, a beacon that held the audience's gaze amid the sea of cool, desaturated blues and greens.

Color theory is a complex subject that has its roots deeply embedded within science, art, and mysticism. Like with all things within this incredible coalescence that is the art, the craft, and the science of making motion pictures, there is far more than can ever be held within a single point of view. Explore all you can, within all subjects that you both feel drawn toward and repulsed from.

Remember that while a good film school can indeed show you what it is you need to know, the results of some of the most successful artists, craftsmen, and mystics within this field are within arm's reach at your local video store.

Environment (The Importance of Choosing Your "Exposure")

"Being a good reader is one of the keys to being a good writer."

— Unknown

The cinema, videos, television, art, music, radio, video games, and Internet that we expose ourselves to play huge parts in shaping our mental and emotional states (and these *directly* affect our physical state). They shape what we feel, what we think, and how we feel about what we're feeling and thinking.

The media tells us what is funny and how to be cool. It shapes the way we sculpt our interactions with other people. We are *inundated* to such a degree by what we choose to tune in to that our creative choices can't help but resonate with the stimuli that we allow to envelop us!

NOTE

> It is surprising just how much human behavior is shaped by the desire to produce results that will be perceived as "cool" by one's peers. The affectation of specific speech patterns and the purporting of specific thought patterns are influenced deeply by the one goal that doing so will make one "acceptable" to a specific target group.
> Think about it.

What we take into us directly shapes our decision-making processes. Watching a certain genre of films shapes your predilections to align with certain filmic motifs. Listening to specific music shapes both our underlying emotional state and our definitions of what we are capable of identifying as good music. Watching television conditions one to "internalize" the conventions used in broadcast media (television formulae being *significantly* different than the ones that produce successful cinema).

We are products of our environments! What you put into you is what you get out of you (mentally as well as physically). The wonderful thing is that we can choose to consciously choose what we allow into us! If you have a specific target in mind for your work, surround yourself with the "best of the best" of that genre. You will begin to "internalize" the results as your standards for success. Producing results that meet those standards will begin to structure your own internal decision-making process to allow you to create more and more freely within and expand upon those standards for success.

So while someone may have never gone to film school and can't explain in a dissertation exactly why what he's seeing is "successful," everyone *already* has a gut feeling about something that works for them. As you craft your own film, you'll get that gut feeling about your own film! By exposing yourself to high-quality filmmaking, your "gut-level" responses will direct you more and more to the decisions (both conscious and subconscious) that will result in similar levels of success within your own works.

I'm not downplaying the importance of a good education, but not everyone has either the means or the time to study filmmaking at one of the *good* film schools. The successes of the absolute best filmmakers in the world are waiting for you at your local video store. They are there for you to *study!* They are waiting to teach you! All you need is the true desire to learn how to see what it is they have to teach!

Books on Filmcraft: The Foundations of Understanding

The ability to produce greatness first begins with an ability to understand what makes something "great." We can all identify something that strikes us as "great." But how did the creator of that work go about sifting through the myriad decisions he *could* have made, making the decisions he *did* to produce that "greatness"? You can watch thousands of films and read hundreds of books, but until you begin to understand what to watch for, it may be years before you can understand the craft that creates a work that pulls you in.

Books are your best resource to beginning your understanding of the actual craft that shapes the filmic decisions that go into visual storytelling. (Bear in mind that not all books on the craft of filmmaking are created equal! Some are pale parrotings of true masters' works. Ask someone who truly knows their stuff what they recommend *before* filling your head with something that may end up hampering your progress!) Books tell you what to look *for*, how to *plan* shots and sequences so the viewer loses himself within the film. Books tell you how to let your audience fall into your story, while the actual craft that created it remains completely invisible to them.

The following books are on my required list of reading for anyone interested in CGI filmmaking. They each explain vital, *specific* parts of the filmmaking process that cannot be covered adequately within the pages of a book of this scope. Together they offer the understanding that creates the most memorable performances and powerful stories and the tools and conventions that create the most effortless works of cinematography. *The Artist's Way* helps you find what you'd most like to be doing and helps keep your artistic fires alive during times of self doubt. My own books take readers from not knowing a darn thing about 3D CGI and brings those who do

the exercises up to a point where they can build and animate in LightWave almost anything they can imagine.

- *Film Directing Shot by Shot: Visualizing from Concept to Screen* by Steven D. Katz
- *To the Actor: On the Technique of Acting* by Michael Chekhov
- *Audition: Everything an Actor Needs to Know to Get the Part* by Michael Shurtleff
- *The Artist's Way: A Spiritual Path to Higher Creativity* by Julia Cameron
- *The Writer's Journey: Mythic Structure for Storytellers and Screenwriters* by Christopher Vogler
- *LightWave 3D Character Animation* by Timothy Albee
- *Essential LightWave* by Timothy Albee
- *Cinematic Motion: A Workshop for Staging Scenes* by Steven D. Katz

These are the original sources for the tools, techniques, and methods that are integral to the craft of filmmaking, the art of CGI, the skills of acting, and the beauty of simply allowing oneself to be the creative individual that one can be. They are the books that are most greatly responsible for me being able to do what I do. They are within arm's reach on the bookshelves and tables in my studio. I strongly recommend that they find their way into yours as well. (*A book can only help you if you read it and explore its exercises.*)

Books tell you *why* a certain kind of cinematic transition is successful. They explain *how* to interlink the different shots of your scene through different camera positions to tell your story. They explore the conventions that have been used for years to *successfully* tell stories within this visual medium.

Books are extremely helpful in building within you the ability to understand what it is you are seeing. However, it is in doing your "homework" that you really begin to receive those flashes of brilliance that shape you as a filmmaker. What is that homework? It is simply to watch films and make your own! As you watch and work, identify what you're seeing on screen as the teachings you have learned in books.

NOTE

Audiences are *trained* by what they watch, and all filmmakers were at one time part of the audience. New conventions are developed (the "MTV quick-cut," "extreme steadycam," etc.), and you must know these too (even if you choose to avoid them). Every filmic technique you are exposed to becomes yet another tool in your toolbox to create the exact emotional space you want your audience to exist within. (Even though you may *think* you'd never use a specific kind of tool or technique, you'll be very happy that you learned about it when the time comes when that tool is the only tool for the job you need to do!)

Understanding tradition allows you to make your decisions in an educated manner, even when those decisions are in the *breaking* of those traditions! The result is a work of art that is built upon the strong foundations of education and constructed with power, intelligence, and passion!

The absolute best book I've ever come across, in terms of a *genuine master* explaining the true craft of every aspect that a director needs to know about making a film, is *Film Directing Shot by Shot* by Steven D. Katz. (I've run across at least one "pale parroting." Don't be fooled by imitations!) From in-depth examinations of storyboard sequences from groundbreaking feature films (like *Blade Runner, Citizen Kane*, and *Empire of the Sun*) to actual examples of patterns of camera placement used in shooting dialogue to evoke certain, specific feelings in the viewer, this book is a must-read!

To the Actor by Michael Chekhov and *Audition* by Michael Shurtleff both focus on *acting* and how to craft a powerful performance. As a CG filmmaker, you are the director, you are the actors, you are the cinematographer, director of photography, producer, and often grip, gaffer, and production assistant all rolled into one. Even if you have animators working for you who create the performances of the characters, books like *To the Actor* and *Audition* will help you communicate with your actors/artists to get *exactly* the performance you are looking for in the shot.

Essential LightWave teaches you the actual, practical skill set of someone who has been a studio LightWave artist for between five and eight years (it teaches you all the skills you need to know to use LightWave to make your own feature film, should you be so inclined). If you're new to CGI and want the most "bang for your buck" and the least amount of frustration (and a software package that *follows through on its promises*), take it from a guy who has been around the block a few times: LightWave is the *only* 3D package that has stood up to the "Tim test."

LightWave 3D Character Animation and/or *Fundamentals of Character Animation* are books that show you how to create feature-film quality character riggings and how to put yourself on the path to creating feature-film quality animation. Feature-quality character animation isn't difficult; it just takes time. More importantly, it takes someone showing you the "tricks," someone who has actually done feature-quality animation to show you how *you* can achieve feature-quality results. I wrote these books so that *anyone* can make the choice to do what is needed to become a feature quality animator.

The Artist's Way by Julia Cameron is by far the book I recommend more often than any other. Writers, directors, musicians, painters, sculptors, poets, physicists, chemists, mathematicians, architects, bankers, accountants, programmers — all can benefit from the exercises (which seem more like games than "exercises") that Cameron has worked into this book. One of its greatest assets is its ability to help you find out what you'd *like* to be doing and to truly realize that doing whatever that is relies solely on a simple choice in *allowing* ourselves the *freedom* to do it.

Books give you access to the knowledge, the points of view of master artists and master craftspeople that we may never have the opportunity to meet in person. What you do with that access is a choice that lays entirely within your jurisdiction. A book can only help you if you let it — if you *read* it. Books like those I've recommended here can do the most amount of good if you do the exercises within their pages.

It's simple: Do the work, get the reward. How much do *you* want to be a filmmaker?

Films

If you're planning on making an action-adventure film, surround yourself with the best action-adventure films that you can find. If you want to make a drama, stock your video shelves with the best dramas that you can find. The same thing applies to comedy, "art films," romance, and any other genre you can think of.

Because we are all so heavily influenced by our environments (where we work, eat, sleep, and play and the media to which we allow ourselves to be exposed) only allow in the very *best of the best*. Make a stack of these films, and be sure to get exposure to them each and every day. If you don't have the time to watch an entire film every evening, watch ten minutes of it each night. The important thing is that you are constantly surrounding yourself with *good* films and their influence is enveloping. With such constant reinforcement of the results of others' *good filmic judgment calls*, you will find that your own decision-making processes are heavily influenced by the same.

As a filmmaker, you need to "experience" films a little differently than the rest of the masses. Sure, let yourself be swept away by the emotions, visuals, and sounds the first time (or times) you see a film. But then, if you find the film inspiring, commit yourself to understanding *what makes the film successful*.

NOTE

> The best way to see the actual art of filmcraft within a film is to watch the film with the *sound turned off*.

A film's soundtrack (score, sound effects, etc.) has often been called "the invisible actor," and with good reason. Sound surrounds us (even without surround-sound), pulls us in, and gets us emotionally charged about what is going on on-screen. This is great for an average audience member who wants to be swept away into the experience of a film. This isn't so good for a filmmaker who wants to be able to examine the director's and director of photography's choices of staging, editing, lighting, framing, lens usage, etc.

When watching a film with the sound turned off, you are able to disassociate yourself from the action on-screen and focus on the materials that you've learned by reading your books about filmmaking. You can see more clearly the director's and editor's choices of how long a shot was held after the actor completed his dialogue before transitioning to the next shot. You can examine the subtle facial expressions of the actors, the way a set was lit, and exactly how edits were organized. It is a simple trick, watching a film without sound, but there is nothing more powerful in helping you begin to understand how the book learning actually translates into *practical filmmaking*.

In addition to watching the films that are the best of your film's genre, be sure that your "research list" is heavily flavored with *classics*. (My definition of a "classic" is any film, regardless of when it was made, that is both enjoyable and a great work of filmmaking, regardless of genre. Films on my own list of classics are *Alien, Star Wars* (episodes 4-6), *Casablanca, To Kill a Mockingbird, The Iron*

Giant, The Secret of NIMH, Babe, Blade Runner, Crouching Tiger, Hidden Dragon, Lady and the Tramp, The Hudsucker Proxy, The Road to El Dorado, Rosencrantz and Guildenstern Are Dead, The Majestic, and *The Cradle Will Rock.*

Now, there are also the films that "the experts" think are good. The fact that you or I may or may not *enjoy* them is secondary to the fact that they were/are *groundbreaking* or an example of mastery in an area of filmmaking. (True, there are aspects of "The Emperor's New Clothes" in what "experts" consider "good filmmaking," but even understanding that herd mentality is important to identify and develop *your own personal opinion*.) It is important to get exposure to these films to understand both their filmcraft and the reasons why the experts view them as "masterworks."

It may be hard for a modern audience to connect with the rather stiff acting of Hitchcock's *Rope*, but its filmcraft in showing an entire movie as if it were one, long reel makes it a must-see! The ways in which Hitchcock hid the fact that film "cans" rarely run longer than ten minutes is absolutely brilliant, even by today's standards.

Death of a Salesman is very difficult for many audiences to watch. But it is the powerful acting and the masterful direction of both performance and editing that make it such an emotional challenge. What makes it a masterwork is exactly what makes it difficult for some to watch!

I, personally, am not a fan of *Being John Malkovitch*; however, the majority of experts rave about the work. I can identify and agree with many of their points, even if I do not personally enjoy it as entertainment.

This brings up a very important point: Beware of using the blanket statement, "I don't like." When you use the phrase "I don't like," what is actually being said is, "I don't understand." Whether you are content to exist within "I don't understand" or to learn all you can about a work or genre and *re-evaluate your judgment from a position of understanding* is a choice that is entirely up to you. You may find educated reasons that affirm your initial feelings, or you may find a deep and powerful love for an entire other "world" you never knew existed.

DVD Commentaries

The thing that finally converted me from a devotee of laser discs to being a fan of DVDs was the director commentaries. (If you're even slightly interested in filmmaking in *any* capacity, drop the $60 U.S. and get yourself a DVD player. It'll be one of the better $60 you've spent in the pursuit of filmmaking.) If you haven't listened to a "full-length director commentary," imagine sitting in a screening room with the top brass of a production, listening to them reminisce about all that went on during the production.

Some special edition discs are coming out with more than just the top brass talking about their experiences on the film. *The Fellowship of the Ring* special extended DVD edition has separate full-length feature commentaries by the director and writers, the design team, the production/post-production team, and the cast. Some special editions (like *The Fellowship of the Ring*) also come with hours and hours of *extremely educational* documentaries outlining individual pre-, post-, and production tasks, problems, and solutions.

You can learn an immense amount by sharing the experiences of those who have gone through the process.

NOTE

Of all DVD commentaries, the ones I've found most helpful to a novice filmmaker are *Alien, Highlander* (the first feature film), *Ronin,* and the special edition of *The Fellowship of the Ring.*

Research

There is a great distance between *fantasy* and *falsehood*.

As you mindfully fill your creative well with quality material, you also want to be doing the research that will aid in making your film believable. Even fantasy films base their strengths in establishing an all-permeating "reality" that their viewers can both understand and relate to.

Surely you've surely heard the phrase "God is in the details." Well, here is where you delve into those details. This is your time to be a kid in a candy store. Everything you ever wanted to know about the things that happen in your film is now your job to discover!

If you're doing a film where your characters will be using guns, take a course on learning how to *safely* handle and use the guns that your characters will be using. Learn what is proper gun etiquette and what is not. The handling of firearms will be vastly different between the good guys and the bad guys. A "good guy" may be trained to keep a magazine out of his semiautomatic handgun, always keep the weapon in a gun safe, store the ammunition in a different location from the firearm itself, never leave the weapon with a round chambered, and never have his finger on the trigger until he is ready to actually pull it. "Bad guys," however, don't follow these same rules. A friend who has worked closely with actual felons told me that felons usually find their portrayal with the storage and handling of weapons to be more or less imbecilic. I was informed that if a bad guy has a shotgun by his bed, there will *always* be a round chambered; if he is feeling significantly confident, he *might* have the safety on. (All the extra actions, gyrations, and sound effects just make those experienced with actual working environments react with disgust over the fact that yet another filmmaker is trying to talk about something he knows nothing about.)

If you're going to be working with swordplay or martial arts, find someone who knows what they're doing to help you understand the techniques. They can help you define the styles for the individual characters based upon their physique and personality. From personal experience, "the real thing" is far more breathtaking than almost anything that someone who doesn't know what they're doing could ever concoct.

If you're working on a film where military tactics are used, find someone who can teach you what proper military procedures for a mission of that nature might really be!

For instance, I've been told that pilots are trained to use the word "niner" instead of "nine" so that the number isn't confused with the German word for "no."

Of course, if you are going to have your characters speaking with an accent, make sure you get the accent correct. Either hire an actor from that country or an actor well-trained in dialects, or dive into the books *Foreign Dialects* or *American Dialects* by Lewis and Marguerite Hermann.

Making your film adhere to strong anchors in reality does two things. For one, it lets people who really know how to do what you're portraying in your film leave your movie feeling both *respected* and *satisfied*. And two, even people who have never seen or experienced a thing will still be able to identify the "correctness" of watching a skilled master perform something correctly. To a master, every motion has a purpose.

The greatest stories, however fantastical, always ring strongly with elements of the "truth." It's what gets an audience wondering if that's maybe the way things "really" are or might be. (How did *you* feel after you first watched *The Matrix*?)

There is also the motif in storytelling of "the domino theory of reality." This means that if you start with something completely "real world" and then, through a series of completely plausible events and reactions, lead into something completely fantastic, your audience will go there too, right along with your characters.

Whatever story you are telling, you need to have your audience feel that you know what you are talking about. The more *research* you do into your subject, the more *details* you work into your finished piece and the more *believable* your completed work will be. Perhaps only one person in a hundred thousand may be able to identify *all* the minutiae you have woven together to create your world, but to that one person, as well as to every other viewer, you will have created a real world in which your characters live and breathe.

Chapter 10

Screenwriting

The art of *screenwriting* has the same "shroud of mystery" around it as nearly everything else in filmmaking. With code words for simple concepts and strictly defined formatting, it's easy for a newbie to feel overwhelmed. Don't. Screenwriting is one of the most *intuitive*, free-flowing forms of writing that you'll ever find.

Treatment

> "Just fax me the treatment."
>
> — nearly everyone

Treatments are the written representation of the ultimate core ideas of a film. They condense your wall of sticky notes into a *single page*. Much more than just a "Hollywood calling card," they help you fine-tune the story and its flow before you get into the "down and dirty" of writing the script.

NOTE

A *treatment* was best described to me as imagining someone on his deathbed trying to tell the most important story he's ever told before he dies. A treatment is short and "grabbing" and hits only the high points.

Treatments also have the same air of mystique about them that scripts do. There are classes, seminars, books, and more that you can explore to help you figure out how to write a treatment that sells.

In my experience, a good treatment is a treatment for a good story that is well-written and engrossing. (*Selling* a treatment is as much a matter of luck and timing as any "gamble," which is the whole reason for taking independent filmmaking into one's own hands!) If you've got a good handle on basic writing skills (and a good thesaurus), writing a *well-written* treatment is simply a matter of inductive reasoning (reasoning from the specific to the general).

Treatments have this rap of being tough to write because most treatments are written *backward*. When you try to fit the "meat" of an entire story (or script) into a single page, it's a painful process! You don't want to lose a single, beautiful detail of the story, and so the treatment *feels constricted* (and it is)! (This is a huge issue for treatments that are written *after* the screenplay has been completed.)

The *simple* solution of letting your treatment feel expansive is in letting the process that creates it actually *be* expansive!

From what I've been able to tell, a lot of big productions have the same problem with their entire productions as many folks do with writing treatments. They work backward. They have a *result* that they want, and they try to figure out what kind of work will produce that result.

Big studios want a big hit (the result), and so they set about trying to *fabricate* all the bits and pieces that "smack" of the truth and honesty that usually result in such a hit (the work). This is why (on more films than I am at liberty to mention) the "mid-production-jitters" result in major rewrites halfway through production. While this is going on, animators nervously sit on their hands, watching their hard work get tossed out the window. All the while, the film's due date remains hard and fast. (Being subjected to this does wonders for morale, as I'm sure you can imagine.)

What the studio bigwigs don't seem to understand is that you must do what you *love* — deeply, passionately, more than anything else in the world. That *truth* will yield something that will connect with audiences because they will sense the love, passion, and honesty that was integral to creating the work! Films created from those centers of truth, passion, and honesty are works that people want to experience again and again (like the phenomena behind *The Lion King*, *Mononoke Himé*, *My Big Fat Greek Wedding*, and *The Fellowship of the Ring*).

Three Words

With screenwriting, I find that it is best to start your work with the most distilled concept of your story. This is the seed, and you let it grow and expand from there. Working from the "seed" will help you to understand your story better, having been able to purify it into the smallest space possible. With each step of the process, from seed to treatment to script, your story will be imbued with the sense of freedom that comes from *freedom!*

This first step in the screenwriting process begins very simply. It begins with *three words*.

Tell your story in three words.

Describe your story with three words that fit it better than any other three words ever could.

In order to do this, you *really* have to understand your story. You can't be ambiguous about anything and still have those three words resound with the core feeling of what you envision your story to be.

These three words should reverberate with power! They should resound with the single, core idea of your story. Usually, those three words are the most powerful when they describe the truth of a feeling rather than an event. When you hear the three words, you should have no choice within you but to nod your head and say to yourself, "Yeah… that's it!"

For example, someone may have a romantic story and think that the three words that represent it are "boy meets girl." To that, I'd have to say, "Yeah? And? What of it?" In the story it may be true that a boy does indeed meet a girl, but those three words leave a listener like yesterday's oatmeal.

"Love is sweet," as trite as it may be, is better than "boy meets girl." But maybe it's not *that* kind of "love." How about "love is *bitter*" (or even more intense, "love is hate")? You get the idea.

The three words that describe *Kaze, Ghost Warrior* (for me) are "honor is life."

One Sentence

Now you've got the three words that describe the absolute core of your story better than any other three words ever could. (Because finding the perfect three words forced you to really understand your story, settling on them was probably a bit more challenging than was originally thought.) Let the story breathe a "sigh of relief" as you let it expand into one sentence. (Run-on sentences are cheating and don't count!)

Like the three-word exercise, this one sentence needs to capture the very essence of the core of your story. Nearly every word must resound with the marrow of your story. (You'll probably spend a lot of time with your nose buried in a thesaurus.) The end result is an even clearer, *expanded* understanding of the story you are creating.

The one sentence for *Kaze, Ghost Warrior* is: "A ronin exacts justice for the anguished while avenging his own death."

One Paragraph

When you are able to let your story expand to fill an entire paragraph (of about 100 words), your writing will be able to exude another "sigh of relief" as more overall information is included. Still powerful, with almost every word still exactingly selected to most accurately fit the feel of your piece, this one paragraph allows you a bit more space to fill in some details.

The one paragraph for *Kaze, Ghost Warrior*:

> In a distant world's feudal past, a masterless warrior tracks down the murderers of the Imperial family, the same men responsible for his own death. Driven by honor, his quest throws him headlong against those who dominate through villainy, fear, and intimidation. An "avenging angel" for the tortured, the story unfolds in *Kaze, Ghost Warrior*.

Remember, you're painting with broad strokes here. The one paragraph is almost completely without *specifics*; there is nothing in it that "slows the reader down" by asking them to think too much about any one thing.

One Page

Then, following the same "formula" that you used to expand your one sentence into an entire paragraph, you let that paragraph expand into an entire page. You still want to keep *specifics* down to a bare minimum, but you are able to let yourself be a bit more "painterly" with your writing. (See what we're doing? If telling the story in one page is the act of allowing ourselves the luxury of being able to fill an entire page, the feelings of freedom and expansiveness will come right through the words!)

NOTE

You want the story to almost feel like it is sliding off the page as if it were Teflon. You want your one page to be an easy read (with almost every word carefully selected to portray an exact emotional focus).

Each sentence needs to *entice the reader to read the next sentence*. You can be successful in this by just using your imagination. Pretend you are someone who has never met you before, who has never heard this story, and who may or may not have the time to listen to your description of it. Read each word "aloud" in your mind as you read your one page. If at any time you notice you feel "lost" or you find your attention wandering, you know you need to retouch that part!

In your one page, you create a *distillation* of the core ideas of your story. In doing so, you've created a treatment! By letting your work *expand* into one page, your work reads with much more power and freedom than if you had worked *backward* trying to *condense* the story into one page!

The treatment, as I use it in filmmaking, is just part of my process of never going backward:

1. Start with a story idea that you can believe in for six months (or however long it takes to make it into a film).

2. Use that story idea to create a script that you can believe in for six months.

3. Create visuals that are worthy of telling that story idea.

Little bits and details may change as you go about working on your film. It is perfectly natural for inspiration to strike in production and you suddenly *know* a much better way of telling a part of the story. *But the core idea doesn't change!*

If you don't believe in your story idea, don't make it! Don't think you can fix it later. Fix it now!

> "There's no point in painting a bad drawing."
>
> — Kevin Cunningham

The treatment is your way of knowing exactly what your story is about. You know by reading your treatment "aloud" in your head whether or not you can really *believe* in it for however long it takes to bring it to fruition.

With the treatment alongside you as you write your script, you know if you are deviating from the story idea in a significant fashion. The way I work (and I'm not saying you have to work the same way), once I commit to the story idea, *it doesn't change.* If I can believe in and commit to the story idea, and the *script* and *film* follow that *story idea* and do it justice, there is no reason to change the concept!

Commit to the story idea. Let the treatment be the readable *distillation* of that *idea.* Let the script and subsequent film serve to bring that story idea into a form that communicates it to others through *visual storytelling.* Only when you feel, through and through, that the treatment is something you can believe in for the run of production do you begin writing the script.

Script

Scriptwriting is really one of the most enjoyable styles of writing. With scriptwriting, the vast majority of the *details* that fill the pages of novels are summed up in very terse descriptions: INTERIOR. TAVERN — NIGHT.

You're almost like a stenographer, jotting down the visuals and dialogue from the viewpoint of an invisible observer as the scenes play out in your mind. But this kind of "free-flowing" nature of writing a script can only happen if you aren't fighting with the tools that you use to create it.

I knew several beginning writers/directors who labored using Microsoft Word to format their scripts. All it takes to get them to move over to professional screenwriting software is about five minutes of showing them screenwriting using a tool designed specifically for the job.

Scriptwriting Software (Formatting Your Script)

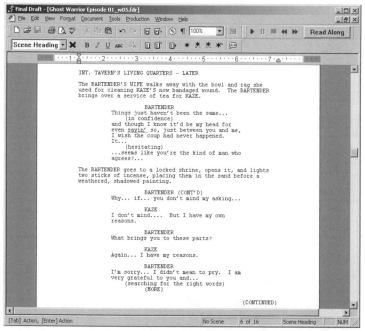

Figure 10-1: The scriptwriting software that I use is Final Draft (available for Mac and PC: http://www.finaldraft.com). It has all the functionality of Microsoft Word as a word processor (with a significantly better dictionary/thesaurus) along with incredibly intuitive control for formatting your script as fast as you can think it "out loud."

One of the many benefits of using scriptwriting software to write your script is the *ease* and *speed* with which you can let the ideas pour out of your head and onto the page.

> **NOTE**
>
> What follows is a basic explanation of the different elements within a basic screenplay. Please refer to a book solely dedicated to the art of screenwriting to find out all the particulars of script formatting.

Scene Heading

At the top of the page in Figure 10-1 is the Scene Heading (still sometimes referred to as a "slug line").

The Scene Heading establishes whether the scene is INTERIOR or EXTERIOR, on what LOCATION, and WHEN the scene takes place.

> **NOTE**
>
> From a Scene Heading element in Final Draft, pressing Enter *automatically* changes the format to Action.

Action

The Action line describes what is going on in the scene. In this case, we "see" the Bartender's wife walking away from Kaze. That, together with Kaze's freshly bandaged arm, leads the audience to *presume* what has just taken place.

> **NOTE**
>
> From an Action element in Final Draft, pressing Enter creates another Action line, while pressing Tab formats the next element as a Character.

Character

Character establishes who is speaking the dialogue that immediately follows.

NOTE

> From a Character element in Final Draft, pressing Enter establishes the next element as Dialogue, while pressing Tab sets the next element to be a Parenthetical.

Parenthetical

A Parenthetical modifies the dialogue to be spoken. "Hesitating," "in confidence," "slowly," "quietly" would all be used as Parentheticals to modify how the character performs the dialogue.

NOTE

> From a Parenthetical element in Final Draft, pressing Enter formats the next line as Dialogue, while pressing Tab sets the next element to be a Character.

Dialogue

Dialogue is what is spoken by the characters.

NOTE

> From a Dialogue element in Final Draft, pressing Enter formats the next element as an Action, and pressing Tab sets the next element to Parenthetical.

One of the nifty things about decent scriptwriting software is that it remembers the pattern of who is speaking. If you have multiple characters speaking in sequence in a scene, Final Draft remembers who spoke last and *automatically* sets the next character to speak from the established pattern of speakers!

Some scriptwriting software also includes the ability to have your script read aloud to you, assigning different voices to the different characters! The Read Along and VCR-like buttons in Figure 10-1 control the computer's "performance" of the script.

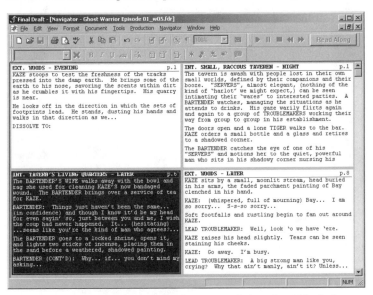

Figure 10-2: Another major benefit of programs designed specifically for creating works of visual storytelling is their ability to show your scenes as a series of "virtual Post-its" that you can rearrange even more easily than your wall of sticky notes!

NOTE

One of my secrets for proofing my writing is having it read aloud using TextAloud MP3 by NextUp.com using their releases of AT&T's Natural Voices (http://www.naturalvoices.com). I find it much easier to spot mistakes, typos, and confusing phrasings while having my work read aloud by what sounds like a professional reader. (My current favorite Natural Voices voice for proofing my writing is "Audry," who speaks in UK English.)

NOTE

One more benefit of using scriptwriting software is that should you ever need to change the formatting of your script (say, into a stage play or a "Cole & Haag screenplay" or the specific format Warner Brothers wants screenplays submitted in), doing so is a simple matter of clicking through a few menus. Final Draft comes with a plethora of different formats and allows reformatting in milliseconds!

Scriptwriting software may seem like a luxury to someone just getting into the field, but to someone who has gone through the process, it is simply a wise choice for eliminating frustration by using the proper tool for the job.

The Reasoning Behind the Formatting

Why the rigid adherence to formatting in screenwriting?

Script formatting is about more than just making it easy to see which character is saying what. Formatted in adherence with industry standards, the average script page will "time out" to about one minute of screen time.

Look closely at Figure 10-1 or at Chapter 5, which contains the entire shooting script for *Kaze, Ghost Warrior*. Dialogue has huge margins (about two and one-quarter inches from the edges of the

page). Dialogue is spoken and comes across much more slowly than the volume of information that can be portrayed in an action. (Actions have their margins at about one and one-quarter inches from the edges of the page.)

The formatting all adds up to a convention that allows people with a lot on their minds to not have to guess about how long any particular script is. If you have a 120-page (correctly formatted) script in your hands, it will be seen in the industry as a *two-hour* film.

NOTE

Like all "rules," there are exceptions. The most common is in action films, where the two words "they fight" could end up being 20 minutes of screen time.

Formatting your script in accordance with industry standards helps organize your thinking. It also gives you a better idea, right at the outset of pre-production of just how large an endeavor you are undertaking.

Dialogue (Hearing Your Preferred Actors' Performances)

There's only *one* "secret" to writing a good dialogue: See what you write as if you are watching it in a theatre, and hear what your characters say as if they are being performed by the actor you dream of playing the role.

You know who you would love to perform the characters you are writing (it's hard not to). Envision one of your characters as DeNiro in *Ronin* or Jeremy Irons in *The Mission* with just a dash of Gregory Peck in *To Kill a Mockingbird*. Whomever you have in your mind as your *ideal* cast, hear the voices of those actors in your mind as you write the dialogue!

When you hear a specific actor's voice attached to a line of dialogue, you instinctively know whether it is "good" or in need of adjustment. (You wouldn't hear Albus Dumbledore say, "Yo, 'sup, G?") Diction, pattern, grammar all fall much more easily into place when you actually *hear* your characters portrayed by people who have already established expectations within you. You *expect* certain performances from an actor. This can make the art of writing dialogue go much more smoothly.

Now, you don't want to simply say, "Well, this character *is* Dustin Hoffman's performance of The Conscience in *The Messenger*." Your character is *influenced* by a performance; he doesn't replicate it. Gary Oldman perfectly performed the Winnie-the-Pooh-like Rosencrantz in *Rosencrantz and Guildenstern Are Dead* and also masterfully played the almost terrifying, substance-abusing DEA agent, Stansfield, in *The Professional*. Similarly, the performance of your character is that of a unique individual, influenced by the same dramatic choices that a specific actor (or actors) would make.

Here are some important points about writing dialogue (note how they all pretty much revolve around the same core concept):

- **Someone else talking about you is far more powerful/believable than you talking about yourself.**

  You're at an "event," and someone walks across the room. The person next to you nudges your shoulder, indicating the entrant and says, "Hey. Have you seen any of his films? He kicks some serious ass." Your response is to hold that with more merit than if the guy entering the room announced, "I make films, and I kick ass!"

  Talking about yourself doesn't work in real life, and it doesn't work in fiction. If your character has to have something about himself known, let it be divulged by someone else or let it be "tricked" out of him by someone else. We tend to believe information gathered in this way much more readily than if it is "volunteered."

- **What you *don't* say carries far more weight than what you do say.**

  A lot more can be conveyed with a *look* than with a line. Michael Shurtleff covers throwaway lines in *Audition*. A throwaway line is a line that an actor *doesn't* say or says under his breath so few in the audience actually hear it. (This is based partly on our own, constant "inner dialogue" and the fact that we frequently *subvocalize* — say things under our breath that others around us aren't meant to hear.)

NOTE

> Often, when working with live action and good actors on set, the actors will simply drop lines, portraying them through "non-verbals" as part of their performance. In animation, nothing happens by chance, so all this must be carefully planned in advance.

An example of establishing a throwaway line is:

```
INT. DEMOLISHED LIVING-ROOM - DAY

A SERVICEMAN walks into a room ahead of his
Clients, stands with hands on hips, surveying
the 'wreckage.'

                SERVICEMAN

What the heck was going on here? Well, it's
doable, it'll just take some work.
```

The SERVICEMAN isn't really *asking* his Clients what happened in the room. The line was written with the screenwriter simply paying attention to the natural reaction someone like the SERVICEMAN would have when presented with something "unbelievable."

The line, "What the heck was going on here," could be *struck entirely*. The SERVICEMAN would react silently, long enough to think the line "out loud" in his head, *looking* like he was thinking that sentence.

Or that line could be subvocalized, (*whispered*, *mumbled*, or *mouthed inaudibly*) before the actual conversation begins. Or, the "What the heck..." part of the line could be animated with lip-sync (but without sound), with the lip-sync trailing off (as, "...was going on here," is "said" only in the character's mind).

- **Sell me, don't tell me.**

You don't emphasize the mass of an object by having your character say, "Gee Bill, this one-ton weight is heavy!" You *show* the effect of the weight on the character (physically, verbally, or whatever).

For the following examples, picture two people standing at the base of a sheer cliff.

This example is weak:

```
                    MACK
This looks like a dangerous climb.
```

We, as an audience, *see* the cliff. We can imagine what it would be like in their position. We don't need someone stating the obvious. (If we were with MACK here, we'd probably look at him and say, "No $#!+, Sherlock!")

This example is stronger:

```
                    MACK
You gonna be OK with this?
                    BILL
        (hesitating, quiet — not
        believing the line himself)
Yeah.
```

```
                    MACK
We can find another way.
                    BILL
No. Let's do it.
```

Here, we have people talking about how the situation impacts them. Through this simple exchange, we read a lot into the characters and their confidence about what they are preparing to undertake. It is four lines, and yet it develops the characters, making them feel even more real to the audience. MACK's focus is entirely on BILL. You *read in* that MACK isn't as concerned about making this climb as he is with BILL doing it. BILL knows this is beyond his abilities, and yet he doesn't want to slow MACK down, and/or what is at the top of the cliff is so important that he's willing to confront the possibility of death to do so.

This small exchange *also* sets up the drama of the two climbing the cliff. The audience knows that BILL is out of his league here. When they reach the top (if indeed they both do), the reward is much more strongly felt and believed for the audience being let in on the fear that BILL has tried (unsuccessfully) to hide!

NOTE

The strongest example would be to cut BILL's first line and the "No" from his second line, letting these things be "said" only within his mind.

With a performance strong enough to carry the subvocalization, the audience is "let in on" something that BILL really doesn't want to say. The battle of emotions within him are more strongly felt through the *silence*. The audience is being treated with respect and with the acknowledgment of the fact that they are intelligent enough to pick up on the acting cues. Audiences can sense this, regardless of their age group, and they will respect *you* for respecting *them*.

"The Zone"

Now, if you've never written a script before, there's something I should warn you about:

Your characters may start talking to you.

When it first happened to me, I was more than a little concerned that I might be totally losing it. I was writing a very intense scene of a feature film within the *Ghost Warrior* world, taking notes as to what I was "seeing" as fast as I could. While my fingers were flying, I noticed (after the fact) that I had actually started having a conversation with Kaze about his fate. This wasn't the "sitting on the sofa and discussing what you'll have for dinner" kind of discussion. This was similar, in a way, to the dialogue with your deity that goes through your mind when you find yourself in intense situations.

Needless to say, I was a little concerned that I might be quickly shaping up to be a prime candidate for the booby hatch.

Thankfully, that afternoon, on NPR's *Fresh Air*, Terry Gross was interviewing playwright Neil Simon. Over the course of the interview, Simon described having *exactly* the same kind of experience that I'd had with Kaze earlier that morning with almost every successful play he'd written. In fact, he confided that those experiences had always resulted in his most powerful screenplays!

You may find that your characters go about completing their "tasks" in ways different than what you had originally envisioned. You may find something seemingly contrary to your story idea taking place as you "watch" the characters live lives of their own. The beautiful thing with writing scripts is that they flow so quickly out of you when you are in the zone that you can easily just watch the characters as they "do what they will." If they end up in a place that you don't want them to be, just rewrite the section where they started deviating from your core idea (or *carefully evaluate* where it is that they *did* end up — there is a good chance there is genius in that little bit of the unforeseen).

To let your characters be *alive* within your audience, they must be alive inside you. You must believe in them, as surely as you believe in yourself. When they are real for you, they will be *real* for others. This is simply the way that storytelling works.

Chapter 11

Pre-Production

Once you have your story, treatment, script, and production design brought to a point where you, the director, have signed off on them (meaning that if they stayed exactly as they are until the end of time, you'd not just be content, but proud to be associated with them), you then officially enter into the wonderful world of pre-production.

The biggest mistakes made by the largest studios have been in entering into pre-production (and production itself) before they are truly ready. (I can think of at least one major animated feature that was all the way through rough animation when the studio executives had the script completely rewritten, forcing nearly everything to be redone.) While it may be oh-so tempting to rush ahead to get to the "juicy" parts, you won't be doing yourself any favors by rushing ahead before you're truly ready to get there.

NOTE

Me? I hate to go backward. When I work for/with a client, I have them actually sign a piece of paper that says that they approve of the work up to that point. This helps to stem the "I don't know what I want, but I'll know it when I see it" crud from on high. (Good leadership is good leadership. Poor leadership should almost be a criminal offense.) If a change is made that reworks work that has been signed-off on, it is not made lightly (nor inexpensively).

Most people and studios don't have the resources to rework a film from the beginning. I certainly don't have either the time, money, or heart to do such a thing. So the system I use allows me to start working with large, easily changeable strokes, much like "blocking in" the underlying values for an oil painting. As I go along, I add more detail and refinement, leaving the pieces in place from the previous "layer," never leaving a layer until I know I can live for all eternity with it being as it is.

Working in this fashion, I never go backward. Things can still breathe, grow, and evolve, but *the core concept remains solid*. The project is in a continual state of forward motion, propelled by the growing confidence of each successive brush stroke.

NOTE

I suppose that if there was a secret to my having been able to turn out significantly higher quality *and* volume of work than what is generally expected in the industry, this simple philosophy and way of working with continual forward motion would be it.

Shot List

The first thing you need to do once you have your script finalized is create a *shot list*. Just like its name implies, this is a simple description of every single shot in the entire film. (The shot list for *Ghost Warrior* is found in Chapter 6.)

The shot list will let you truly see how much work you've laid out for yourself. (Remember, if you feel overwhelmed by the actual enormity of something that you thought was going to be a much smaller project, you can always store what you've done so far and save it for your second or third project!)

> **sq03 sc12**: Med. CU. Kaze opens his eyes and turns toward BT. "...I have my own reasons."

As you can see from the above shot list entry, it is the bare minimum needed to paint a mental picture of what happens in that shot.

Breaking a shot list entry apart, the numbering lets me know at a glance that this is the shot from **Sequence 03, Scene 12**.

The next bit of information tells me that I am "looking" at a medium close-up of Kaze that frames his head and torso. (See the illustration in the following note.)

The rest of the shot list entry describes what goes on before we cut, fade, or dissolve to something else.

The best way I've found to start work on creating a shot list is to sit at my computer or PDA docked onto its keyboard, *close my eyes,* and imagine I'm seeing the movie play out in my mind. I simply type what I see, as fast as I can, not bothering to backspace, edit, or fix what pours out onto the page. When my mental camera cuts to a new angle, I hit <Enter> several times and start blazing away at what new scene plays out before my eyes.

NOTE

Let me once again state that this book isn't meant to replace a book like *Film Directing Shot by Shot: Visualizing from Concept to Screen.* It is meant to serve as an *adjunct* to it, lending my own experience in making CGI films to its incredible wealth of knowledge. If you have the desire within you to make your own films, I suggest that you purchase and *read* that book. It covers the foundations of filmmaking better than any other book I have ever read, including several pages of information on the basic framing heights outlined in the following illustration.

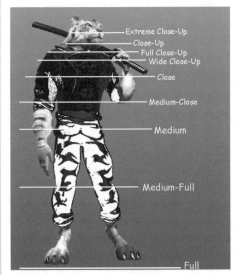

Character shot framing — the basic framing heights for a humanoid character.

When I'm letting this information pour onto the page in this manner, for the *first draft* of the shot list, I don't worry about adhering "to the letter" of the dialogue in the script. All I'm interested in is getting broad strokes down that I can refine once I sit back down and pick through what I've written. I need something on the page for me to reference, and that's exactly what I get from this way of working. It also *frees my mind* from the worry of having to get things perfect.

Once I have this first draft of my shot list, I take a break for a few hours and let that mental focus settle out of me.

When I come back to that first draft, I read through it, making notes about things that work and things that don't. Notes include things like expounding on the action, guiding the story back to the script, notes on angles or camerawork taking place, and adding in shots such as *establishers* (shots that help the audience reference the positions of the players within the scene).

When working through the different drafts of the shot list, if an idea needs to be added, it is, without hesitation. If any idea seems like extra baggage that doesn't serve to further the story, it is struck. (Far easier to do here than later on in the production process, no?)

"Sooner is better than later!"

— Joan of Arc, *The Messenger*

Typing in the changes indicated in my notes and making sure dialogue references are correct gives me the second draft of my shot list. This second draft much more closely resembles the shot list you see in Chapter 6.

Then, after another break to "shake things off" again, I go through the shot list a *third* time, paying very close attention to my gut feelings as I let the words paint the pictures of a film playing

out before my mind's eye, trying to experience this as if watching the film for the very first time. If I get the feeling that I wish something was added (had this been *my* film), I jot more notes. Of course, if something hits me like fingernails on a blackboard (the roll-your-eyes, "why'd the director do that?" kind of feeling), it gets struck.

After the notes and changes get incorporated into the third draft, I feel pretty confident in numbering the scenes (knowing full well that there are still more changes, additions, and subtractions likely to come).

My motif for numbering the scenes comes from an old standard established in the animation industry many years ago. Instead of "acts," the different, major portions of a film are called sequences. (Sequence 01 is the "opener," with Kaze tracking his prey. SQ 02 is the tavern and fight sequence. SQ 03 is the tavernkeeper's quarters. SQ 04 is the glade. SQ 05 is Soshi's place.) Each unique camera placement is a scene (SC) in this motif.

NOTE

When (not "if," *when*) you notice that you need something to go *between* two existing scenes, you tack on a letter to your SC number (like "sq02sc04b"). When you need even more minute additions, you tack on a number, usually starting at ".5" to leave room to insert even more *around* that scene if necessary later on down the road (like "sq02sc04b.5").

Whatever your naming convention is, stick to it! Organization is the key to combating the feeling of being overwhelmed by the contents of Fibber McGee's closet as your production begins to take on a life of its own!

When you go through your shot list after having let it gel over the course of several days and nothing strikes you as needing to be added or removed, you know you are ready to move on.

Scheduling

With your shot list in hand, you can begin to have a good idea of just how long your project will take. There are still many more questions that need answering before you can know for sure the full extent of your journey, but with a reference to each and every scene that you'll need to produce, you can get a pretty good overview of where you are heading.

This is where you truly begin to pull back from the blue sky phase of production (with aiming for the stars meaning you'll at least hit the Moon). Based on what you know that you *can* and *would like* to do, you find yourself retooling both your script and your shot list to suit.

For me, scheduling and *sticking to the schedule* is key to being able to keep my wits about me on an involved project. When I'm knee-deep in animation and I barely know which direction is up (without the 3D software's "handle" giving me a helpful hint), if I can look at my schedule and say, "Yes, I am where I expected to be," I know things are going alright.

Or, perhaps I look at things, and I am not as far as I'd like to be. Either I need to take a more "educated" look at my schedule to see if I was out of line when making it, or I need to stop fixating on things and start getting them out the door!

So, looking at what you know your film entails, knowing your skill level and *sustainable* performance rate (which is about *half* what you think you are capable of), you begin to plan your journey. The following list shows how I mapped out *Ghost Warrior*.

Month 1: Story honing/environmental modeling

- Character, clothing, environmental, and props design
- Storyboarding
- Animatic (animated storyboards)
- Record voices
- Model/surface/light environments

Month 2: Technology solutions

- Fur and cloth simulation solutions
- Enhancements to existing riggings
- Visual effects/compositing solutions
- Audio software exploration
- Facial animation solutions
- Render "pipeline" solutions (getting a scene from final animation to finished movie clip, ready for editing into final version of film)

NOTE

As much as any artist, I would love nothing more than to be able to give each piece of every project the "love" it needs to be as perfect as I can make it. But as a *professional*, I know that isn't going to happen. There are concessions that *have* to be made if a project is going to be completed and completed on schedule.

Were filmmaking a video game, there would be about a 99 percent point deduction for finishing late and a 1,000 percent point deduction for not delivering at all (plus the game console and half your living room would vanish).

If you dream of doing this in the "big leagues," you should be aware of the importance of finishing and finishing on schedule. *Completion bonds* (the legal contracts taken out to ensure the completion of a feature film) are *not* things to be trifled with.

Month 3: Characters
- Model characters
- Surface characters
- Fur characters
- Rig characters
- Prepare characters for facial animation
- Prep "stand-ins" and other procedural adjustments for speeding update rate while animating

Month 4: Pipeline test/refine: movie trailer
- "Proof-is-in-the-pudding" — make refinements to procedures that didn't work as expected and/or that can be improved upon.

Month 5: Animate/render
- Animation
- One machine always rendering; two machines rendering at "night"
- Compose score as animation gets cut into animatic

Month 6: Editorial
- Render scenes not yet rendered
- Finalize edit
- Perform/record/mix score
- Mix audio for "Pro Logic" surround systems
- Redo anything that needs redoing
- Record final on presentation medium
- Archive

This schedule was made from my assessment of the shot list, my own skills, and what I knew at the time of my hardware and software.

For each week, and each day, I made out check-box lists of what had to happen in order for my schedule to be met. Each day's workload could be reasonably accomplished in about ten hours. (Each week left me at least Sunday for contemplation.)

The result of doing this was my being able to make conscious, educated decisions about how I spent my time. I could choose to spend more time on a certain thing, working into the night if I wanted to. I could also choose to finish what I needed at an acceptable level and recharge.

Keeping this kind of focused, aware scheduling meant that I didn't burn through my energy reserves at the head of the project. It meant that through knowing what I expected of myself, I could see the mile-markers steadily moving past me; the entire project was an ongoing series of accomplishments.

NOTE

"Overtime" is always the result of management not doing *their* job, *never* the result of the workers who inevitably make up for it.

Design

Design is one of the most challenging *and rewarding* phases of any animated film. You can begin to look into the eyes of the people, places, and things you will bring to life. It's one of those "blank-page" phases that is best served by picking a direction and just getting started! Hold your longest pencil by its furthest end and just start making marks on a page; it'll lead you to finding the characters, places, and things within those first, amorphous scribbles.

NOTE

Just as a bit of trivia, when I'm working on a drawing or painting of a character, once I have the pose and proportions blocked-in, I always render the eyes as close to finished as possible. For me, if I'm able to actually look into the eyes (the "windows into the soul") of this being that I am portraying, I can tell instantly if I am on target about all other aspects of it that I draw.

It shouldn't come as a surprise that everything in a CGI animated film (like all films, animated or live-action) needs to be designed. Every prop, every place, every person built must have a "road map" pointing you to where they are. Like working with Post-its to help you see your story in broad strokes, even the quickest, most loosely rendered sketches help you know what will work and what won't before you start pushing points in your 3D package.

With your production design reference material close at hand, try to recreate the *feel* that your reference material echoes within you as you design. Always let your pencil roam to find your own angles on things. Be inspired by what you surround yourself with, but *never copy*.

NOTE

Never directly copy another artist's work. Not only is this *unethical*, but with the high-dollar lawyers the studios have at their beck and call, *copyright infringement* yields only unpleasantries. Be aware of the fact that many "real-world" items have their looks, logos, and even their *shapes* copyrighted. In CGI, since we must build everything in our worlds from scratch, we avoid much of the *clearing* process that live action must go through to make sure even a set's wallpaper is not infringing on copyright laws.

Characters

Characters *evolve*, even 3D characters, over the course of production itself. Every angle, every line, every *nonverbal* suggestion of the thinking process that is moving the character affects the way it impacts the audience. It is very important to plan time for this evolution to happen for your characters if they are to forge strong bonds with the audiences who will see them.

Stories, like fine wine, mature over a long time. Some of these sketches, drawings, and paintings come from the earliest iteration of the Kaze story, when Kaze is actually older than he is in *Ghost Warrior*. Some were done even before then, when all I had were *feelings* inspired by dreams that seemed more real than the world in which I awoke. Listen to your instincts, trust them, and save every drawing that you do. Going through your archives once in a while will often flood you with just the things you were looking for.

It seems almost obvious that the key to success in this or any field is to know as much as you can about as much as you can. The more tools and knowledge that you have at your disposal and the more ways you have to *problem solve*, the better you position yourself for reaching your ultimate goals.

In choosing the style for this piece to be my own personal angle on the shamanic, Æsopean, vedic, *anthropomorphic* (the term for blending human attributes into non-humans) vision, the first tool I must have in my toolbox is the knowledge of what these beings' "real-world" equivalents are.

To many, this may seem like arcane knowledge, or that like all "arr-teeeests," I must have some inborn gift to be able to draw, paint, or whatever. Let me make it perfectly clear that the ability to draw is not God-given. The *desire* is. I draw the way I do only because I refused to succumb to the fact that drawing never came easily to me! I just kept at it, doing some little drawing for myself each and every day! That's the key. Compare your work with the masters, and your work will begin to reflect their influence. With books like Glen Vilppu's *Vilppu Drawing Manual* and Richard Schmid's *Alla Prima: Everything I Know About Painting*, the only reason for someone not "being able" to draw boils down to either not knowing about the resources available or not *wanting* to draw.

Figure 11-1: *Lead Dog — Lake of Clouds*. I must understand anatomy to the point where I can paint as accurately as any photograph.

Figure 11-2: *Kemu Yawning*. It is only through an in-depth understanding of anatomy and close, personal, first-hand knowledge that I am able to capture the essence of Kemu in a ten-second gesture-sketch.

Figure 11-3: *Peter Pan*. I must know forms so well that the forms themselves become transparent to the emotion moving through the characters, regardless of rendering style.

Figure 11-4: *Peter Dozing*. I always try to warm up with some quick, free sketches to loosen up both my arm and my mind when I sit down to start drawing.

I knew early on that I wanted Peter Pan (one of my pack of sled dogs) to play a role in *Ghost Warrior*. His personality and how he did everything he did was just too wonderful to not put in the film. His gentle, tentative strength, making the best of all things that come his way, made him perfect to cast as the young male server who gets harassed by Yashin, the lead troublemaker.

Figure 11-5: *Peter Pan Yawning*. It is important to develop your drawing ability in as many styles as possible. Here is a sketch done shortly after the previous one, when Peter was contemplating turning himself over to warm his other side in the sunbeam that was brightening the cabin that day.

Figure 11-6: *A King's Remembrance*. Working from the sketch *Peter Dozing* and having Peter nearby, I did this quick oil sketch. I like the way oil paints let one explore more subtle shading of furred forms, the bristles of the brushes naturally lending themselves to the rendering of fur.

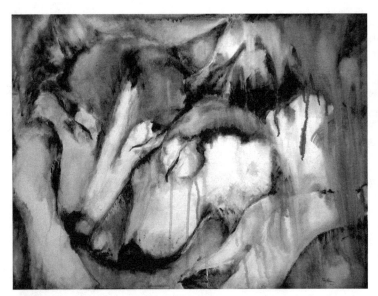

Figure 11-7: *When We Were Sled Dogs*. Sketching in oils can let you be a lot more free with your explorations of forms (more explorations of Peter).

Figure 11-8: *Meditation*. Trying to capture the *feeling* of Peter Pan within a form that doesn't bear his markings. I think this piece is successful in doing this, and so it was time to move on to someone new.

Figure 11-9: *Malamoot*. Joey, another of my pack, exploring possibilities for the bartender, Itsua.

Figure 11-10: …*Grant me Strength*… Exploring more lupine forms.

Figure 11-11: *Solace*. A sketch of the bartender before he settled down to the life of an innkeeper?

Figure 11-12: Exploring different treatments and ways of understanding the patterning in wolf fur.

Figure 11-13: The final sketch for the bartender (now drawing heavy inspiration from Toby, another member of my pack). I really liked the way his sleeves were handled, rolled and almost tied around the elbow, so after experimenting with variants in modeling, I decided to handle everyone's sleeves in a similar fashion.

Figure 11-14: Initially, I had planned tighter wraps and more "blousy" fabric for some characters. After getting dissatisfying results from the cloth-sim, I opted against it.

Figure 11-16: A quick sketch of a generic character.

Figure 11-15: Often, when working on clothing design, I draw a quick body on one sheet of paper. Then using it on a light table, I quickly sketch different clothing tests over that pose.

Figure 11-17: Another pair of quick sketches, exploring different clothing options. The one in the upper left is what became the "uniform" for the enforcers.

Figure 11-18: Changing gears into drawing the female characters.

Figure 11-19: An early, very stylized sketch of Bay.

Figure 11-20: Another version of Bay. The *feeling* is what I'm looking for, even if the style doesn't quite work with *Ghost Warrior*.

Figure 11-21: An oil sketch of Bay (used as the painting in the shrine).

Figure 11-22: Sketches for another female character. Initially going to be the bartender's wife, she was inspired by Rascal, another of my pack.

Figure 11-23: A quick, stylized sketch of Rascal.

Figure 11-24: More quick sketches of female characters playing around with the traditional "mop" of hair.

Figure 11-26: A quick sketch of another of my pack who plays a bit role in *Ghost Warrior.* (Mojo, one of my sled-dogs, inspired the patron who almost gets nailed by the out-of-control chain weapon.)

Figure 11-25: A challenge was once suggested to me (and I'd like to suggest it to you in turn) to take an animal with a strong stereotype and try to draw that animal as something that goes completely against that stereotypical representation. Here, I wanted to draw what was very much a hyena, but at the same time make her gentle, delicate, and very feminine.

Figure 11-27: Young Cerberus, the three-headed puppy of the underworld. The vital importance of *screwing around* is something that a lot of "non-creatives" don't understand about the creative process. It is a rare thing for any artist to just go full-tilt, nonstop for hours on end. We need to take time out, blow off steam, cut loose, and play! It's how we clear the slate and refill the creative energy sources!

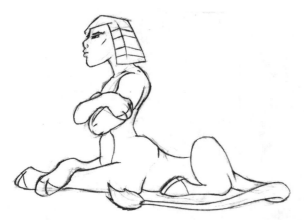

Figure 11-28: It's a sphinx-*taur*... get it? The more emotionally charged your "real" work is, the more important it is to take time out to just be a goof. (As I recall, this image came from around the time I was working on the following two illustrations.)

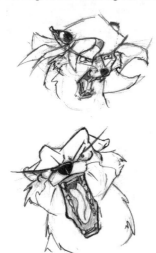

Figure 11-30: *Rage (Wolf Attacking a Caribou)*. Oil sketch, capturing the feeling I wanted to have in certain scenes of *Ghost Warrior*.

> **NOTE**
>
> I've been asked about my decision to not include tails on my characters for *Ghost Warrior*. The reason is simple: I don't have the time to animate them. It takes me about as long to correctly and *believably* animate a tail as it does to animate an entire character.
>
> Sure, they're cool looking and can add a neat, emotional counterpoint to a scene, but I think Calvin (of *Calvin and Hobbes*) said it best when he postulated that a tail is "...like a necktie for your butt."

Figure 11-29: *Faces of Rage*. Exploring the handling of facial expressions of enraged characters.

Figure 11-31: Early, "Bluth-like" sketch of the character who plays Yashin, the lead troublemaker, in *Ghost Warrior.*

Figure 11-33: *Please Don't Die.* More explorations of the emotional palette within the stories of Kaze.

Figure 11-32: *Pieta.* The piece that inspired the *Pieta* scene of Kaze and Yashin in *Ghost Warrior.* (Dedicated to an experience I had while mushing in Alaska's Brooks Range where I was afraid I might lose one of my pack. He lived, thank the gods. This work served as something to help channel the feelings that the experience left within me.)

Figure 11-34: *Losing Someone You Love (When there's nothing you can do).* Exploring the same, within a more traditional animation style.

11-36: Another sketch for Mishka. The inspirations for the characters of *Kaze, Ghost Warrior* are many and varied. Some have come from dreams. Others came from doodles and sketches while enjoying the company of friends at a Chinese teahouse in LA. *Inspiration*, when it hits, can be powerful or subtle. As an artist, as a storyteller, you must be open to its *possibility* at all times.

Figure 11-35: Sketch for Mishka, a character from the initial feature screenplay of *Kaze*.

Figure 11-37: *Tiger*. Kaze reflects more than just the markings of this incredible being.

NOTE

The weather was cold and just a bit too windy for good sketching at the Grand Rapids Zoological Park. Still, I really felt the need to get out and draw from life. The winter away from Los Angeles had not quite turned out as I had hoped it would, and I needed an influx of that magic that can only be touched upon by seeing such magnificence as watching the great cats.

I had heard that there were a pair of tigers at the local zoo and thought this was the perfect time to get out and explore. There was a small group of people huddled by the thick glass that walled part of the naturalistic enclosure for the cats, who pointedly ignored the waving and flashes of disposable cameras. I hung toward the back and prepared my sketching supplies.

The crowd quickly moved on, driven no doubt by the briskness of the weather and the disinterest of the cats. I had started sketching, slowly working through the first awkward lines when I felt something the likes of which I have never felt in my waking life, like a touch of some sort, but somewhere I couldn't quite place, inside me.

The next thing I knew, the male tiger was walking directly toward me, his eyes locked on mine. He stopped only inches from the glass and held my eyes locked in a gaze that was deeper than could ever be painted in words alone. The world itself began to tilt, and I had to reach for the railing — I could not take my eyes from his.

I don't know how long I was held there, though I remember noticing that at some point he had laid down but was still only inches from the glass. I don't quite know exactly what transpired during that time, however long it was (it felt like days, though couldn't have been more than an hour). I do know that when I did leave, I left there with much more in my head and heart than when I arrived — a magic that illumined the fledgling story of Kaze in ways that I am still discovering.

There is magic in even the smallest of events. The practice of art asks only that you become aware of these bits of wonderment as they exist continually all around and through us. As filmmakers, our art is more than just visual; it exists in a place that moves through emotion, time, space, and belief. It is mystery itself. It is something much more than what can be held within a single frame of film. Our art itself is a journey — a journey that is continually rediscovered as the viewer thinks back on, relives, what he has experienced within our touch. Ours is a gift that stays with those we touch, forever shaping their lives in ways that we cannot begin to imagine.

Chapter 12

Storyboarding

Storyboarding is where you finally begin to see your film coming together as visual storytelling. It is like making a comic book of your shot list. Every entry in your shot list is represented by *at least* one storyboard drawing. (Shots with complex character or camera moves are represented by three or more drawings.)

As Peter Jackson put it in the DVD commentary to *The Fellowship of the Ring*, storyboarding lets a director make his movie on an extremely low budget — for the cost of a few pencils and some paper.

Figure 12-1: One of the opening shots to the tavern sequence.

Only Computers Draw Straight Lines

To most professional artists, the most absurd reason why someone *thinks* he can't draw is that he "couldn't draw a straight line with a ruler." To be brutally honest about my own abilities, when I need a straight line, I use computer-aided design software and print the darn thing out.

Unless you're planning a career around being a storyboard artist, don't worry about your boards being beautiful works of art. So long as they convey the pertinent information to those who need to be informed, any rough sketch will do. (If you're doing a solo production, the only one who needs to understand your scribble is you!)

> NOTE
>
> It seems to me that ideas, drawings, and all things creative are like dairy products: Use 'em or they start to get "funky." So, whenever I start working on something creative after having "sat" for a while, I know I can expect to toss out the first three drawings, paragraphs, etc. This relieves the pressure of feeling that I have to match the quality of what I was doing when I last worked in that medium, letting me focus on just doing what needs to get done in the moment.
>
> You may have to work through a number of funky things to get them out of your system. Usually, the longer creativity goes fallow, the more funk you can expect to have to work through. So, if you want to do some really jammin' creative work, it's best to not fret the funk! Just buckle down and start doing what needs doing!

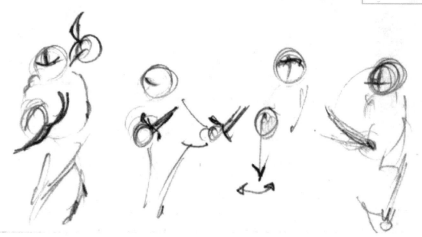

I've found that with the way I work, no matter how in love with any idea I set down in storyboard, when I'm actually working the scene, something better usually comes up while I'm animating. So, with my storyboarding *for myself*, I don't worry about getting things perfect, I just work on trying to establish a contiguous flow of images that represent the core ideas of the story.

Figure 12-2: This quick set of lines, crude though it may be, gives me everything I need to know about the basic positioning of the four attackers and the camera in this scene. It isn't "great art" by a long shot. But it does pin down my idea of that scene enough for me to work with later!

Frame Format

Guess what? If you haven't yet figured out what frame format your picture will be in (see Figure 12-3), you've got to do it now before you can start drawing your storyboards. Makes sense, doesn't it? But for many first-time filmmakers who are beginning their work outside of film school, frame format is often something that has never crossed their minds.

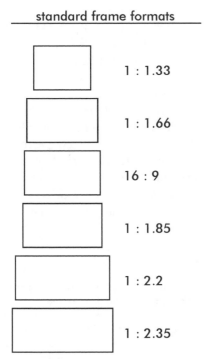

standard frame formats

1 : 1.33

1 : 1.66

16 : 9

1 : 1.85

1 : 2.2

1 : 2.35

Figure 12-3: Standard frame formats.

1:1.33 is the format used by "standard" televisions. It is also known as "Academy aperture."

1:1.66 is the wide-screen format common in Europe.

16:9 is the television wide-screen format. (It works out to 1:1.77.)

1:1.85 is the wide-screen format common in the United States.

1:2.2 is the format for 70mm film.

1:2.35 is the "anamorphic" wide-screen format (where in practical photography, a special anamorphic lens is used to "squish" the image to fit on a frame of 35mm film and another is used on the projector to "expand" it to fill the screen on playback).

My initial choice (reflected in my storyboards) was to do *Ghost Warrior* in 1:2.35, anamorphic wide-screen. However, when viewing my first final-render test, "letterboxed" on a standard television, I found that a lot of the fine detail of fur, eye, and mouth was lost. As an artist, I made the decision that it was more important for me to preserve the artistic composition available within the wide-screen format than it was to preserve the finer details of fur and clothing, and thus went with 1:1.85.

If you want to get the most crispness on a standard television (non-letterboxed), go with 1:1.33. If you are planning on a theatrical release and having the majority of your screenings in Europe, go with 1:1.66 (which can be shown on a screen built for 1:1.185 without worry). If you are planning on a primarily American theatrical release, 1:1.85 is a good aspect ratio in which to work (though it would be helpful to frame your storyboards keeping in mind what can be lost from the image's edges should you be asked to provide a 1:1.66 format version for European theatres). Of course, there is also 1:2.35 ("seriously" wide-screen format) for those who push the envelopes of dramatic framing and filmic compositions.

Resolution

Traditional filmmakers don't have to worry about the resolution of their frame images unless they are planning on having their film scanned (and eventually reprinted) for digital compositing and special effects. We, as CGI filmmakers, have to think about resolution right from the start. The more pixels we have to push, the more tedious things can become (and so very quickly).

Resolutions and ratios:

Format	Frame Aspect	Pixel Aspect	Width	Height
NTSC 1.33	1:1.33	1:1.111	720	480
NTSC 16:9	1:1.78	1:0.833	720	480
PAL	1:1.33	1:0.938	720	576
PAL 16:9	1:1.78	1:0.703	720	576
HDTV 720p	1:1.78	1:1	1280	720
HDTV 1080p	1:1.78	1:1	1920	1080
2K 1.85	1:1.85	1:1	1828	988
4K 1.85	1:1.85	1:1	3656	1976
2K Anamorphic	1:2.35	2:1	1828	1556
4K Anamorphic	1:2.35	2:1	3656	3112

Four factors come into play when determining at what resolution you will be rendering.

1. Computing power (hardware)

2. Plug-in functionality at higher-than-NTSC resolution (software)

3. Storage (hardware)

4. "Realistic" distribution medium

First comes *computing power*: How fast are the systems on which you'll be rendering? Do you have the time to render the resolution that you want in the time that you have? As the number of pixels you are rendering increases, it takes exponentially longer to render. (This proved to be a huge oversight of the first director of *Bugs Bunny: Lost in Time*. When he was fired and I had the directorship settled upon my shoulders, in addition to bailing out the animation, I had to figure out how to have all the frames rendered in-time at 4K film resolution!)

Secondly, some software and plug-ins don't behave as expected as you move away from NTSC resolution or take so long to compute that they become prohibitive when rendering film resolution.

Third is storage/archival. Yes, I realize that nowadays, "hard disk space is cheap." But bear in mind that for every finished frame that you get, you may have ten or more rendered layers that make up that one frame. If each open EXR frame of your film takes up 9 MB, and each RLA or RPF layer that has all those extra channels that make compositing so much better than rendering "in-camera" take up around 10 MB per frame, and you have six of these layers to go into each individual frame, that's about a CD's worth of information that needs to be stored (and archived) for each individual frame!

NOTE

Cover your ASCII!
Every night, you should be creating at least incremental backups of your work, and you should keep one copy of that backup *on-site* and at least one other copy *off-site*. This makes it so you have at least some chance of not losing your data if bad things should happen. You never know what can happen, from a simple hard drive crash (which happened on Babylon 5's *Thirdspace* — thank goodness for parity in striped RAID arrays) to fires, floods, thefts, vandalism, or even an ill-fated cup of coffee.

NOTE

Immediately after completing the modeling for *Ghost Warrior* before moving into the actual animation of the trailer itself, a series of ice jams breaking compounded the powerful force of water coming off the glaciers that feed the mighty Tanana River. (Picture the Mississippi, but moving at 10-15 knots during *normal* times and filled with glacial silt that will drag you to its bottom in no time flat should you fall in with any scrap of clothing on.) The Tanana overflowed its banks for the second time that year, flooding the little stream that my cabin in Salcha stood next to. Silently, the waters rose so fast I could see the change, but I was absolutely powerless to do anything about it.

Feeling very much like those battling the darkness at Helm's Deep, I received a call from Salcha Rescue that we were to evacuate.

Between my first run out to save my dogs (my Dodge Ram 4x4 was already spinning dangerously in silt-fed mud with the adhesion power of epoxy) and my return trip for my equipment, the bridge had been completely washed out. The part of the road that I *could* drive through was covered in swiftly flowing water about 2.5' deep. The only way across the torrent was in a neighbor's amphibious hunting vehicle.

With my computer equipment wrapped in garbage bags and balanced on my lap, the second trip saw us nearly swept downstream as wave after wave of silt-laden water crashed against the edge of the makeshift rig. Finally, the wheels caught on the gravel bottom and we began to swing toward the far shore.

Once the equipment was safely aboard my truck, I made a mental note to always keep current backups of my work.

Even in "the lower 48," one never knows when the unexpected might happen.

This photo is of the 15-meter wide "stream" during the midwinter flood earlier that year. The ambient temperature was −35°F, and yet with the force of the Tanana pressurizing the water from under the cover of ice, it became "overflow," super-cooled running water that at the point this photo was taken had already risen eight feet. All the "mist" you see is actually steam as the water was rapidly evaporating into the arctic dryness.

Lastly, make a good, educated decision about the medium in which your finished piece will be presented. You may indeed have the power and storage to produce 4K frames for your film (your software and plug-ins may indeed be perfectly stable and functional at that resolution), but if you are most likely to only showcase that particular work on DVD or video, don't kill yourself doing film resolution. (Sure, it would be nice to have your work backed up at film res, just in case some wealthy benefactor or distributor decides they'd love to see your work on 35mm, but make the conscious decision as to whether this is worth the effort.)

Rendering at film resolution takes immensely longer than rendering at video resolution. Compositing at film resolution takes immensely longer than compositing at video resolution. The current cost to print work to film is what will unfortunately keep a lot of independent filmmakers from having their films actually printed to film. (At the time I was shopping around, the average cost for having *Ghost Warrior*'s 22 minutes printed to 35mm with optical audio was about $12,000 U.S. for the first print and $1,000 for each additional print.)

Tools of the Trade

When you strip away all the technological "niftyness" that we have at our fingertips to create these works of art, when you examine the final render itself (projected on either the large or small screen), the art is still comprised of a series of colored shapes resting on a two-dimensional plane.

So, really, when it all boils down, the only thing that separates our work from the works of other artists working pigments onto two-dimensional planes is the fact that our "paintings" move. That's it.

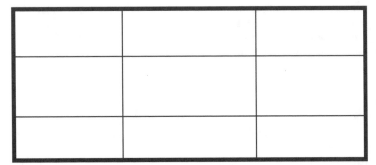

Figure 12-4: The *"rule of thirds."* Compositions are usually strongest when major elements fall on these lines.

With all the same rules of layout and design, the rules of *composition* that have applied to painters for thousands of years still apply to the two-dimensional plane on which our images are shown.

What's great is that the very best in "static" visual storytelling is all around you whenever you visit your local comic shop! Comic books are fantastic reference materials for storyboarding (regardless of whether you are a director or storyboard artist, and regardless of your level of skill at drawing). The comic book industry is *always* exploring new and exciting ways of framing panels and layering important visual information within a frame!

NOTE

The following illustrations are just different camera angles of the *exact same* pose! Notice how with changes of framing, composition, and camera angle, the same poses seem to tell different stories!

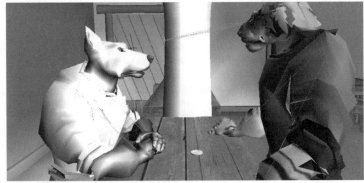

Figure 12-5: *Balance.* A composition that is split (or "weighted") evenly usually denotes a feeling of solidity.

Figure 12-6: *Un-balance*. Tension is created in this framing; it feels that Kaze has backed Itsua right up to the edge of the frame.

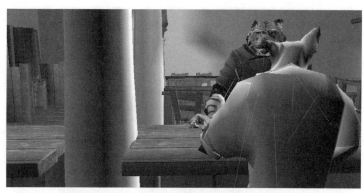

Figure 12-8: *Even rhythm*. The even, vertical nature of the elements within this shot makes for a very solid feeling for the viewer.

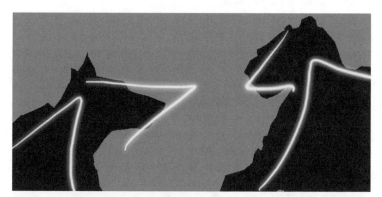

Figure 12-7: *Triangles*. Wedge shapes focus the viewer's eye and expectation of motion from their widest end to their narrowest. They are like *arrows*, directing the viewer's eye from one important point of interest to another.

Figure 12-9: *Syncopation*. Here, elements are staggered along *all* axes (including the z-axis). There are still strong vertical elements with the columns echoing the characters, but they are offset with the angles of the wooden support beams and the bottom of the Persian arch.

Figure 12-10: *Atmospheric perspective.* Fading elements into a layer of *fog* helps viewers place visual elements in "3D space" with respect to one another. (Because only places of extreme temperatures are devoid of atmospheric moisture, renderings of all other places benefit from even an "unnoticeable" bit of fogging.)

Figure 12-11: *Depth of field.* This works like atmospheric perspective by letting viewers identify relative positioning along the camera's z-axis based on varying degrees of edge softness.

Figure 12-12: *Silhouette.* The single most important tool that we have as visual artists is a strong silhouette. Eliminate all other points of reference, and a strong silhouette will still let your viewer identify what is going on, both physically and emotionally.

Figure 12-13: The *long shot. Long* shots are shots that show the maximum amount of the environment within which your characters are working. Often, they are used as an opening to a sequence to help the audience establish where everything and everyone is in relation to everything and everyone else. So, the "super-long-show-where-everything-is" shots are known as *establishers.*

Figure 12-14: *High-angle*. High- and low-angle shots are more "artsy" and extreme than your average shot. Both create dramatic effects of perspective and wonderful angles from linear elements (like the bar in this shot) that so often find themselves lining up with a frame edge otherwise. High-angle shots are often used to make a particular character look diminutive, as if being seen from the eyes of someone bigger or more powerful. (Often, in "Gen X" vids, these angles are pushed even farther by rotating the camera on its bank, or local z-axis, known as "Dutching" when done with a real-world camera.)

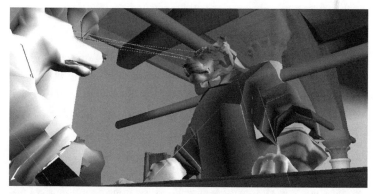

Figure 12-15: *Low-angle*. Like the high-angle shot, it coaxes some wonderful lines and perspective from the elements within a shot. Most often used to make a character seem bigger or more imposing, as if the camera represents someone much smaller and less powerful than the main character in the shot.

NOTE

I've been asked that with all the 3D work I do, if I still paint. The answer is yes, at least once a week.

My work in 3D, working directly with the mathematics that govern light and shadow, has greatly helped my understanding of what I'm seeing when I want to recreate a scene through a series of colored shapes on canvas. My work painting has helped me immeasurably when it comes to 3D.

As a painter, it is my job to create single frames that tell entire stories at a glance as patrons walk by in galleries. It is my job to create strong, narrative compositions that reach out and grab the hearts and imaginations of those who meander casually by while talking among friends. I have to manually apply the colors, lighting techniques, surfacing techniques, and edge techniques that 3D compositing software allows me to do almost without thinking. Because of this, I feel I have a better understanding of what goes into making art than I ever would have otherwise.

The result in *Ghost Warrior* is that each and every frame is exactly as I would want it to be were it a painting. Every effect of light, color, composition, edge, and shadow is what I would like to see in a painting that would take a week to a month to create were I rendering it by hand on canvas.

Almost Animation

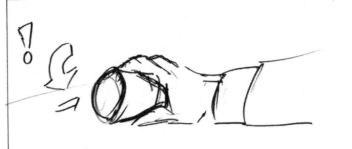

Figure 12-16: In this shot, a Troublemaker slams down his shot glass, tips it on its side, and presses his fingers down on it, "snapping" it so it spins off-screen.

In storyboarding, sometimes you run into a complex shot that needs more than a single image and a description to be told. Multiple frames are especially needed if you frequently find yourself looking at a board and wondering what was in your mind when you drew it or if the scene will be animated by someone else.

Storyboarding these shots sometimes means doing quick sketches of what might be the key frames for that animation.

The shot illustrated in Figure 12-16 would be difficult to convey in just a single frame or description. Drawing it as a series of three frames lets me flip between them and see if the action I had hoped for is working.

Don't shy away from doing multiple drawings for scenes with semi-complex or complex action in them. When you cut them together in a video editing program and let them play out at real time, you can see if your plan is working or if you need to go back and make changes. This is just one more way to work in broad strokes first while changes are still quick and easy.

In Figure 12-16, you'll also notice arrows and exclamation points. Storyboard artists use every visual convention they can think of to indicate action or emotion. Arrows are common tools to indicate action and movement of both characters and camera. The more clean and readable the arrows, the better the storyboards! As you can see, my arrows (and drawing for the adjacent storyboards) are pretty crummy. Because I'm the only one who has to work from them, even these rough scribbles work just fine for my purposes. If you can understand your own scrawls enough to convey what you need to convey, even if you feel you're terribly "illustratively challenged," you can still manage storyboarding your own film just fine!

Action

Filmmakers have honed the skills of portraying storytelling through the visual medium of film for over 100 years. Conventions of "marrying" shots and angles to tell a narrative have been devised, abandoned, and rediscovered.

Going to film school is a very good way to learn a wealth of information. Books that focus almost entirely on these techniques, like *Film Directing Shot by Shot*, are beyond measure of their value for the information they contain. But remember, the *results* of all these years of the actual practice of filmmaking is available at your fingertips for a few dollars at your local video rental store.

The trick is to watch the films without getting sucked in (as they do when they are doing what they should). A secret to being able to do this is to *watch movies with the sound off.*

It sounds simple, doesn't it? Watch a movie with the sound muted, and you can begin to really see the art of filmcraft used in *creating* the work. But that's exactly how things are.

The way to learn quickly from these masterworks, like *Alien*, *Blade Runner*, *Star Wars* (episodes 4-6), and the like, is to get yourself a playback device that you can (safely) pause and step-frame through sequences and scenes.

It is simple. Just find some portion of a film that you really find moving, and step through it, quickly sketching the *placement* of what you're seeing. (I keep a stack of preprinted storyboard "blanks" that I've had xeroxed in a folder by the TV, just in case something really moves me and I want to understand how it was done.)

Even though the human mind will try to find a narrative context among any series of images, your visual storytelling will be much better served by understanding how the masters worked their magic. All it takes is a single-frame VCR or DVD player, a pencil, and a pad of storyboard blanks for you to begin to understand that magic yourself!

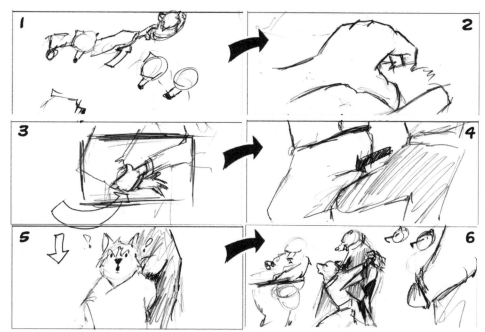

Figure 12-17: This is the part of sequence 2 where the Male Server gets kicked to his knees as the Lead Troublemaker tries to get a reaction from Kaze.

After step-framing through many fight sequences in other films and knowing the sequence of events that a martial artist would undertake to perform the move, I sketched the sequence of storyboards shown in Figure 12-17. The sequence of shots seems to work well on paper, reading like a comic book, but the only way to know for sure if this series of images would really work for a viewer is to edit them together in a video editing program. (I use ToasterEdit, part of the VT[3] suite.) Doing this is known as creating an animatic or Lecia reel (see Chapter 14). It creates a movie from my storyboards, a movie that for all intents and purposes is a quickly drawn, perfect representation of what the final film will be.

Creating an animatic is the *only* way to know for sure if your storyboards are really telling the story you want. This is *pre-visualization!*

Chapter 13

Technology Solutions

When you actually begin to move into production, you want to be able to focus 100 percent of your attention on getting the best performance and best look out of your scenes. You don't want to be fighting with your software or hardware. So you enter into a time where you are exploring your technology solutions. This is the time when you push your potential tools much harder than they will be pushed in production itself to find out what succeeds in giving you what it promised and what falls to pieces.

For hardware and software, this is where you pull the "blue sky" phase of ideation into the real world of what can actually be done. You may find yourself having to rework some points of your story because of things that may not work as well in practice as in theory. Or you may find some speed optimizations or certain programs that outperform their marketing (rare, yes, I know, but I found that in Digital Fusion, LightWave, and the other parts of the VT[3] suite), letting you rework your concepts to allow for the increased ability now at your fingertips.

This is the part of pre-production where you set aside time to explore all the neat things that you've heard from friends, from colleagues, and over the Internet. You explore these cool, *potential* tools and press them to their limits to see if they'll do what you need them to do under the high-pressure environment of full-fledged production.

A nifty plug-in may work fine for doing the test scenes, but may fall apart or slow animation to a crawl with your high-res characters or cause crashing when rendered over a network renderer! You've got to test all these situations and scenarios *before* you get into production.

Your one goal this time with technology solutions is to find out what works. You may find a way to script together two things that were never meant to go together but produce the perfect result for what your film is needing. Results are all that matter here; "style points" are virtually nonexistent. After all, the audience will never know how "Rube Goldbergian" the production pipeline may have been; all they will see is the final product.

Knowing as much as you can about as many things as you can is your greatest asset in this part of pre-production. Even if you have teams of development people working for you, if you know what they're talking about (and you know what *you're* talking about), you can lend your creativity to their process and help them achieve things they might never have thought of on their own!

If you are a small studio or a one-man show, the importance of knowing how to sift "$#!+ from shinola" cannot be understated or underestimated as you set up the pathway every single frame of your film will travel to its final place in your film.

You cannot be afraid of your tools. Like a good general, you have to know what each part of your production force (human and non-human) is capable of doing under pressure. You have to know ways of achieving your desired results even when it may be "logically" beyond your team's abilities. The phrase that describes this process in action is *applied creativity*. This is both knowing how to find out what needs doing and being able to get done what needs to be done.

Through your testing of personnel, software, hardware, and the bits and pieces that connect them, you are establishing a "pipeline" through which each and every frame of your film will flow until it becomes a part of your finished film. You will have to know what this pipeline can accommodate, how much pressure it can withstand, where it is most likely to "spring a leak," and how to fix problems with and within it, big and small, while it is still in use!

It's an exciting time, full of experimentation and discoveries. Once production starts, like the crew on a space flight, there's no turning back.

> "Once you're off the ground, you have committed yourself and your passengers to making a successful landing."
>
> — old pilot's saying

NOTE

Always bear in mind that one can't plan for everything. But what one *can* do is build up enough knowledge to implement the creativity needed to find out how to fix what needs fixing when the need arises.

Beware Big Words

I want to really drive home the point that you really, *really* need to avoid (don't touch with a ten-foot pole) anyone (and anything) that is hooked on using "big words." You know the type. These are the people who make themselves seem smarter by making their listeners feel dumber.

Look, if you can't make yourself understood by a seven-year-old, you don't understand what you're talking about yourself!

I've heard of more productions that have been killed (or almost killed) by the hiring of "big-word" people because producers assumed that "buzzwords" or "tech-speak" equated to *real knowledge*. When things got hot, those people didn't know the first thing about how to do what they said they could do. (Remember Lt. Gorman in *Aliens*? Something like that.)

Here's a big hint to all the Hollywood producer-types out there: The ones who truly know their stuff let their work speak for itself! The ones who know their stuff can explain it and make it sound simple.

NOTE

Like runners in a marathon, the one with the easiest, most understated stride is the one to bet on winning. The one who really looks like he's working hard will probably never make it to the finish line.

However, the current system of Hollywood rarely allows for "reality" to be seen through the salesmanship of being "Hollywood." But as with any system of habits and patterns, this "hard-sell" behavior can be modified by the people with the power (like you, if you're making a film) to recognize and *reward* those who truly know their stuff.

This happens by making anyone that you are considering working for you explain to you in plain English, in ways that you, or anyone, can understand exactly, what they do and how that can help your dream become a reality. No acronyms, no tech-babble — just plain, simple English that a seven-year-old would be able to understand.

Hardware

Don't believe for a microsecond that a computer is "just a computer." Granted, with the power of even one of today's "meager" systems, one can work wonders with a well-coded 3D package. If the hardware that you currently have is the hardware on which you'll be working, that will play a major factor in what you'll be able to do render-wise with your story. However, if you have the resources to purchase new, dedicated equipment, *research, research, research!*

Start at the Source

If you already know the software that you'll be using (or are considering using), give those software manufacturers a call and *ask them directly* what hardware specifications they recommend. See if you can get them to be as specific as possible, even down to the manufacturer of the boards themselves (with more and more companies leasing out their technology, like nVidia and their graphics cards, this becomes ever more of an issue).

Compile notes on both "best case" and "bargain basement" options. Once you've collated your notes from the software manufacturers (who aren't going to try to sell you hardware), *then* start contacting vendors. When you know more about what you're

talking about with the salesmen, you stand a better chance of making good decisions.

One rule of thumb to follow is never purchase anything immediately. Always let at least one night pass before making any kind of commitment to purchase anything. Collect your notes (and yourself) and make a decision based on rational thought, not on the "neuro-linguistic programming" techniques that sales staff frequently use. (*Neuro-linguistic programming* (NLP) is a technique that basically uses hypnotic training and methods to get the listener to do what the speaker wants him/her to do.)

"Home Brew"

One option open to the PC and UNIX crowds is to build your own computers yourself. For the technology-inclined, it's a tasty prospect to save some cash and know exactly what goes into a system and what to expect from it.

But, with making your own film, short or otherwise, you will be pushing your hardware far beyond what is needed for writing an e-mail, far beyond what is needed for playing your favorite first-person shooter or massively-multiplayer online video game. The kind of processing that goes into rendering 3D will work your microprocessors like they've never been worked before. So, the low-end processors of the same generation that are sold as "family-oriented," "lite" versions (lacking things like enhanced floating-point operations that aren't needed when just composing e-mails) will be far slower than their higher-end counterparts.

Floating Point

This is just a note on the difference between the full-fledged versions of microprocessors and the "perfect for family," "lite" versions.

3D CGI is the art of mathematics. (The 3D programs just give us a nice, usable interface to this artful math.) Floating-point calculations are, in essence, extremely precise mathematics. A microprocessor that has the ability to accelerate and streamline these calculations will be much faster than a "lite" microprocessor that has to do things the "long way." (You can think about this in terms of someone using a calculator racing against someone using a pencil and paper to do long division.)

If you're in doubt as to the math capabilities of a particular processor, talk with your local hardware dealer. Processors and chipsets change so rapidly that talking with someone who's business it is to know about the "latest and greatest" is the only way to know for sure if what you are getting will fit your needs.

Dual Processors

Most programs that a "normal" person would run, like a word processor or a spreadsheet, would never take full advantage of a system that has two microprocessors on the same motherboard. In fact, going into your local computer shop, you'll probably get some strange looks at first when you ask for a dual-processor main board ("Why would you ever need that?").

Almost all 3D packages and compositing programs *do* take full advantage of this parallel processing. What is absolutely amazing to

me, and still dumbfounds me, is the speed increase of today's processors *specially designed for parallel processing*.

> **NOTE**
>
> Both AMD (American Micro-Dynamics) and Intel have specifically designed processors intended to be used in multiprocessor server systems. If you are going for a multiprocessor system, make sure the CPUs (central processing units) are rated for multiprocessor use.

For *Ghost Warrior*, I brought in a commercial that would pay for the system upgrade I wanted, moving from an "older" AMD Athlon 1GHz to a dual, Intel 2GHz. When comparing render times using only one processor, the speed increase was a factor of 1.5, exactly what I expected from my previous upgrades that doubled the processor's clock rate.

When I kicked in both processors, rendering with multi-threading active, I was floored to find the speed increase to be just under a factor of 7! I checked my experiment carefully and upon retesting got the exact same results. I even found that while rendering on only a "single thread" (only using one processor) when I was asking the other processor to do something like play a movie or slide show of pictures, a similar exponential speed increase was evident too.

A solution offered by someone connected with the Arctic Region Supercomputing Center was that since the CPUs were *designed specifically* for *parallel processing*, like ARSC's own parallel processing *supercomputers*, the same kind of optimizations were taking place.

Whatever the reason, this "happy accident" allowed me to further expand the complexity of my work with *Ghost Warrior*. It also made me a serious fan of multiprocessor machines!

Compatibility

Some people have said that with all the stuff that goes into computers, built by umpteen different companies across the world, it's a minor miracle that they work at all. Because of small variances between companies, even when working from the same specifications, sometimes bits and pieces of a computer won't work, or work well, with other bits from other manufacturers.

The long and the short of this pedantic pain in the posterior is that it allows hardware manufacturers to hide behind the fact that if a bit of hardware wasn't specifically tested with their own bit of hardware, they don't have to feel ashamed that it doesn't work. I've found several companies in my own computer-building escapades that conveniently hide behind the phrase, "Oh, that video card isn't tested to go with our motherboard" or "You need our special power supply that costs almost eight times as much as a regular power supply."

So, before you start spending your hard-earned money, research, research, research! Call manufacturers directly if you need to in order to find out exactly what kind of memory (does it need ECC, error-checking memory), video cards (what brands *aren't* supported), and the whole nine yards of what you will need to put your system together. It may seem like extra effort at the beginning of a project that you really want to be diving into, but let me tell you from experience that trying to run a production on a computer that you want to mash up into little-bitty computer meatballs is a level of hell I'd wish on no one.

Running a production is enough stress without the added stress of your computer locking up sporadically. Doing 3D CGI, we're pushing these machines as hard as they were ever meant to be pushed. What we're doing with them is so far beyond what most normal people do that it isn't even funny. Pushing them this hard, we find all the "weak spots" and they sometimes (virtually) tear

loose at the seams with explosive force under the extreme pressures of the average production environment.

I have been very happy with my AMD. It is still very much in use as the "second" machine on *Ghost Warrior*. My reason for making my primary machine an Intel was partly curiosity for not having used an Intel processor in four years and partly the fact that the VT[3], my choice for video input/output, was approved only on a specific Intel chipset.

Prebuilt Systems

There was a time when I thought of build-it-yourself computer components like Legos® for adults. Now, however, I don't have time to "play" with computers; I just want the darn things to do what I paid for them to do. (Do you ever have the feeling that if your computer were an employee, you'd have fired it long ago?)

Buying a system prebuilt by another company that *specializes* in the specific kind of system you need (*not* the low-dollar places you find on price-comparing, Internet meta-search engines) can often be well worth the extra money that it might cost over building a system yourself (or having anyone not versed in the specific needs of 3D CGI build a machine for you). When you figure your own time as money and know how much you'd like to be paying yourself (you'll often find the ability to know that if your machine isn't working as it is supposed to, that you can call "tech support" and get things fixed), you may find a huge savings in going the prebuilt route.

Dual Monitors

If you've never worked with dual monitors while doing 3D CGI before, plan to treat yourself to doing so now. Video cards that support two monitors are very reasonable, as are monitors themselves.

It may seem like a luxury to those who have yet to have their paint package open on one monitor and their 3D package open on the other, but once you start working with "dualies," you'll never want to go back.

Most programs, 3D and otherwise, allow you to "undock" your menus, moving them around or even letting them float unattached over some other area of the screen. With dual monitors, you can maximize your working space by having all your "helper windows" on your second monitor!

Again, of course, each video card has its own driver that tells a computer how to handle using two monitors instead of just one. I've tried both the ATI and the nVidia high-end graphics cards and personally liked the way nVidia handled dualies best. (Which isn't to say that you might not like the ATI way better. Find someone who'll let you work on their machine *first, before* making a purchase that you might feel inclined to return!)

Flat Panel LCD vs. CRT

I work with one flat panel LCD monitor and one cathode-ray tube (CRT) monitor. I find the LCD screen to be easier on the eyes when doing fine detail work or writing, but depending on how high or low in my chair I am sitting, the monitor's colors change. So, I have my left monitor, the CRT, "color-corrected," so when I'm doing print work, I can know that what I'm seeing on the monitor is going to be very close to the output I see from a print.

Another thing that most people don't think about as a difference between LCD and CRT is that I'd never dare use dry erase markers on an LCD monitor. Dry erase wipes away perfectly from my CRT. Why would someone ever want to use dry erase markers on a monitor? As an animator, I'm always using different-colored dry erase markers to help me track elbows, heads, knees and whatnot; it lets me view my progression of frames the same way I would if I were animating on paper.

One thing to bear in mind about LCD monitors is that you very much get what you pay for. You can find inexpensive LCD monitors, but I've found these to be blurry and almost maddening for the precision required for doing 3D work.

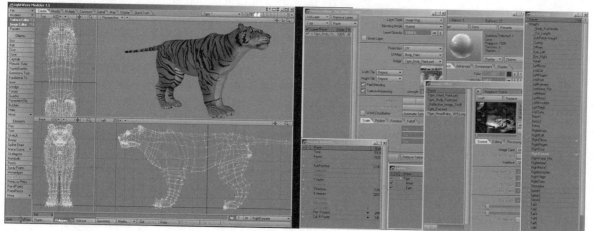

Figure 13-1: Having moved the clutter of all my helper windows to the right monitor, I can model with an unhindered view on the left!

Broadcast Video In/Out

You need to think about what you will be using to play your work to a video (TV) monitor and "digitize" any reference footage that you may be shooting. Even if you are planning on working at film resolution, you can use video resolution as a quick way to do "offline" edits that you can view right on your computer or video monitor, exporting an edit list (EDL) for your film resolution software to mirror on the film resolution footage.

There are many different brands of professional, "pro-sumer," and consumer video input/output cards available. Their prices range from under $50 to well over $5,000. Curiously enough, price isn't necessarily the determining factor in the quality of these boards. Research, and knowing beforehand what you need your card to do for you, is the only way to sift through the plethora of possibilities available to you.

My own choice for *Ghost Warrior* was to go with the NewTek VT[3] Film and High Definition hardware/software suite. It is billed as being a "TV studio in a box." In this day and age of nearly everything and everyone overselling themselves, I thought, "Sure, maybe a small studio." I was completely unprepared for the scope, depth, and forward-thinking nature of this combination of hardware and software. It far exceeds what is used to broadcast the NBC feed and produce live newscasts at the NBC affiliate I was a producer for when I first moved to Fairbanks.

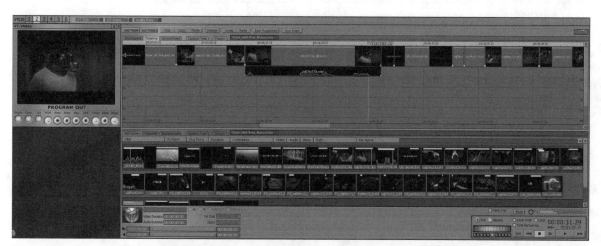

Figure 13-2: This is Toaster Edit, shown loaded onto one of the *six* "desktops" that can be instantly switched between in the VT[3] suite. (The use of multiple desktops allows you to have every tool you want open and still keep your monitor clean and clutter-free.)

(The cross keyer in the upper right of this image lets you key-out multiple colors by painting them into the vectorscope area.)

Figure 13-3: This shows an example of the VT[3]'s *keying* capabilities. The *background generator* is creating a four-color background (on the *main* monitor) over which the image of Kaze is *chroma-keyed* (removing the "green screen" from behind him — seen on the *key* monitor). A *downstream key* of the text "Ghost Warrior" is composited over the resultant video (useful when doing live broadcasts). Chroma-keying in VT[3] is as easy as dragging an eyedropper from the *keyer* onto the green or blue screen in your video footage.

Figure 13-4: This image shows the VT[3]'s audio mixer, real-time waveform monitor and vectorscope manual capture controls (it also supports batch, timecode-based capture), digital disk recorder, and its interface to control an external SDI, Firewire, or other controller-based VTR.

Probably the single most helpful thing about the VT[3] suite is something that is so small and innocuous that it might go unnoticed unless one has tried to learn other video systems: Each and every tool's on-screen interface looks exactly like the "real-world" tool that it replaces. Why is this important? Two reasons: One is that most real-world tools have been honed and developed over years and years to be as "intuitive" as possible. Secondly, if you know how to use the real-world tools, you already know how to run the VT! (It took me all of about an afternoon to feel comfortable driving the VT with the same skill level I'd used when manning a real-life Betacam, Grass Valley, Fostex, and other real-world audio and video equipment.)

However, the most impressive thing about the VT is that *all of it works in real time* (when you are running it on a recommended system). It doesn't bat an eyelash when running *eight streams of uncompressed, broadcast-quality video at once!* Its chroma-keyer (and multi-color key, "cross-keyer") do every bit as good a job as any hardware-based keyer I've used (as evidenced in Figure 13-3 where Kaze's fur is perfectly separated from its "green screen" background). It has real-time special effects, color correction, image manipulation, blurs, fades, wipes, dissolves, positioning, overlays (over *both* prerecorded and live, incoming streams of video — using the optional SX-8, you can switch between up to 24 live video inputs), and the ability to play video forward, backward, and slow or fast (just to list some of what it can do).

The video editor that the VT suite comes with is probably the fastest, most intuitive editor I've ever worked with, supporting all of the VT's other special effects and tools. It's like the designers thought ahead to what people might someday need when they find themselves in a bind. For instance, undos and redos *persist between editing sessions* (and optionally when you save to different named revisions as well)! This means that you can come back to your project weeks later and have just as many options to undo as you did

before you saved (the default number of undos for Toaster Edit is 100)!

Couple that with a real-time waveform monitor and vectorscope, the ability to do real-time "character crawls," (like end-credits after a show), *and* an animation-enabled, resolution-independent, multi-layered, pressure-sensitive paint program (called Aura) that shows its display in real time on (or keyed over) your video out, *plus* a license of LightWave. In short, I was just floored. It's rare to find that much really good stuff (that actually does *more* than what its marketing says it does) all rolled into one package.

It should be noted that the VT[3] production suite gives you *lossless*, component, YC, and composite NTSC/PAL video in/out and comes with its own software-based editing suite, audio mixer, scalable 8-input video switcher, waveform monitor, vectorscope, chroma and luma keyer, multiple-color "cross keyer" (that both work in real time on *both* captured and live footage), virtual monitors that support *underscanning*, *zebra*, and the flagging of "off-limits" colors, optional support for *serial digital interface*, Firewire, batch capturing, background generator, and character generator. The VT[3] suite also comes with full versions of New-Tek's Aura (imagine Photoshop but with animation capabilities, a full-fledged scripting language, and the ability to instantly see what you paint on your television monitor — regardless of resolution, with a solid background or *keyed* "downstream" over live or captured footage — in addition to seeing your work as you'd expect on the computer monitor) *and* LightWave!

(Pardon the above lengthy sentence-paragraph, but it is the only way I can think of to give even a glimmer of the "Holy cats! It does this too" feeling I experienced when going through the VT suite for the first time.)

What amazes me even more is that while LightWave alone is $1,500, the entire VT[3] suite (which *includes* LightWave) is only $2,700. That means that for less than twice the price of LightWave alone, you get LightWave and all the tools of the VT[3] suite that let you play, view, edit, and adjust your CGI film in broadcast-quality video in ways that not even a $60,000 Avid suite can match!

Storage/Backup

The amount of storage and backup space that you'll need is determined by the length of your film, the number of layers used to create each frame, and the resolution at which you'll be rendering. Hard-disk space is much less expensive now than it has ever been. Even the high-speed, video-approved (meaning that they won't try to recalibrate themselves when you're trying to read or write video to them) SCSI drives are reasonable for most budgets nowadays.

So, my comment about storage is to plan in advance for how much space you might need and make sure you get at least half again that amount (amount_you_get >= 1.5 * amount_you_need) before you begin production. This saves headaches later on down the road.

You can combine, or *stripe*, several drives together into what the computer will see as one huge drive (usually done with SCSI drives because you can "chain" up to 15 ultra-SCSI drives to one ultra-SCSI controller). This allows you to get faster performance when reading and writing from and to the "striped array" and lets you set up *parity* that will enable some measure of data recovery, should one of the drives of the "RAID array" go bad. (Ask your friendly, neighborhood computer technician how.)

But the only true way to "cover your ASCII" is to back up and back up regularly!

The "standard" method of backing up data is backing up to tape. Exabyte and DLT (digital linear tape) are the "old standbys."

I tried something new with *Ghost Warrior*, backing up to CDRW and later to DVD-rewritable.

DVD rewritables, both the drives and the media, are much more inexpensive now than tape drives and media and can hold gigabytes on a single disc. There are many different formats of DVD write-once and rewritable drives out there, including +/– R and +/– RW. Each specification behaves differently, allowing for a little more or a little less data storage and a higher or lower probability of being able to have their discs played on a home DVD player. Up-to-the-minute research and comparison shopping is the only way to know which tool will suit your personal needs.

My own methodology for backing up is to do a *full backup* each and every week (making a copy of that disc to keep in an off-site location). I also do *incremental backups* every single night after I make notable changes to my work. (*Incremental backups* just save the files that have been changed since the last backup, while *full backups* save everything.)

"Color me paranoid," but I keep my in-house backups in a locked metal cabinet and my off-site backups on my person whenever I go out. I've worked too hard bringing my dream to this point to risk losing it. I see it as a measure of respect for both myself and my dream to protect it to the best degree I can at all times.

Mice/Tablets

You'll be doing a lot of computing over the course of your film, so treat yourself to the best ergonomic mouse available. If a few dollars now will save you the possibility of pain, downtime, and possible surgical costs of a repetitive stress injury later, it is so very worth the expenditure.

Personally, I prefer to work with a tablet whenever possible. I find that the angles and motions of using a Wacom stylus to be much easier on my own joints (but remember, everybody's different). Where I notice this the most is in "pulling points" while modeling. Being able to just tap the stylus down and drag a point is much easier on my hand, wrist, and arm than the "click-hold-drag-release" needed when using a mouse.

The Wacom I still use on a daily basis is the old 12"x12" that I bought from the studio I did my first "animated storybook" animation work for. It was well-used then, back in 1995, and it has held up and performs beautifully to this day. Something not often thought of until you actually use the daylights out of a tablet is that the little plastic nib of the Wacom stylus has held up incredibly well. I've only had to swap nibs twice (from its included packet of about seven) in my entire time of using my Wacom heavily on a daily basis for eight years.

UPS

Oh, let me sing the praises on high for the wonders of a good uninterruptible power supply! "There ain't nuthin' better" than to be working away, and when the lights go dark and the music goes silent (for whatever reason), your face is still lit by the cheery glow of your monitor as you think to yourself, "Boy, it's been hours since I last saved. Without this UPS, I'd be up a creek without a canoe!"

Seriously, even in the best of places, tiny power outages that can freeze a computer aren't uncommon. When most artists really get "in the groove," part of that groove is to forget about time and saving your work. While most software packages let you activate an auto-save feature, most artists don't because that tiny, almost imperceptible "hiccup" as the computer automatically saves your work gets really irritating when you're in the groove.

The more powerful the machine you have, the more "juice" it takes to power. I purchased my first, "light-duty" UPS when all I had was the "old" AMD. With the AMD, I could run about 20 minutes on the UPS' battery before having to shut down. Now, with the dual-processor Intel and the dual monitors on the same UPS, I have a maximum of three minutes before the battery dwindles.

If you can afford it, it is a good idea to have a good UPS on every one of your "render nodes" as well — and of course, on your render server also. This way, if the power does go out, if it isn't longer than your UPS' batteries last, you won't have to worry about restarting your render farm!

Anti-virus/Firewall

Oh, what a pain in the *butt* it is to have to have a *virus-protection* program and a *firewall* running on one's machine nowadays. As good as these protective programs are, they still add time to logins/logouts and program starting, and they take up compute cycles that would be much better used in rendering masterpieces.

I don't know why people write viruses. Maybe they feel powerless in their own lives and feel that this gives them some kind of anonymous power over others. Maybe they think they'll be "cool" if they frustrate other people. Maybe they're jealous of the success that other people have.

Personally, from the amount of time and data loss and frustration ("pain and suffering," in legal terms) viruses have caused, it astounds me that there aren't more class-action lawsuits when someone gets caught causing frustration and/or pain to someone else by writing or modifying a virus or worm.

But, all Kaze-like opinions aside, it's a sad fact of the times that we've got to cover our ASCII in all ways possible, and that means getting the very best in virus and hacker protection available. There are many good anti-virus software packages out there and many good firewalls (Internet security tools) in both hardware and software. (With the rise of "always-on" Internet connections like cable modems and DSL, you need to protect yourself from the numerous intrusion attempts made every day, even when just connecting through a dial-up connection.)

CG Software

Now we're at the part that most people think of when they think of doing a CGI film — the 3D software (the "front ends" that control the magnificent maelstrom of mathematics that control the hue, saturation, and luminosity of the pixels that make up each and every frame of your film).

Each of us has our own preferred ways of working, and each software package's unique quirks will more directly appeal to some more than others. I've been "around the block" and have made my own decisions as to what is *good for me* and what is not. Because I've seen a lot of the dirty underbelly of the world of CGI, I can't promise to be impartial, but I can promise to be honest.

I can't go over every package available, but I can make clear points about the packages that I have chosen to create *Ghost Warrior* and the reasoning behind those choices.

There is so much out there in terms of 3D and compositing software that all one can hope to do is make a moderately educated decision about what to use. Seek out people who approach problem-solving as you do, and ask them about their experiences with the packages that they've used. Ask them about what they wished the software did that it doesn't do without coding one's own scripts. (I've never been able to find the value in purchasing a piece of software that I need to rewrite in order to get it to do what I paid for it to do; it's like hiring an animator and then having to animate half of each of his scenes myself!) Ask which parts of the 3D software package saved them time, what "foresightful innovations" the program implemented.

What you want to do in selecting any program is find functionality that works so well with the way you, personally, problem-solve that the program itself seems to "disappear" as you work, evoking the feeling that you are directly working with and within the works of art you are creating. It may sound esoteric, but it happens each

and every time a digital artist begins to "get into" his work on a well-crafted combination of hardware and software (just as it does every time a traditional artist starts to sink his hands into his medium of choice).

NOTE

The creation of most art (filmmaking and CGI included) is like the magical blending that happens in a live jazz jam session.

Before the music starts, each artist knows bits and pieces, "riffs," that can be played through all scales and in all ranges of his or her instruments. Each artist knows how to *listen* to what is going on around him to direct his own decisions.

When the music begins, all the technical training, all the "riffs" and scales, vanish into the domain of the subconscious, letting the artists go on "autopilot," as they just listen for what *feels right*. The skills that they have honed to such high degrees let their fingers execute perfectly the elusive combinations of "weight" and "timing," so they can remain almost an outside observer to the experiences that they are participating in creating.

Every skill that you develop with your CGI software and every control you memorize lets you forget about the running of your program while you work. Like the jazz artist, you simply *feel* that something is right, and your training lets your hands execute the combination of controls to enact that thought into form. You remain as an outside observer, watching your work develop through an almost "eternal now," as amazed as any theatregoer at the magic you played a part in bringing into this world.

Only the best software allows for this kind of spontaneity, of this kind of freedom. Each software package is as unique as the individual ways in which we think. But not every software package has the strength to let you forget that you're working on a computer. Research well, and choose wisely.

Character Animation

Use the correct tool for the job.

It is common for the biggest studios to use one software package for character animation and another for facial animation. That's what was done on *Ghost Warrior*, but even if you decide that you'll use your 3D package for doing both, I strongly recommend thinking about character animation and facial animation as two separate steps.

If you are able to *sell* your scene through the character's actions, postures, poses, and movements *first*, *before* you get into any facial animation, then the facial animation will be "icing on the cake." This simple-sounding concept is a cornerstone to crafting beautiful, believable performances. Knowing that if, with your character's face a stiff and static mask, you are able to still *feel* the core emotions within a scene, you've done your job as an *actor*, and an equally powerful performance with facial animation will boost the impact of the scene exponentially.

Research

My own research for the appropriate CGI software for the way I work has been an ongoing process of continual evaluation since I started practicing as a professional animator. I now take the marketing "glitz" and "glam" for what it is — salesmanship, nothing more. Like being wary of "big words" from potential employees and partners, I focus my evaluation solely on what the program is actually capable of.

My choice in using LightWave for *Ghost Warrior* follows a long path where I departed from using the software for some time while using Maya, Softimage, and 3D Studio Max. I came back to it with renewed respect after having delved deeply into those other programs and, in that education period, having seen just how much

LightWave is capable of, how much creative *freedom* it affords, and how rare it is that software actually delivers on what it promises.

Of the other three professional CGI packages mentioned, I rank Softimage higher in some respects than LightWave, but its cost for the complete package that had everything I needed was out of my range of "do-ability." So, while I admire Softimage highly as a fantastic platform for character animation and its Mental Ray as a rendering engine, LightWave comes out on top in the Timothy Albee "bang-for-your-buck" competition.

NOTE

In addition to the purchase price of character animation and rendering software are two things that are somewhat like "hidden costs," not immediately thought of to the noninitiate. They are the cost of plug-ins (programs that fit, "Lego-like," onto the 3D package enabling extra functions, like cloth or fur) and the cost of additional render nodes for rendering your scenes across a network. (Render nodes are usually command-line programs that do nothing but render your frames on idle machines or on machines set aside specifically for rendering — known as a "render farm").

Plug-ins that are made for different programs usually cost significantly more for Maya and Softimage than they do for LightWave and 3D Studio Max. (I have not been able to get a satisfactory answer as to whether this is because it is that much harder to code for Maya and Softimage or simply the practice of taking advantage where advantage is to be had.)

LightWave offers an unlimited number of render nodes, *free* with the purchase of the program. There are also *free* render node controllers (like Lightnet by Joe Justice and Spider by Station X) that offer huge enhancements over LightWave's own internal control for network rendering.

Character Modeling

I use *subdivision surfaces* to do my character modeling (subpatches in LightWave terms, mesh smooth in 3D Studio Max terms). Thankfully, most 3D CGI packages support a form of this sort of modeling, which yields a very good-looking character, very quickly.

My techniques for character modeling are explained in detail in *Essential LightWave*. These are techniques that I've used in modeling characters in LightWave, Maya, *and* 3D Studio Max on numerous productions. So even if you are using another 3D CGI software package, that section of *Essential LightWave* will *still* give you important information about subdivision surface modeling techniques for both human and non-human characters alike.

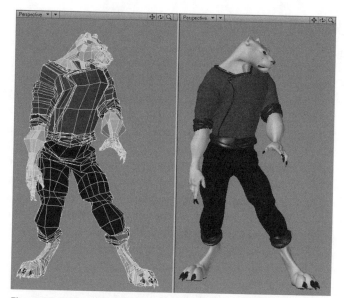

Figure 13-5: Through the magical mathematics of subpatch modeling, the low-resolution *cage* on the left (only 5,087 polygons) automatically becomes the high-resolution subpatch model at the time of rendering (shown here at a resolution equivalent to about 67,128 polygons).

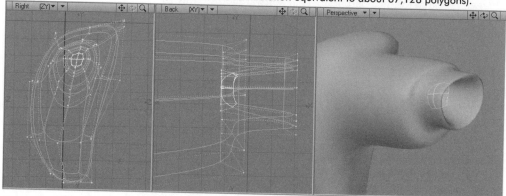

Figure 13-6: The images on the following pages are from *Essential LightWave*'s chapters on body and facial modeling.

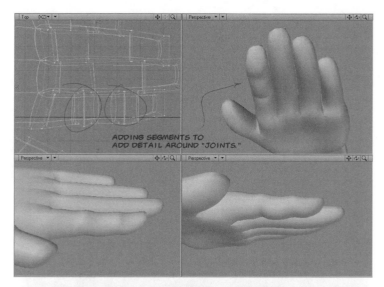

ADDING SEGMENTS TO
ADD DETAIL AROUND "JOINTS."

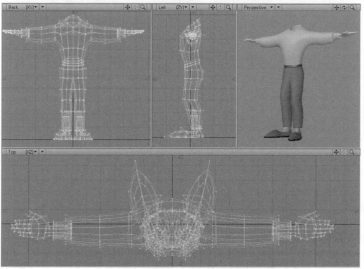

NOTE

Subdivision surfaces come from developments made by Pixar that, in essence, takes a polygonal object (made up of either three- or four-sided polygons) and recursively splits each face into smaller and smaller arrays of *quad* polygons. The math that controls this *subdivision* process tries to make each iteration *smoother* than the last.

LightWave was one of the first packages to implement this kind of modeling at the time, calling the process *metaforming*.

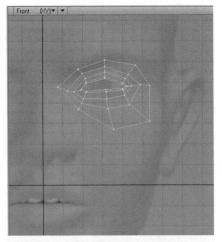

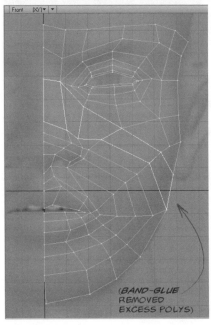

(BAND-GLUE
REMOVED
EXCESS POLYS)

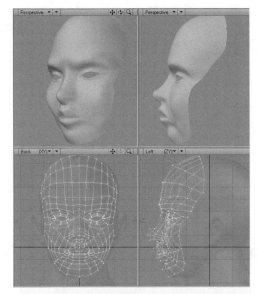

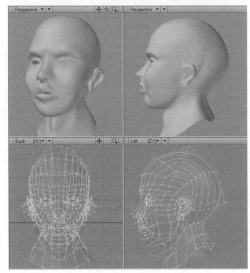

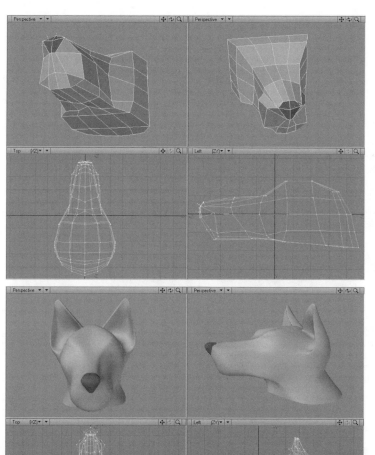

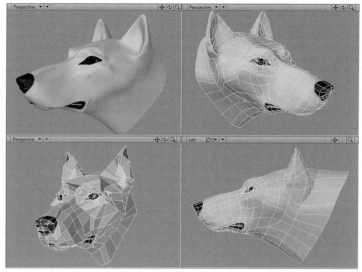

Character Rigging

A good rigging allows for good animation.

It's hard to be an artist if you're constantly fighting your tools.

> ### NOTE
>
> I may seem to breeze over this section, but keep in mind that it took *half* of my 350-page *LightWave 3D Character Animation* book to cover all that is needed to know how to properly create feature-quality riggings. (That book already assumes a fairly complete knowledge of the 3D package, established in the 400-page *Essential LightWave*.)
>
> So let me again state that this book is about how these elements were put together to create *Ghost Warrior* — elements you may already know, elements you may have yet to learn — flagging areas of importance that one might not notice until one has already taken that journey for oneself.

For the layperson, a rigging is a set of controls that moves a character like the strings and bits of wood inside a marionette. Most riggings on the CG program's *IK* (inverse kinematics) engine provide smooth movement from pose to pose as the animator positions hands, feet, and torso, and the IK takes care of the elbows and knees.

My one rule of thumb for riggings is: *Let the computer only do the barest minimum to make your job easier.* Anything more, and you will probably be disappointed, as the computer makes bad decisions about the poses and motions you are trying to achieve. While it's tempting to try the programs that allow for varying degrees of working with computer-controlled *synthespians*, I find that as one becomes more and more accomplished as an animator, the less and

less these "time-saving" tools actually save any time at all. As an animator, you actually "see" or "feel" the way you want your character to look and move. The program that drives the synthespians isn't inside your head and can't know what you see, and so you spend hours trying to get automation to do what would take minutes to do by hand.

In the books *LightWave 3D Character Animation* and *Fundamentals of Character Animation*, I get into the moderately tedious process of creating the base for the riggings that I've used in *Ghost Warrior* and provide an understanding of how they work so you can create your own. I'll just go into a brief explanation here of what a CGI rigging is for the casual reader.

Figure 13-7: This is Kaze when viewed at low-resolution animation settings ("dialing-down" his polygon count for animation greatly increases how many frames per second I can see while I'm actually animating). You can think of a computer model almost like papier-mâché stretched over a wire frame.

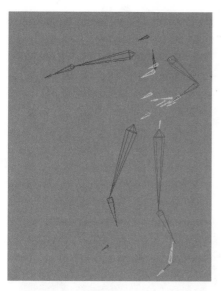

Figure 13-8: This is the collection of *bones* that fits inside Kaze's "skin." Through a precision process called *point weighting*, each intersection of the mesh that makes up Kaze's skin is told to move when a specific bone moves.

Figure 13-10: With IK properly set up, Kaze's hands, feet, and torso can be moved, and his arms and legs bend like "real" arms and legs. (I'm just moving Kaze's torso in this illustration, leaving his hands and feet where they are.)

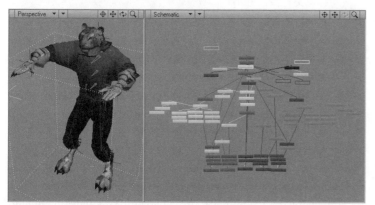

Figure 13-9: The bones and other items that control the position of this *skeleton* are laid out in an *iconic* fashion so an animator can quickly select exactly the control he needs to move or rotate to put Kaze into the pose that he sees in his mind.

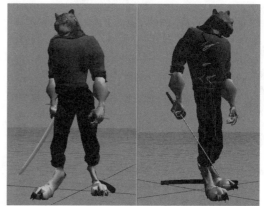

Figure 13-11: So, using these controls, I can pose Kaze in any way that I can imagine.

Figure 13-12: In testing my riggings, I move Kaze through *extreme* poses, like this tight crouch. If everything looks believable, and there are no "jitters" (caused by either poor IK computations or a poorly created rigging), I know I can use this rigging for all other characters of similar proportions.

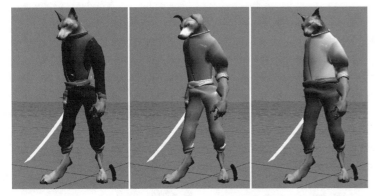

Figure 13-13: Once I've got a rigging I can trust, I use Kaze as a *base to create all my other characters*. This way, using the techniques of *rig swapping* (explained in *LightWave 3D Character Animation*), I can almost instantly have each of the characters rigged! I can have any character perform any other character's animations!

By using Kaze as a base for all the other characters, thickening some things here, thinning other things there, and pushing and pulling points in muzzles, ears, and bodies, I was able to build all 22 characters from Kaze's base form within *Ghost Warrior* in just

under one and a half weeks. That includes all surfacing, including application of each character's unique fur patterning!

The last thing I do before moving on to working on the building blocks of facial animation is create a *stand-in* character and scene for each and every one of my characters. Stand-ins are *extremely* low-polygon-count models, made up of boxes and low-poly spheres and cylinders. These super-low-resolution character placeholders let my video card handle scenes with almost ten characters in them before beginning to slow down.

Figure 13-14: The stand-in model allows for *extremely* fast updates while animating with many characters on-screen at once! Most of the tavern scenes and all of the fight scenes were done using stand-ins.

When I'm ready to render a scene that I've animated with a stand-in character, I simply use the "character swapping" technique (again, explained in *LightWave 3D Character Animation*) to replace the stand-in with my actual character model!

Character Animation versus Motion Capture

Now, here's a note on using motion capture. One might think that as an animator, I'd be against motion capture. Quite the contrary.

In perfect alignment with the "use the proper tool for the job" mindset, if a scene can be more quickly and perfectly animated using motion capture, then by all means use it (if you have access to it). Scenes perfectly suited to motion capture are scenes where characters *recreate reality exactly.*

While there is no motion capture in *Ghost Warrior*, and I believe strongly that a well-trained animator can *usually* produce better results faster than motion capture, there are some animations that call for motion capture. The first thing that comes to mind is the scene in *Star Wars: Episode II* where C3PO is moving along the conveyer belt and has his head removed. That must have been a bugger of a scene for the animator to work, and it still doesn't read exactly right. A better solution would have been to motion capture a hinged, wooden mannequin collapsing. It would have resulted in a much better-looking animation, infinitely faster.

One thing to keep in the forefront of your mind if you ever do use motion capture is to have your mo-cap actor use props that are the same *relative mass* as ones that the CGI character would be using in the film. If your character is swinging about a heavy machine gun, have your mo-cap actor swing about a 60-pound prop, weighted and balanced the same way as the machine gun. If your character has big, heavy boots, go out and get some of those anklet weights and strap a few sets to your actor!

Animation is all about weight and timing. Audiences can instantly pick up on a character not counterbalancing himself properly to compensate for the weight that an animated scene implies. They may not be able to know exactly why something in the scene doesn't *feel* right, but they'll be able to instantly pick up on the fact that *something* is off.

Puppetry

Something that I'm surprised hasn't made a bigger crossover into the realm of CGI is puppetry. There is a magic to puppetry that just doesn't come across in even the best animation. This magic has much to do with the subconscious movements puppeteers make during a performance, things that are sometimes "worked to death" when an animator spends weeks on a scene.

I saw a presentation by Jim Henson's Creature Shop where they rigged one of the controllers they had used to control an *animatronic* (robot-actor) device to inputs to a modified motion-capture setup. The results were amazing. They were able to capture the performance, the director was able to make comments, and the puppeteer was able to nail exactly what the director wanted the second time through. Weeks worth of animation were completed in all of about five minutes.

The really amazing thing was that there was *beautiful* subtlety and sensitivity to the captured puppetry performance. The captured performance read with the kind of depth of acting that it would have taken a master animator to pull off in traditional CG animation.

I imagine that if these kinds of puppetry motion capture riggings were available to the general public that high-quality character animation would be much more accessible to the hobbyist animator. In the hands of truly skilled puppeteers, I can only imagine what kind of performances this could create.

> ### NOTE
>
> Isn't it funny that with all the power of CGI that Yoda as a puppet is far more *believable* than he was in *Star Wars: Episode II*? This has to do with the sensitivity of the subconscious actions that Frank Oz's performance imbued into a model of latex and cloth.

So while this is, at the moment, just a pipe dream, because of what I've seen from Henson's Creature Shop and the results I was able to achieve with Lip Service that uses a kind of performance capture for its facial animation, I think that puppetry of this kind is something that could open the doors to some truly amazing performances with a fraction of the work.

Facial Animation

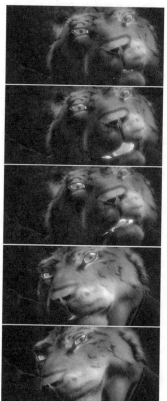

Facial animation, with the right tools for the job, is one of the most enjoyable parts of character animation. When you've got the characters in your scene already giving powerful performances, the added touches that come with well-done facial animation make the *read* (how the scene touches a viewer emotionally) all the more powerful.

There's no "secret" to doing facial animation, really. It's all just a matter of breaking a task down into a series of *next logical steps*. Following the steps (and using good tools), facial animation comes together almost by itself.

Figure 13-15: KAZE: What makes you think you stand a chance now?

Building Blocks

You first start with your character's basic *facial mask*. Create *selection sets* that will allow you to quickly isolate parts of this *mask*, like inner ears, outer ears, eyebrows, eyelids, eyeliner, cheekbones, lower jaw, upper jaw, lower lips, upper lips, teeth, gums, and tongue. (You can get even more specific, but I find that this list gives me all the control I need, without getting too stuck in minutia.)

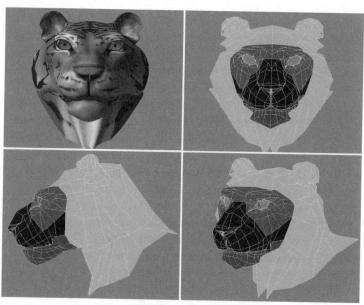

Figure 13-16: Kaze, shown in the upper left in his "high-res," *subpatch* "rendering" mode. ("Subpatches" is LightWave's name for its real-time subdivision surfaces that allow me to "dial up" and "dial down" how many polygons a mesh has in real time for animation and rendering.) The other three quadrants show the "low-resolution" *cage* that is automatically subdivided at the time of rendering to create Kaze's smooth, high-resolution "skin." The different colors on the cage represent my four largest selection sets: head, eye-mask, upper muzzle, and jaw.

LightWave allows me to have many different kinds of selection sets, isolating subpatch surfaces, polygons, or points. Using combinations of these selection sets to add to or remove from my current selection, I can quickly isolate exactly the parts of a character's face that I want my tools to affect. (See *Essential LightWave*.)

Each 3D package has its own way of working with morphs and the actual act of morphing, the process where the points of the base object are moved to match those of the target object. This depends on both the base and target objects having *exactly the same number of points* and, even more importantly, *having those points in the same order*.

Every point, or *vertex*, you create in a 3D package is stored in a kind of database, with a number assigned to it. This is how the 3D package keeps track of where everything is within its virtual world.

If *point order* gets mixed up somehow (usually by removing, adding, and/or cutting and pasting from either the target or the base object but not the other) and say, for instance, the point at the tip of the right ear is point number three in the base object, and point number three in the target object at the corner of the left eye, you've got a problem. When these two objects are morphed, even though they may have the same number of points, the object turns "inside out" as the tip of the right ear tries to become the corner of the left eye.

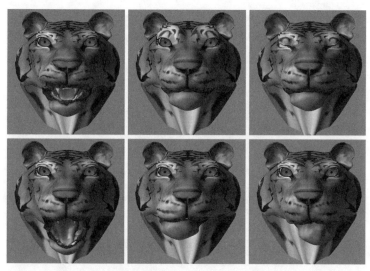

Figure 13-17: Having isolated parts of a character's face so I can "pull" specific points without touching others, I start to build the facial shapes that I will use as *morph targets* for the facial animation. (More specifics on these *face shapes* in just a moment.)

There are two distinct schools of thought as to how best to create these facial morph targets for facial animation: the lowest common denominator and some assembly required.

In the *lowest common denominator* way of working, each individual part of the face that can move has targets created for it in every possible way that it can move. This results in *precise* control over every aspect of facial animation, but it can be time-consuming to manipulate the often more than 100 controls that must go into a single expression.

In this way of working, each side of the head would have separate controls to raise and lower the upper eyelid, lower eyelid, right cheek, left cheek, the outer and inner sections of each eyebrow, each cheek sucked in or puffed out, the rear, mid, and front sections of the lips and mouth, etc. Its *precision* makes it my favored way of working when I have the luxury of time. It isn't quick, but it lets an artist create any facial expression imaginable.

The *some assembly required* method of facial animation involves putting together (partially) preconstructed facial expressions to get something that looks not too much like it "came out of a can." It doesn't allow for nearly as much control as with the lowest common denominator method, but it is passable and *much* quicker.

Common face shapes in the some assembly required method would be surprise, scowl, snarl, smile, frown, scoff, etc.

For *Ghost Warrior*, I opted for something that fell about halfway between the two methods. I needed to get my facial expressions done quickly, and I also needed them to have a great range of flexibility and diversity. So I built some predefined expressions like "smile" and "frown," which both affect the lips, muzzle, cheekbones, and lower lids of the eyes (using separate targets for left and right sides of the face — *asymmetry* in animation is one of the simplest keys to making something look "real"). I also built specific morph targets to bring the corners of the mouth forward or stretch them tightly backward and to rotate the ears in specific directions.

Figure 13-18: This is the list of the different morph targets that I use in *Ghost Warrior*, grouped and shown with their animatable slider controls. (The one tab not shown is the *LS* tab, created specifically for dialogue animation in Lip Service; I'll show that one in just a moment.)

Figure 13-19: Using these controls, a character can be brought through a whole range of believable expressions and emotions!

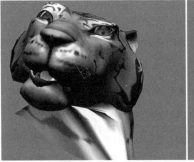

NOTE

How do you figure out what to model as a morph target? *Look in a mirror!* Act out your character's scenes and watch the contortions that your own face goes through (or watch a performance by the actor that most inspired your character). Take notes as far as what parts of the face are doing what!

You can also "reverse engineer" expressions. You know that you'll need your character to smile, so looking in a mirror, you can figure out what parts of your face move and where they move to in order to create an expression that reads as "smile."

Lip Service

It is a rare and wonderful thing to find someone who has "thought outside the box" and has the ability to implement their thoughts into a workable tool and made that tool available to others. *Paradigm shifts* — the kinds of things to which those buried in their comfortable, habitual ways of working might look at and say, "why would anyone ever want to do things *that* way?"

Aaah, but those are the areas where true genius can be found — not in following the paths that others may take but in following one's own sense of inspiration to create the things that you, personally, would enjoy most. This philosophy applies both to films and the tools that create them. That is what I found in the incredible, virtually unknown program called Lip Service.

NOTE

Unfortunately, at the time of publication, Lip Service only directly supports LightWave and only runs on Intel machines. However, its animation interface writes out an ASCII file to be read in by the plug-ins that drive the actual morphing in LightWave, so it would be possible for a good scripter to make it work with any 3D package.

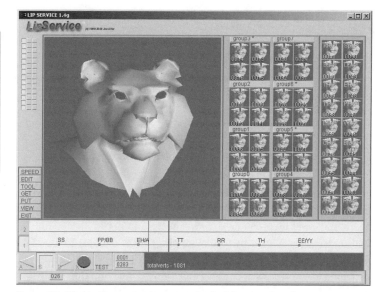

Figure 13-20: Lip Service is a program for facial animation that was years ahead of its time. Having used it, I wouldn't want to work on a film without it. It's that good!

Lip Service consists of an external program that runs outside of LightWave and plug-ins that let LightWave read the ASCII file generated by the external program that contains all the information about which morph targets to apply to the face's base form. Within Lip Service's external program, an animator loads the base model and the different morph targets and sets the speed of the animation (film, NTSC, or PAL) and the audio track (which automatically specifies the length of its scene file).

Dialogue

When a character mouths the words spoken by an actor, the animator starts his work by listening carefully to the prerecorded dialogue track (*scrubbing*) and noting where each of the different parts of speech (*phonemes*) are. (This is sometimes known as "slugging" the dialogue.) In the "old days," this meant taking an exposure sheet and penciling in the sounds, holds, and whatnot while running a reel-to-reel tape backward and forward. Once the *x sheet* was properly marked with the dialogue notation, the animator would then sit down at his desk and animate to his notation, only finding the results of his animation when he shot his drawings and played them back with the dialogue track.

The first great thing about Lip Service is that an animator no longer needs the intermediate step of working on or from an x sheet to do his dialogue! The second great thing about Lip Service is that an animator gets *instant feedback* as to how his dialogue is shaping up just by pressing the Play button! (You can play an animation backward as easily as playing it forward. Playing an animation backward is an old trick to quickly spot trouble areas.)

Using keyboard commands in Lip Service, an animator "step-frames" through his scene, hearing each sound that plays out over each frame and watching the already-assigned morph targets do their work on the cage. Where each sound "peaks," or hits the main part of the facial shape that makes that sound, the animator just clicks on the appropriate phoneme face shape at the right side of the screen (see Figure 13-20), and it is inserted in the dialogue track below the display window.

Using Lip Service, I was able to quickly add, remove, and change dialogue shapes faster than I've ever been able to before. To be able to simply press Play and see *and hear* my work play out on the character's actual cage was tremendous in letting me know if what I was doing was what I had in mind!

Now, all that I've described thus far would be well worth the price of admission for an animator who's done CGI animation the old-fashioned way of moving *morph sliders* based on hand-written notes on an x sheet. But the thing that really knocks me out is how Lip Service handles *performance*.

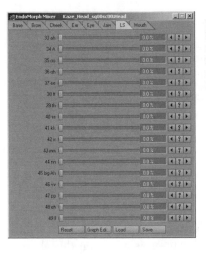

Figure 13-21: This tab shows a listing of all the different phonetic morph targets created for Lip Service (along with the slot number into which they fit in the Lip Service program).

Performance

Remember my comments earlier in this chapter about how nifty puppetry is for recording the subtle, subconscious movements that really give life and sparkle to a scene? Well, that's where Lip Service really blasts light-years ahead of anything else I'm aware of on the market.

Figure 13-22: Looking back at Figure 13-20 of Lip Service's interface, you can see eight groups of four poses each (*performance groups*, labeled 0-7). This is a closer view of one of those groups, featuring the different ear positions for Itsua.

Lip Service's real magic happens once you've got your character lip-syncing to the dialogue track. You click on one of the performance groups, and then when you click the Record button, your animation plays out slightly slower than real time as Lip Service turns your mouse into a motion-capture input device.

Figure 13-23: With a performance group active, the four corners of the display area are assigned to the four separate morph targets of that *group* (in this case, Group 0, morph targets clockwise from top-left, 02, 01, 03, 04).

Having your mouse centered in the display area when you are recording a performance group will leave your model as it is in its base form. Moving your mouse toward a corner will gently blend the associated morph targets into the base form.

The results are stunning, eerily *real*, and hands-down the fastest way I've ever, ever received feature-quality facial animation.

NOTE

I'm a fast animator at feature-quality work. In a comparative test, it took me about a day to animate with all the subtle nuances of life Kaze's line, "I was better than you *before* I 'died.' What makes you think you stand a chance now?" Using Lip Service, I got the same quality result in just over 15 minutes.

Touch-up

While Lip Service is amazing, it isn't *perfect*. There are still a few areas where I'd like to see some specific enhancements if I had my druthers. But it gets me to a point where all that remains are the "Timothy-Albee-perfectionist" stuff that perhaps no one else will ever notice but make the performance on-screen exactly what I've seen in my mind and heart.

So, once I've got the performance *nearly* perfect in Lip Service, I bring the facial animation into layout (via the plug-ins that read the Lip Service ASCII file) and make some minor adjustments with the morph mixer slider controls shown earlier. In a few minutes, I've got the scene reading the way I want, and I move on to what needs doing next!

Character Modeling

Having proven to myself that the tools I've chosen for character and facial animation can give me what I need within the timeframe I have set aside for working on scenes, I can then move on to modeling the rest of the characters and environments.

The great thing about LightWave is that if I simply "pull points" from an existing model to make another (elongating the muzzle, reshaping ears, applying a different "paint job"), all of my prior hard work with rigging and facial morph targets is *preserved* in the new model! So, having all of Kaze's facial animation morph targets working as they should, pushing his points to become, say, Itsua, then Itsua needs only a cursory checking-over to make sure all his facial morph targets work properly as well.

This is the only "secret" to me being able to have done what I've done in so short an amount of time. It's just another permutation of the "never go backward" mentality (you know, of working a script you can stand proud with, from a story you can dedicate yourself to, etc.). Building and rigging Kaze, making sure he works *perfectly*, exploring and fine-tuning the controls, weight maps, surfaces, morph targets, and facial animation software leaves me with a *base* from which to start the other characters where they are already 80 percent done.

NOTE

A life-drawing student is instructed to not start drawing immediately at the beginning of a pose that lasts for five minutes or longer. The student studies the model, gets to know visually the "lay of the land," gets a feeling for where things might be challenging. With a clear knowledge of what lies ahead, he is able to quickly surpass the students who have begun immediately and find themselves struggling with unknowns.

This kind of planning can benefit nearly every situation.

So, working from Kaze's base form, all 21 other characters were modeled and surfaced using the techniques discussed in *Essential LightWave*. I tend to stay away from hand-painted textures in my models wherever possible, leaning much more toward mathematical, *procedural textures*. I like procedurals for two reasons: They can be "zoomed-in-on" as much as one likes, and they don't break up into pixels, and they can be quickly changed to look like something completely different with a few numerical changes to their inputs and still retain the *feel* of how they looked before.

On the characters' skins, which defined their fur patterns, where I did paint textures, I tried to keep these as simple as possible. Simple, quick, and *interchangeable* was the name of my game.

By using one texture map layout for all characters, after painting about the third character, I began to know exactly where each bit of "paint" would be applied on each character's skin. Painting the maps went extremely quickly this way, much more quickly than having a new map layout tailored for each and every character. That way, I only had to learn the nuances of one UV map layout!

Figure 13-24: Here you see the hand-painted, UV texture map used for Kaze's head. If the UVs look strangely like a wolf's profile, it's because I wanted the elongated muzzle shape of a wolf for the UV map for all characters so I could squeeze more detail into characters that did have more canine muzzles. All characters use this exact same UV map layout for their head texture maps.

Figure 13-25: For painting textures, I found after a little "noodling" that even though I was painting textures in NewTek's Aura paint package, the Photoshop file format best suited my needs for texture painting. Aura and LightWave both support the Photoshop file format's ability to save and load images, retaining their multiple working layers. This let me quickly explore and experiment without the worry of ruining what I'd done that I liked. It also let me have the grid layout layer *visible* at the click of a button for painting and *invisible* for saving and using in LightWave.

Sets and Lighting

Now we get into an area where a background in stagecraft comes in handy. In working on sets for theatre productions, you learn volumes about just how much you can get away with when a set is is well lit. It would take thousands of pages and illustrations to convey what you could learn by volunteering to work on just one stage production. So, let me strongly suggest finding a local theatre troupe that is getting into building sets for a production and lending a hand. I'm sure they'll be grateful for the extra help, and you'll come away with volumes upon volumes of information!

Modeling

Modeling the sets for *Ghost Warrior* was very straightforward. After deciding on the art direction for each location (based upon my *production design* "wall o' inspiration"), I just built sets "thinking out loud" in LightWave to scale for the average two-meter-tall character.

NOTE

If you are interested in tips on how to quickly model interior sets, a whole chapter in *Essential LightWave* is dedicated to the "tricks" involved in modeling interiors. These three images are the results from the book's exercise on interior set modeling.

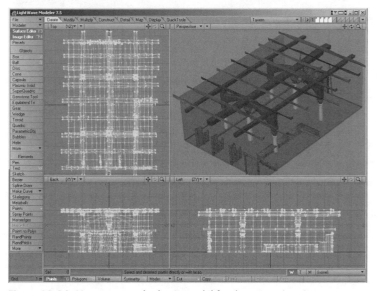

Figure 13-26: Here you see the basic model for the tavern interior.

Figure 13-27: These are the furniture pieces that fill the tavern. Each model was built by using pieces from the previously built model: The table became the chair, which became the stool. Working this way, not only was it much faster, having already assigned and painted UV maps for the table, but all the pieces look as if they exist within the same "world."

Figure 13-28: This is the texture map that I used for all things wooden on the tavern set. It is made by combining a few digital photographs of the front steps to my cabin. I use the lights and darks of this image to create the highs and lows of the bump map that makes the wood seem to have dimension to it. I also use it to affect the procedurals that color the wood and make it appear shiny in some places and dull in others.

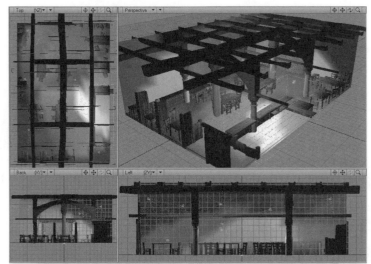

Figure 13-29: Then, like an interior decorator, I move the "furniture" into the set, arranging until it makes both aesthetic and logical sense.

Figure 13-30: The set for the tavern's back room.

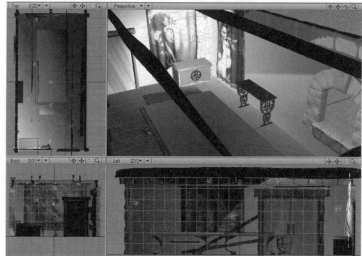

Figure 13-31: The set for Soshi's chambers. For the design for this set, I blended a lot of influences from various parts of the world, including my own paintings as "tapestries" on the walls, which spoke of the underlying motivations that would appeal to the "marginally publicly acceptable" side of Soshi.

Lighting

My own preferences for lighting scenes, sets, and characters will forever be influenced by my upbringing with my grandfather directing and acting in productions at the Ramsdell Opera House in Manistee, Michigan. I love the richness of theatrical lighting — the history that has gone into developing techniques to make the actors and sets still read as vibrant, three-dimensional objects that can be seen equally well from the fifth balcony as from the first box seats.

As I mentioned at the beginning of this section on sets and lighting, the absolute best way to learn about lighting and set building is to volunteer to help with a theatre production. However, the core of theatrical lighting can be broken down into two basic tenants.

- To make any object read as three-dimensional from a distance, it must be lit on one side (with respect to the viewer) with warm light and on the other side with cool light.

- To keep an object from blending into the background, at least one edge of it must be lit so that its contrast is far greater than any contrast in the nearby background.

These two axioms have led to the individually controllable banks of red, yellow, blue, and green lights above a stage and the "bright-white" spotlights hung at the top edge and just audience-side of the *proscenium* (the "arch" that separates the stage from the auditorium) for *rim lighting*.

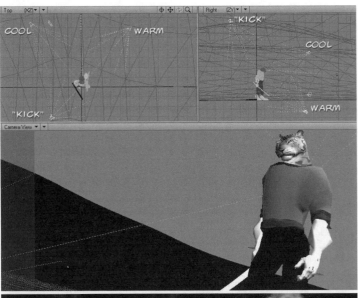

Figure 13-32: Kaze, lit on *screen right* (in the camera view) by a cool, moonlight blue light of an intensity value of 200 percent. Low and on *screen left* is a warmer light with an intensity value of 69 percent, suggesting *bounce lighting* from the grass. High on *screen right*, almost *behind* Kaze, is a white light with an intensity value of 300 percent to add a brighter "rim" around Kaze's *screen right* side, helping to "kick" him off the background.

Really, that's my only "secret" to lighting. Any object that needs to be seen by the audience is lit with this three point lighting motif.

Before signing off on any set model, I quickly lay out a series of (shadow-mapped) spotlights, based on the *storyboarded* suggestions where the characters will be. I know that for each individual scene in actual production, I may need to make small adjustments, additions, or subtractions, but this base lighting model gives me a good, quick place to start!

Visual Effects

Here's where testing really comes into play. From online research and talking with other filmmakers, you may have an idea that a particular plug-in is just the thing for you and your film. In actual *testing*, you may find that, in truth, it comes close but doesn't quite fit what you need (like my diving into the cloth simulations). Or, you may find something that far exceeds your expectations, letting you push the visuals of your film into new areas that before had been only wishful thinking (like the discoveries I made with Sasquatch, the fur simulation).

This is where you find out what is possible in the realm of visual effects, and you tailor your film's look accordingly. This is where you find out what *you*, personally (or your team), and your software packages are actually capable of. You need to take strong stands as to what is *good enough* to allow into your production pathway. Things must keep running smoothly during production so you can keep your focus on getting done what needs to be done.

Cloth

I originally wanted to make use of cloth (*soft-body dynamics*) simulations for *Ghost Warrior*. I tried a few ways to cut down the calculation time required for the simulation and in the end, decided to abandon the cloth simulation in favor of "good old-fashioned" bones moving the clothing exactly the same way they move the characters' skin.

Figure 13-33: The first method I used for cloth simulation was the "old standby" of replacing the character's body that is covered by the clothing with medium-resolution "collision" spheres that would be *invisible* to the camera, but that would give the illusion of something *inside* the fabric by "colliding" with it during the calculation of the simulation.

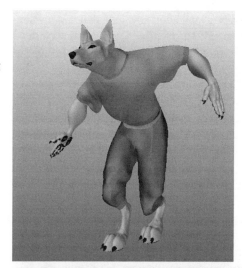

Figure 13-34: The results of this simulation were breathtakingly beautiful in motion. However, the time it added to *approve* each scene was more than I felt I could afford, so I sought out new answers.

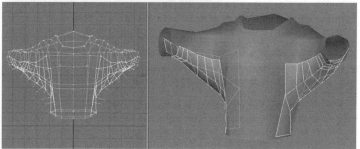

Figure 13-35: Another solution I tried was to do away with the *collision spheres* entirely and using the *cloth simulation* on only the parts of the garments that one would expect to hang loosely. (Shown highlighted here on the low-resolution cage used to calculate the simulation; after the simulation was approved, its solution would then be applied to the high-resolution final render, subpatch version of the clothing.)

NOTE

At the time of publication, calculating the *cloth simulation* is generally done *last* after all the animation has been brought to the desired level of perfection using the "invisible" collision surface model. Then the simulation is run and the computer figures out how the "cloth" would react to the *collision surfaces* inside it as the collision surfaces go through their animation.

The simulation is figured by pretending that the cloth is made up of hundreds or thousands of little springs, each affected by gravity, wind, and whatever collision surfaces they come in contact with. It is a brilliant way of simplifying the actual mechanics of "real" cloth, but it is still very, very complex. As such, it can take a long time to run the simulation, especially if the cloth becomes pinched between two collision surfaces.

In the end, as neat and clever as using cloth simulation was, in comparing two scenes, one with the simulation and one just using bones to move the clothing, I didn't find the results to be cool enough to merit the extra time and effort involved in using the simulation. My solution was to hide the fact that I *wasn't* using cloth dynamics by my choice of camera angles and by using it *only* on the scenes where I absolutely couldn't get away without using it.

Fur

Working with Sasquatch, the fur simulation from Worley Labs (www.worley.com), was an absolute joy. I remember a time not too long ago when thinking a 3D renderer could produce good-looking fur was like thinking one could find the end of a rainbow. To go from fiction to *fact* in a few short years is truly exhilarating!

Aside from just being really darn excited that fur can be done at all was the wonderful experience of working with Sasquatch, the primary fur simulation package for LightWave. This is a program that is so well put together, so open-ended, so forward thinking that it soundly puts to shame other fur simulations that I've used in LightWave and other 3D packages.

The long and the short of using Sasquatch is that it quickly gave me *exactly* what I was looking for (and when you're talking about something as complex as perhaps a million individual fibers in a character's pelt, that's something)! From quick and easy ways of using UV texture maps or model-based vertex maps (where each individual point in a model is assigned a percentage, much like what is used when telling which points to move with which bones) to control things like fur length, density, clumping, and curling to the beautiful look of its default settings, it showed incredible foresight on the part of its creator.

However, the one, tiny bit of the software that was more impressive than anything else, something that an artist who has never tried to use another fur program would most likely just take for granted, was the way in which it figured how the direction of fur *flows* over the skin like water! This tiny feature alone saved me about a week per character in the furring department.

Figure 13-36: A closeup of Kaze, showing the fur flowing backward from his nosepad, cascading around his eyes and over his head, exactly as it does on a "real" furred being.

I found a "trick" that might be over the heads of those who don't already know a fair amount about fur simulation — using the result of rendering the skin to derive the shading on the fur. (If this *is* over your head, don't worry. It'll be here if you ever need it.)

Normally, the fur simulations take care of figuring out every aspect of how the fibers of fur look, including the casting and receiving of shadows. Because there are so many individual "hairs" in a furred being's pelt, the calculating of self-shadowing and the receiving of cast shadows can often make a render take up to ten times longer than without self- and cast shadows (depending on the complexity of the lighting setup that your scene has).

So, my theory was that if one figured out which kinds of shading were affecting the skin that was "growing" the fur, those colors could be "extrapolated" into the fur itself and yield good-looking shadowing without having to have the fur simulation worry about all the shadows from each individual strand of fur.

LightWave has the ability to *bake* the shading of an object to a UV texture map (or a vertex color map, frequently used in video game work). So, I created a special UV map of the characters' skin that represented each polygon individually (as opposed to the UV map I used to paint the fur/skin, where left and right sides overlapped so they would be perfect copies of one another).

Then, having created the UV map that will record the shading information before each scene is sent to *final render* (see "Render Input/Output" later in this chapter), I render a quick, very low-resolution pass through the scene to let the Surface Baker plug-in create a series of images that fit the shading map (shown in Figure

13-37) that records how the lights play across the surface of each character's skin throughout the scene.

Then it's a simple matter of assigning the sequence of images that the Surface Baker generates for each character's skin to color that character's fur and sending that scene off to be final rendered.

The end result is a reduction in render time from about 18 minutes to just under *57 seconds!*

It is through discoveries like this — reducing the render times of using fur to 5.2 percent of what is "expected" in "industry standards" and still yield beautiful results — that made *Ghost Warrior* possible.

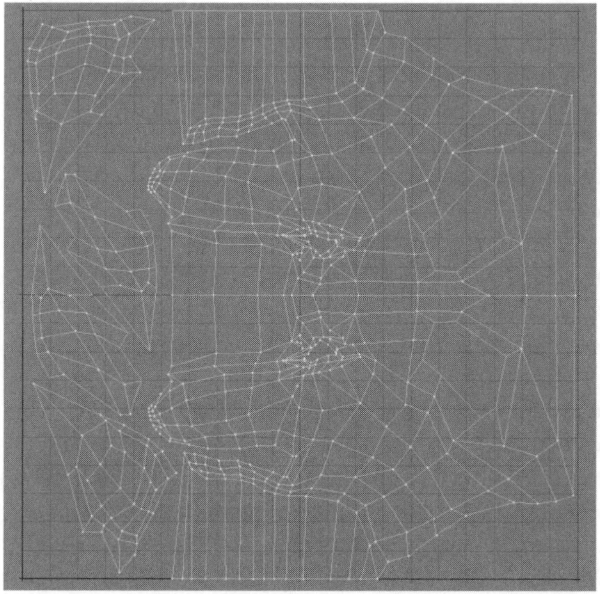

Figure 13-37: Here's the UV map used to "capture" the shading falling on the skin. I have all characters using the same *map*, so like the "painting" UV map shown earlier, the UVs have the elongated muzzle of a canine to hold the detail that the canine characters have in that area. Making the UV map "one-size-fits-all" makes a lot less work for me.

Figure 13-38: Here's how one of those baked shading maps looks.

Post-Production Software ("Compositing")

A common misconception of beginner 3D artists is that everything must be done in the 3D software itself and in one take. This would be akin to taking a photograph with a disposable camera, having it developed at the local one-hour photo place, and calling it "good."

If you've played around in a darkroom, you know that half of the beauty that comes out of a good photograph happens *after* the negative is developed! You cup your hands under the enlarger to let more light hit the photographic paper in some areas more than others ("dodging" and "burning"). You play with how long the paper stays in each chemical bath or bypass certain baths altogether.

Your compositing software is like the photographer's darkroom. Within it you take a good initial image produced by your 3D package and turn it into something that can only be defined as art. You add layers, you soften edges, and you accent your work with glows and highlights and depth-of-field effects. You do all the things you would do to "pretty up" an image in a paint program, only a *good* compositing program does the work of applying these "retouches" to every single frame!

Digital Fusion

A large part of being able to pull off the *look* of *Ghost Warrior* lay in me being able to find a compositing program that let me "sketch" in my 3D package and quickly and easily bring those "sketches" up to something presentable without having to re-render in the 3D package! That's the beauty of using a *good* compositing program. You can let yourself get your 3D final renders "close"; they don't have to be perfect!

> **NOTE**
>
> The phrase "God is in the details" has an art school cousin: "The first 90 percent."
>
> This means that it is only in the last ten percent of the labor put into an artwork that it really starts to look good. If a piece takes an artist 100 dedicated hours total to complete, that work would look "not bad" for the first 90 hours.
>
> It is in the last ten percent of the total time spent on an artwork where the piece really begins to sing!

The part of 3D that really takes the time is in the last ten percent, when you already have most everything roughed in and are noodling the final details to make everything look exactly the way you want it to. Unfortunately for 3D, usually by this time in the process you've got to be working with the complex final surfacing shaders, the fully ray-traced shadows, refractions, and reflections; you need to work with all the really time-consuming stuff for the computer to "think about" as it draws. So, each time you render to test your work, you're having tea for maybe 20 minutes while the computer "thinks" about the smaller and smaller changes you're making in your hunt for perfection.

With a good compositing program in your arsenal, you can instead save each rendered layer of each individual character or group separately from the background, separately from the shadows, separately from the items in the foreground. Then, in the compositing program, you can adjust the coloring and contrast of each and every layer, effectively *relighting* parts if necessary to produce the result that you're looking for. The great thing is that with each *layer* within the compositor already rendered, it takes but a moment for each of these changes and modifications to be calculated!

With a good compositing program, the eight hours it would have taken me to bring a scene to perfection in my 3D package takes perhaps 20 minutes.

I judge compositing programs on four criteria: 1) How quickly can I piece my work together? 2) How good are the post-processing effects? 3) How fast does it render? 4) Does it read and write the file formats I want to work with?

I had enjoyed using another compositor for many years, had gotten to know it well, and had learned to work around its quirks. But for *Ghost Warrior*, I made the move to Digital Fusion.

> **NOTE**
>
> Digital Fusion comes with courseware (in addition to its user's manual) that walks you through the kinds of things you might be asked to do on a production. This kind of teaching got me up to speed on it in about a week of evenings.
>
> There's more to Digital Fusion than we can even hope to discuss here. So, if you'd like to see for yourself, you can download the time-limited demo version (Mac, PC, and Linux) and slightly abbreviated courseware from http://www.eyeonline.com. Like I said, I've not seen its equal. If you're serious about making a film, download Digital Fusion, and put it through its paces. I think you'll also be impressed.

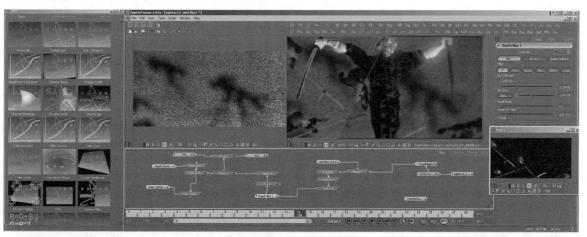

Figure 13-39: Digital Fusion has beautiful *post effects*, blazingly fast workflow, complete resolution independence, multiprocessor background rendering-while-you-work, multiple floating views (each with the ability to be color-corrected to your specific output), resolution-independent painting, the ability to compare "before" and "after" on a single viewport, and such forward thinking as I've rarely seen in a package (just to name only a few of my favorite things); I've yet to see its equal.

Here are some things you can do with a good compositing program:

- Adjust color balance of individual layers.

- Add effects like glows, "sar-filters," and real-time particle effects.

- Add fog and depth of field in real time using an image format that supports z-buffer.

- Blur and/or "soften" certain layers or portions of layers to control where the viewer's eye is drawn (just like in a painting, areas of sharp definition and contrast draw a viewer's eye to them).

- Adjust the color and opacity of shadows when working with an image format that supports shadow buffers.

- Re-texture map and even relight entire scenes when using image formats that support surface, normal, and shading buffers.

- Add motion blur in real time when using a file format that supports motion buffers.

- Track and stabilize/destabilize footage (great for using a single background frame with a foreground movie that has camera movement).

- Add lens-warping effects and camera shake.

- Simultaneously output different resolution image/movie formats, specifically color corrected for film, VGA, NTSC, and PAL formats.

Now, all the above points are neat and vitally important to creating a feature-quality look in your final output, but something that *still* makes my head spin is the ability of a good compositing program to be able to merge layers based on where each pixel is within three-dimensional space. This is called *depth merging* and was pivotal to saving weeks of render time, especially in Sequence 4, the "Moonlit Glade."

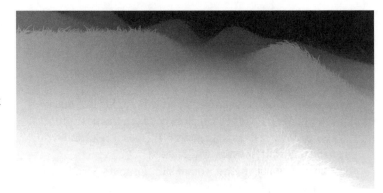

Figure 13-40: A z-buffer (also known as a *depth buffer*) is nothing glamorous. It is basically just a grayscale image that records a grayscale value for every corresponding pixel of the full-color image.

Figure 13-41: This is the "full-color" image of the grass that goes along with the z-buffer shown in Figure 13-40 (shown here with the shadows cast by Kaze already composited into the grass).

Figure 13-42: This is the plate (another name for a layer) of Kaze, also with its own z-buffer (not shown). Pay close attention to his screen-left foot and screen-right knee between this illustration and the next.

Figure 13-43: The final *depth merged* composite. Based upon comparing which z-buffer pixel was "brighter," the compositing program "nestled" Kaze's foot and knee *into* the surrounding grass!

By using depth merging, I was able to render the characters *separately* from the grass layer, letting me fine-tune the subtleties of lighting on each quickly in Digital Fusion. In a pinch, it even allowed me to render a single frame of grass for the background,

compositing the character plates in afterward! (On average, the grass backgrounds took about two minutes to render. This is very good, speed-wise, but rendering only one frame for the background, on a 300-frame scene, saved me *almost ten hours of rendering time for that one scene alone.*)

Image File Format

LightWave can read and write files in almost 40 different kinds of file formats. Digital Fusion can also read in and write out 40 different kinds of file formats. Choosing which one I wanted to work in was part research and part "executive decision."

There were two key features in the file format: 1) The ability to hold image data in *floating-point color space* and 2) the ability to hold *extra buffers* (like depth and shadow).

Floating-point color space is important when working with film, which is much more sensitive to subtle changes in colors, lights, and darks than the phosphors of a TV or computer monitor. What most laypeople think of as "24-bit, true color" actually refers to an image that has *eight bits per color channel* (eight for red, eight for green, and eight for blue, possibly eight bits for an alpha channel). So in professional terms, the .jpg off the Internet of the sunset over the Brooks Range is actually an *eight-bit color* image.

Floating-point color space stores the information for each pixel in a way of recording numbers that allows for extreme precision. Values in the "normal" scale between "black" and "white" are very precise decimals that amount to values between 0 percent and 100 percent. With floating-point color space, values can go well below "black" and well above "white," which allows for images that will undergo large amounts of *color correction* to maintain their integrity, as in *Ghost Warrior.*

So, after experimenting to see how easily my 3D package could save the RGB, alpha, depth, shadow, specular, and my own "special buffer" channels to varying types of floating-point file formats, I more or less arbitrarily chose the .flx file format. LightWave could read and write "flexible format" images with ease, as could Digital Fusion. The files weren't tiny, but they weren't prohibitively large either. In the end, it came down to an executive decision.

NOTE

The one drawback to using an image file format that had more depth than the "normal" eight-bit images was that I could only view the images from within Digital Fusion and LightWave. My favorite image-viewing program couldn't begin to make sense of them. It wasn't a huge deal, but it was a little irksome before I got used to having to drag files into Digital Fusion to check the renders.

"Pipeline"

The *production pipeline* is the path your work takes from when a scene first starts to be worked on to the final output, ready to be sent to *editorial* to be cut into the final version of the film. If you're simply taking the rendered frames directly out of your 3D package as your finished product, this "pipeline" is a simple thing, consisting solely of your 3D package and whatever network rendering you have set up.

However, if, like most professional productions, your work goes through a compositing process before it is ready to be called "good," then the pipeline starts getting a bit more complex. The more complex your pipeline, the more important it is to establish exactly what it is before production starts and figure out *contingency plans* for those "minor emergencies" that can creep up during production.

For those who are more inclined to organization and procedures, the concept of a production pipeline is almost second nature. You have to know how much work there is in store for each scene and exactly what needs to be done and how to get that work done. If you don't figure this out early on, the probability for completion is slim.

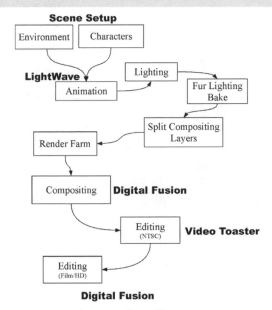

Figure 13-44: This is the pipeline that the visuals for *Ghost Warrior* followed. Knowing with each and every scene exactly what had been done to them and exactly what still waited for them helped to make sure that nothing got lost and helped to keep things from being too overwhelming during production.

Asset Management

Asset management means that you know exactly where everything is that you need to do your work. You know each item is *current*, and you know that each item is *safe* (like those woodshops that have the outline of each tool traced on the pegboard).

It may sound retentive, keeping everything ultra-organized, but when production really gets flying, you don't have the time, desire, or energy to go sifting through Fibber McGee's closet to find the one tool you need.

Professional production houses often go so far as to have a system that prevents two people from modifying the same item at the same time. These systems require each "thing" to be *checked out* to be worked on and then *checked in* when done. This way, nothing is lost — nothing is left to chance.

In its simplest sense, like on *Ghost Warrior*, asset management simply means having a rigid directory structure from which you never deviate. This structure lets you find exactly what you're looking for, even when you're not quite sure what you need.

All props are stored under Objects/Props with separate subdirectories for Furniture, Weapons, Table Service, and Decorations. Any images needed by each individual object is stored *with* that object so should I need to move that object for any reason, I know that by taking the object's subdirectory, I have everything I need.

Each character and its pre-rigged, ready-to-go setup scene (including each character's stand-in scene) are stored under the same subdirectory under Setups/Characters, named for that character. Like all other objects, any images needed by that character are stored within that subdirectory as well.

Every setup scene that has all the information for each set/environment is stored in the same way. These *scene setups* are created before production begins, so I can take a look at the scene number that I'm working, load up the environment for that scene, load in the appropriate character or stand-ins, and get working! This allows me to not have to *think* about what I'm doing while I'm doing it. Almost like a kata, one trained move flows effortlessly into the next.

The scenes for the individual shots are stored first under a Scenes\Work\sq##\sc##\ directory. Knowing that any scene within that tree is a work in progress, when each of the layers is split from the main working scene (backgrounds, characters, shadows, etc.), those scenes are saved to a final directory under Scenes\Final\sq##\sc##\. So, I know that any scene under the final directory tree is completely done with my noodling and ready to be sent to the render farm!

Scheduling

Making a schedule and keeping to it is the only way to complete a project of the size and scope of making a film (short, feature, or otherwise). To be honest, I was never a fan of doing things "by the book" until I started making my own films.

NOTE

In April of 1992, my dog team and I mushed 60 miles through the Brooks Range wilderness, about 100 miles north of the Arctic Circle. My destination was a friend's cabin on Chandalar Lake. As night fell and the blowing snow hid all but my first two ranks of dogs, I had no real way of accurately judging time or distance.

Not knowing how far I had gone or how far ahead of me the cabin was (or even if I was still on the right trail) made the experience almost overwhelming.

Filmmaking isn't quite as much of a life-and-death activity as mushing the Alaskan wilderness, but it can be overwhelming without some way of measuring your progress. Good scheduling gives you the ability to know where you are on your journey, regardless of what the journey is.

Make a plan, and stick to it. Allow only forward progress by not changing that on which you have signed off.

When, in my own schedule, it seemed that I was beginning to lag behind, I found what corners I could cut with the least amount of visual impact to bring me back up to "on schedule." I found two key ways of doing this:

- Move a longer shot in closer up.
- Use multiple cameras for scenes that "fit together."

When you can move the camera for a shot intended to show more of a character closer to that character so less of him is being shown, less of the character needs to be animated! It's an old anime trick, but it's extremely effective. This "trick" can alter the *feel* of your storytelling, and there are some shots that simply have to be full shots. But when you can avoid having to animate all of your character, this is a great way to save time.

Just like in a live-action film, you can cover certain scenes from multiple camera angles and piece them together later in editing. For the fight sequence part in Sequence 4 that appears in the trailer, I didn't have time to animate all the action I would have liked. So, I animated *one* "skirmish" but animated it very carefully. I then "hung" eight cameras around the two characters and rendered that one fight from eight angles. In editorial, I was able to make that one fight read like three.

Now, along with scheduling, there is planning. I find that I don't like doing many different things at once. I much prefer to dedicate myself to doing all of one kind of thing before moving on to doing something that requires a different part of my mind. So, whenever possible in *Ghost Warrior*, I loaded up the render queue with scenes and then spent days doing nothing but animation. I'd like to have done all the animation at once and then moved on to doing all the lighting and other required bits for sending a scene to the render queue and then focused only on doing the compositing work, but under my six-month schedule, I had to make some allowances. Still, the plan of having something always rendering was, for the most part, realized.

Render Input/Output

This part of the pipeline is like asset management for your rendered files. Files that come out of your 3D package need to go into a place that only holds files that need to be run through the compositor. Files that come out of the compositor need to be held in a place that only has *final footage*. If, like on *Ghost Warrior*, you are editing at multiple resolutions, you need to make sure that your "on-line" and your "off-line" versions are stored separately and in a directory structure that makes sense (like, FinalFootage\sq##\ sc##\Film\ and FinalFootage\sq##\sc##\NTSC\.)

Once a scene has gone through the pipeline and has produced *final footage*, ready for editing, it (and all of its rendered layers, frames, and whatnot) needs to be removed from the server to free up space and reduce clutter. These were archived on CDRs and stored for safekeeping.

Render "Farm"

Different third-party programs exist for every 3D package that control the *render nodes* that do nothing but render your 3D scenes. Many of these commercial render controllers can work with several different software packages.

A feature that I first experienced during my *Babylon 5* days that I have grown to love is the ability for the render controller to "watch" a directory for incoming scenes. When a scene is saved to this incoming directory, it automatically drops that scene into its active render queue. This simple little feature can save time and hassle when you've got your mind busy with other things.

Some render controllers will even watch a computer for activity, "gracefully" bringing a computer into the render farm when it has been idle for a predetermined amount of time and "gracefully" bringing it back out when someone starts using it again. These higher-end commercial render controllers can even run as a Windows service so they can be working even if no one is logged into the machine. These kinds of render controllers are great for intranets where you want to make good use of every possible compute cycle!

One thing to remember when you're needing to work and render at the same time is that on a dual-processor machine, one processor can be dedicated to helping you animate and the other processor can help your render farm plow through the scenes in your render queue. The command-line render node for LightWave uses only one processor, so on a "dualie," you can have one of

those working away in the background while you're using the other processor to work!

> ### NOTE
>
> On my PC, I just made a "shortcut" to that *incoming* directory (for the render-node controller) in the Send To menu that is available when right-clicking on a file. So, after saving a final version of a scene, I simply chose Save As again, and when presented with the File dialog again, I right-clicked on the file that I had just saved and chose Send To the *incoming* directory for the render controller.

■ ■ ■

If you're planning on making a film of your own, remember that *technology is changing every day*. But while technology changes, the *logic* behind making it work for your needs will almost certainly stay the same. Good management is good management, regardless of whether you are managing people or processes.

If you are reading this section purely for entertainment, I hope I've been able to shed a bit of light on the "inner workings" that I had to have in place before I could start animating on *Ghost Warrior*.

In short, the *only* way that *Ghost Warrior* could have been completed to the level of *quality*, within the *budget*, and within the *time frame* it has been is thanks to LightWave and the VT[3] suite (both from NewTek), Sasquatch and G2 (both from Worley Labs — Sasquatch for the fur and G2 for the real-time rendering and extended surfacing it offers), HD_Instance (from Happy Digital — used to quickly and easily create the sometimes hundreds of thousands of "cloned" elements in some scenes), and Eyeon's Digital Fusion. I hope it is clear that these findings came from extensive exploration and dissection, having *extensively* used most 3D, compositing, and editing products available in production on many past projects. It is only through the proper tools that an artist can fully realize his or her abilities.

Back in the late 1990s, I pitched the idea of one of the *Kaze* feature films around Hollywood. I had very positive responses from meetings with executives from Twentieth Century Fox, Sony Pictures, Nickelodeon, Pressman Films, and BKN (among others). The executives loved what they saw, and they loved the story, but they couldn't believe that a CGI feature film of that scope could be made for $8.9 million when CGI features were expected to cost *at least* $60 million. (I was actually told, on several occasions, to increase my budget by at least $20 million in order to be taken seriously, but as *Kaze* is about *honor*, about doing the right thing when doing the "wrong" thing would be such an easy way out, there was no way I could do this.)

I find it amazing that with the evolution of technology, as *Kaze* migrated from LightWave 5.6 to 6.x, 7.x, and then to 8.0, as plug-in creators developed new and more powerful tools, and as I learned Digital Fusion, that with technology as it stands right now, *a single animator* can far exceed the level of quality intended for the *team* that had been planned for the original *Kaze* feature film in the same 18-month production schedule (extrapolating *Ghost Warrior*'s six months into 18).

Technology will only improve. *Software* will improve; the advancements of LightWave 8 over version 7.5 are greater than any other upgrade in LightWave's history. *Hardware* will improve; 2 GHz machines are as prevalent and inexpensive as 366 Hz machines were back in 1997. *Techniques* will improve; the IK riggings LightWave enables wouldn't have even been fathomable when I did my first CGI short film.

While animation will always need a human's artistic soul to guide it, the *technology* allows for greater and greater realizations of the artists' dreams. Faster, more intuitive, and more elegant, it is the *tools* that enable an artist to realize his or her vision.

Without the tools selected for its creation, *Ghost Warrior* would not have been possible.

Chapter 14

Pre-Visualization

Pre-visualization is all about getting the most clearly defined image of your film possible *before* you start working on the parts that take a lot of time and/or money. "Pre-vis" is where you put all your storytelling ideas through rigorous testing to make sure that the story elements and ideas all do what you think they will to the best that can be done without actually going through all the work of making the film "for real." Pre-vis is the last place where you can make changes to your story without causing major problems.

Pre-visualization has always been a part of animated feature filmmaking, cutting storyboards together into an animatic into which the finished scenes are cut as they are completed. Live-action filmmaking has recently jumped on the idea as well, and it has resulted in significant improvements in the storycrafting of films like *The Fellowship of the Ring*.

NOTE

I like to do pre-vis while I'm working on figuring out which tech solutions will work for me — so on *Ghost Warrior*, this and the previous chapter were done simultaneously.

Actually, I like to always have a couple things going that I can jump onto without breaking stride. If I feel like I'm burning out on something, I can always take a break and do something else for a while.

Animatic

Your storyboards and production design reference material are actually your first forms of pre-visualization. But because filmmaking is an art that moves through time itself, just thumbing through a booklet of still frames doesn't do a whole lot for giving a feel for how the still images will feel once assembled into a movie.

An *animatic* (also known as a *Lecia reel*), is where you use video editing tools to cut your storyboards together so they play like a slide show. It's almost like watching your movie made up of strong poses that are held for the duration of each scene.

Figure 14-1: ToasterEdit lets me easily lay together the scanned storyboard frames into an animatic with amazing speed. Real-time positioning and animation of the scans, instant cross-dissolves, layering/compositing, audio editing, and an unlimited number of tracks for both audio and video are all playable instantly with the click of a button (no pre-rendering required).

and in my observation, it all comes down to personal preference. In the end, it is all about the *gut feeling* the filmmaker has about seeing the move he wants to see.

Now, this isn't to say that there haven't been certain conventions established by the filmmaking industry about how things "should" go together, like dissolves representing a transition of time, while cuts represent a continuation from the shot before. However, I am a huge supporter of the "If-it-works, go-with-it" mentality of getting things done.

As I cut each sequence together from the scanned storyboard frames, I time each storyboard with a stopwatch. I imagine watching the movie play out in my mind, timing how long each storyboard/shot lasts in my mind. This gives me a very good place to start in figuring how long each scanned storyboard frame should last in my ToasterEdit project.

Once I piece together enough frames, I play the animatic, making notes as to where it feels like storyboards need to be held longer or shorter. Because each storyboard frame is held on screen for a certain amount of time, there is a *rhythm* established in the relationship of the lengths of the held images. In this, filmmaking is truly like music. There is a *rhythm* to everything, and every artists' individual preferences for certain rhythms create the specific *feel* of a specific filmmaker's work.

How do you know how long to hold something on-screen before cutting to another shot? Everyone has their own opinion on this,

NOTE

If you want to see how specific effects were achieved through the rhythm of editing, the easiest way is to step-frame through a sequence of shots that make you feel a certain way and count how many frames each camera angle had dedicated to it.

Being a visual person, I used to digitize successful sequences and cut the footage apart in my video editing program to get a visual rhythm of how long each cut was lasting. Longer cuts were represented by longer stretches in the editor's timeline. (See Figure 14-1 — storyboard frames that take up more time are represented by a longer "bar" in the editing timeline.)

It is only through studying successful pieces that had a powerful effect on you that you will understand how to create the same effect on others. Rhythm is a *gut-level* thing. It is *jazz*. I'm not sure it could be taught in books or in schools. Rhythm is what you get by experiencing your own life and being in tune to its own play and interplay of events.

Laying just a few visuals in at a time, put the *scratch dialogue* .wav tracks in when necessary (which we discuss in just a moment). I could only *guess* at the "correct" timings (relying heavily on the stopwatch). I soon had a small part of the sequences complete and ready for testing. Letting the completed parts lay and taking notes, I'd then go back and "slip and slide," stretch, and rearrange the bits and pieces until they created within me the feelings I was looking for.

Once I had larger sections done, I'd play through them as well, evaluating how the longer sequences made me feel and taking notes on the changes. Always going by "gut feeling," in a few days, I had *Ghost Warrior*'s animatic completed.

> ## NOTE
>
> The scriptwriter's rule of thumb: *One script page is equivalent to one minute of screen time.*

I had a specific target length for my film: 22 minutes. So, in editing my animatic, I had to make sure the animatic itself was exactly 22 minutes. Most people making their own short films won't have to be so retentive about hitting a specific mark, but if you do, this is the point where you find where you can trim and/or stretch things and still preserve the overall integrity of the film and its rhythm.

With *Ghost Warrior*, everything timed out to almost exactly 22 minutes on the first pass. So, with a minor change or two, I was at my mark exactly, and by referencing how long each storyboard was on screen, *I knew exactly how long each animation needed to be!*

> ## NOTE
>
> With an animatic, while you're polishing animation on a scene, you can test how your work *flows* with the pre- and post-scenes by cutting the preview of your work directly into your animatic! The most beautifully animated scene does the film no good unless it *flows* from the previous scene perfectly into the scene that follows.
>
> When you have *finaled* scenes out of compositing, you cut them into your animatic as well. Then, when you're done with animation and compositing, most of the work of editing your film is already done!
>
> This process of continually updating your animatic with animated scenes in various stages of completion is a form of pre-visualization that extends almost to the final completion of your film. What was once "just" a way to get a feel for the flow of storyboards and timing of scenes becomes your work print, which itself is honed into the final print of your movie!

"Scratch" Audio Track

As you're building your animatic, you've got to start thinking about the *sound* for your film as well. If your film has dialogue, it's obvious that you'll need to record that dialogue for your speaking scenes. But even now, early on in production, you need to begin thinking about the *sound design* for your film.

Most filmmakers start with a temporary audio track that they know will be replaced as things move toward their final stages. This is known as a *"scratch" audio track*. Having this scratch track helps immensely when making judgments on the timing and flow of scenes in your animatic.

NOTE

Music and sound effects drastically affect how long scenes *feel* to an audience.

With my first, fully CG short film, *The Spartan Martian*, I knew in my heart the kinds of timings I wanted. I had studied the works of Chuck Jones' Warner Brothers shorts to the point that I could almost recite their timings from memory.

My first screening of *The Spartan Martian* was done before the music and sound effects were added. Colleagues who were also in the animation industry gave me some comments about some holds lasting too long. (Without the music and sound effects to carry the gags, some holds *were* too long!)

When I screened the film again the following week (this time *with* the final sound mix), the sound carried the holds just like the Chuck Jones' classics! Those who had commented about the holds being too long at the first screening recanted, saying that with the music and sound effects, the timings were perfect!

Dialogue

There are two ways of doing dialogue in an animated film. The common way in the U.S. is to have the voice actors record the final versions of their lines first, from which the animators will work to create the lip-sync. The more common way in animé is to work from temporary dialogue tracks and have the voice actors record the final versions while watching the finished animations play on a monitor.

I wanted to give the second way a try with *Ghost Warrior*, but it just didn't click with me. As an animator, I felt more comfortable, more *safe*, animating from a dialogue track that I knew wasn't going to change. I knew that each and every subtle phoneme I animated in Lip Service was going to be reflected in the performance of the dialogue recording and vice versa. This was important, especially because of the different dialects used by the different characters.

NOTE

If you find yourself animating a "foreign" dialect (or language), clearly listen to how the sounds are being produced by the speaker's mouth. If possible, watch a video of the actor saying the lines. More than just facial expressions, a video of the actor will help you find the subtleties in *embouchure* (lip shape) and tongue positioning that create the subtle variances in "sound shape."

One of the great things about *Foreign Dialects* by Lewis and Marguerite Hermann is that it has drawings that show the mouth and tongue positioning as the specific, "foreign" sounds are produced.

This leads to a bit of a strange revelation about speaking "foreign" languages: If you speak a foreign language with the correctly affected "foreign" dialect, you'll sound a lot more like a native speaker of the language, even to true native speakers.

Sound Booth

Sound travels a lot more than most of us realize. Sound bounces off hard surfaces, reflecting this way and that, giving the listener *subliminal* cues as to the "shape" of the environment around him. When you listen to voices recorded in your average house with an inexpensive microphone, you'll hear the sound bouncing all over the place, giving the recording a distinctive "echoey," hollow feel. This kind of ambience makes a dialogue recording almost unusable. Dialogue is best recorded in a very controlled environment, a *sound booth*, in which sound is *absorbed* after one "bounce" at most, leaving the recorded voice "clean" and "dry."

Access to a sound booth is a luxury that most folks aren't going to have. Yet, you really need a very specific kind of acoustic environment in which to record dialogue so it doesn't sound echoey and hollow. After experimenting with hanging thick blankets around a space and unplugging heaters and other noisy appliances (not recommended during the Alaskan winters), and still not getting satisfactory results, I tried recording in the cab of my truck and was very pleased with the results!

Figure 14-3: The interior of the sound booth in which the voices of *Ghost Warrior* were recorded. The large translucent disc is a popper-stopper (explained in just a moment). It is suspended from the same shock-absorbent material to which the microphone is attached (a polar-fleece "dog bootie"). You see the edge of the "el-cheap-o" Radio Shack microphone just to the right edge of the popper-stopper, suspended from the bootie's Velcro strap that holds the bootie on the dog's paw. The "mic stand" is a standard ruler, counterbalanced with a small case used for holding CDs while on road trips. (Isn't your mind just screaming, "Heck, I can do *that!*" Well, that's the whole point! *Everyone can do this!* The trick is to work around the "mystique." Use the tools you've got that'll do the job you need to get done.)

Figure 14-2: A kind of sound booth that everyone has access to! The small interior space is padded on ceiling and floor with sound-absorbent material — the only "hard" surfaces are the windows which angle the sound to be sucked right into the seats (cloth seats work best when using your vehicle as a recording booth).

Recording in a vehicle gives you a good acoustical space, but the construction of cars and trucks lets a fair amount of outside noise in through their frames. You'll find that with a moderately sensitive microphone, you can pick up the Harley-Davidson a few blocks away, the dogs howling down the street, or the airplane 2,000 feet above. But dude, it's a *car!* You can *drive* to a place where it'll be quiet enough for you to record your dialogue without picking up extraneous sounds (and hopefully not get "picked up" yourself for having arguments with yourself in your car). Or, like I did, you can record late at night or first thing early in the morning.

MDLP

Figure 14-4: Sony's *MZ-N707* "MDLP" is a USB-enabled, re-recordable digital audio device that allows up to five hours of storage space on a single, two-and-a-half-inch minidisc.

The "LP" part of the MDLP is an advanced form of *audio compression* that lets one record up to five hours on a single, two-and-a-half-inch minidisc. While the audio perfectionist can detect "boiling" of sounds like cymbals and the letters "S" and "F" in the five-hour LP4 mode, the two-and-a-half-hour LP2 mode is nearly perfect, especially for the sounds used in human speech.

So, with the one drawback that the software that comes with the consumer-end minidisc player/recorders only allows USB data transfers from computer to MDLP (and not the other way around), I had found my sound acquisition medium.

"Popper-Stopper"

Certain sounds, like "P," "B," "D," "K," and "Ch," force compressed air out of your mouth at high speeds and easily up to a distance of eight inches. These air currents overpower the "compression waves" that carry sound to the microphone. Recording someone speaking these sounds close to an unprotected microphone will result in awful-sounding "pops." The solution is to put a fine screen-like material between the speaker and the microphone that won't dampen the sound waves but will catch and deflect the air currents coming from the speaker's mouth.

This is just what a "popper-stopper" does. You can buy one relatively inexpensively (usually for under $30), but you can make one for even less (usually for under $3). Just get some nylon stockings and an embroidery hoop (I chose one that was six inches across) and stretch the stocking over the hoop like you were going to do some counted-cross-stitch.

Figure 14-5: You position the popper-stopper in front of the microphone, but not so close that it will touch the mic. You can then rant, rave, bluster, and blow as forcefully as you want. The microphone will "ignore" all but actual sound waves from that direction.

Voice "Disguising" Tricks

If you're limited in the voice talent you either have access to or can afford, you or your actors may find yourselves playing multiple roles in your film. The *best* way to disguise your voice to sound like someone different is to let yourself *be* someone different through method acting (see *To the Actor* by Michael Chekhov).

There are, of course, other ways of having your voice sound different than the one you use every day, but these techniques all build on a strong foundation of acting. (If you don't *feel* different, you won't *sound* different; you'll just sound stupid.) So, while this small list of "tricks" can help alter the acoustics of your voice, don't rely on the tricks alone.

Dialects

Using a "foreign" *dialect* is the most obvious way to disguise your voice. But today's audiences are *sharp*. They are worldly and wise. *They know a bad accent when they hear it*. Do yourself a favor — don't insult your audience by "copping" a cheap accent.

If you do find yourself needing to do a dialect, there are four things I can offer as suggestions that may be of some help:

- Get professional help (no, not from a psychologist). If you can't find or afford a good dialect coach, at least get a book that specializes in teaching the *understanding* of both the sounds and the motivations that shape dialects. (Understanding the motivations help you sound different by helping you *feel* different.)

- If you need to record a voice lower than your normal speaking voice, record that dialogue as the first words you speak, the first sounds you make, first thing in the morning.

   I find that during the night, my vocal chords relax significantly.

They stretch so that my normal baritone has much more of a "bassy" feel to it. When recording Kaze, I'd have the truck all set up to record the night before. I'd stumble out of bed and right into recording Kaze to get his low, rumbling whisper.

- A common thing for voice actors to do for certain voices is plug one nostril as they talk for certain "adenoidal" voices. It may look weird in the sound booth, but it gives a distinct, nasally sound that helps separate this voice from your "real" voice (used for Yashin's voice).

- Another common thing for voice actors to do is to pull out their cheek. This can give either a kind of Droopy or Vito Corleone sound that also helps to set this affected voice apart from your own (used for Soshi's voice).

NOTE

One more reason to like the book *Foreign Dialects: A Manual for Actors, Directors, and Writers*, by Lewis and Marguerite Hermann, is that in addition to all the other things that I've mentioned before about the book, it *also* goes into an understanding of the "general mindset" of the speakers. It even provides you with a practice monologue (written both in "plain English" and with the dialect sounds spelled out) that is a "typical" mindset of a speaker of that dialect.

The secret to doing good dialects is like the secret to doing good impressions. If you're able to actually "get inside the head" of the speaker, and walk, think, and move as they do, the sounds that come out of your mouth will be very similar to the dialect you want.

Temporary Score

As mentioned before, the *temporary score* is the music that you lay into your animatic to help you get a better feel for flow and timing. This will also help you figure out what kind of music you will want to have composed for your final piece; you'll be listening to it a lot over the course of production. *This is music you must replace with your own original or commissioned score before releasing your film!*

NOTE

> Without even mentioning the legal issues, the moment you start being an artist yourself is the moment you absolutely need to start respecting other artists' copyrights as sacrosanct. If you don't want other people pirating your work, *don't pirate others' yourself.*

This temporary score will help you *get in the mood* of your piece every time you're watching your animatic/work reel. As you grow accustomed to hearing the different musical bits with your piece, you'll probably feel the need to change pieces here and there. You are narrowing in on the final feel for the music that you will eventually create. When you compose the final score or purchase the royalty-free *loops* you will string together in a program like Acid Pro or Cool Edit Pro, you'll know the different feelings and nuances that you need your tone poem to elicit.

Foley

Adding sound effects, or *Foley*, is a good way to help solidify your work even more into something that takes on more and more of the shape of a real work of filmmaking.

Since I hate doing things twice that could have been done right the first time, I rarely ever work Foley into the animatic with the idea that it will only be temporary. Foley sounds are easy and fun to get and often prove to be a great little break from the rigors of production.

Anything that makes noise will do. Some old favorites are recording the sound of a plunger in a toilet for "gurgley-bubbly" sounds or stringing silverware or other metal items on fishing line, wrapping the end of the line around an inexpensive microphone, striking the silverware for beautiful ringing gong and chime sounds.

Get creative and have fun!

Pre-Visualization

The term pre-vis, in today's feature film market, usually refers to creating your movie (in part or in whole) in an ultra-low complexity CGI form. Directors have come to rely on this "hyper-animatic" to work out the minute details of scenes on which it would be costly to make a mistake. Since it allows for a director to problem-solve nearly every aspect of storytelling within the film, some directors are now doing their entire film in pre-vis before shooting a single frame of actual film.

Doing pre-vis requires about 80 percent of the work and attention of actually animating for final without the reward of a nice, "correct" animation and polished render when you're done. As an already accomplished animator (and an artist whose motto is "Anything worth doing right is worth doing right the *first time*"), I felt that if I was going through all the trouble of building these mock sets, hanging the temporary lights, and posing the character through the scenes, I may as well be "doing it for keeps." For every

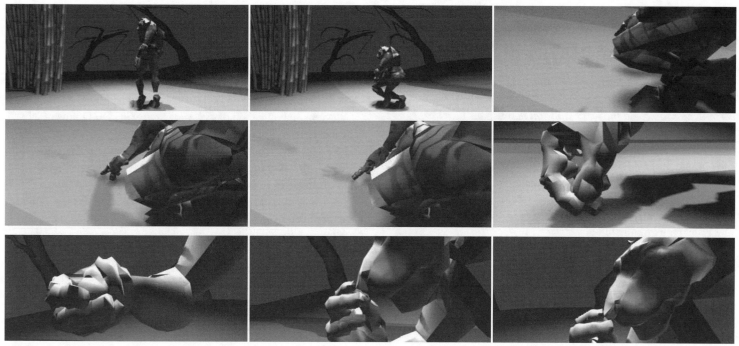

Figure 14-6: Pre-vis for the opening sequence of *Ghost Warrior*.

pre-vis panel I could finish, I could quickly dash out about ten storyboards. As you've seen, those storyboards aren't works of art; they weren't nearly as "tight" as the pre-vis panels, but since I'm the only one who needed to make sense of them, they did just fine.

NOTE

WARNING...Pre-vis is a great idea *if* you've got the time to do your movie *twice* (and/or you've got the money to hire someone else to do it for you). Most places that do pre-vis do so with "fresh meat" right out of art school, paying them a fraction of what real animators make. It's a way for the newly graduated to get their foot in the door, and it's a way for studios to take advantage of hungry artists willing to do just about anything to get into the film industry.

With all that said, there are indeed situations where I'd recommend someone doing their own pre-vis for their own CGI film. The first and most important would be if you felt that you needed to learn more about filmmaking before you could accomplish what it is that you've set out to do. *This would be much the same as doing a series of films in order to achieve the level of skill needed where you were 70 percent sure you could make the film you had in your heart.*

Making a film in pre-vis is, for all intents and purposes, *filmmaking*. Sure it may not have the slick look and the polish of the animations, models, and special effects, but all the *planning* and *management*, all the things that are needed to bring *any* film to completion, are every bit a part of pre-vis. You learn a whole lot when you're doing something of the size and scope of even a short film only a few minutes long.

Pre-vis is also very helpful for people who need to "think out loud" about things like camera angles, lighting, and the like. You build confidence as you gain experience. I can clearly remember my own starting-out days when I had little idea about the "best" angle(s) from which to shoot or light a scene. So, even if you're a wiz at animation, doing a little pre-vis can help you gain confidence in setting cameras and hanging lights.

Lastly, though it's a concept I find hard to imagine, there are some people who just hate drawing. If you absolutely hate drawing, I mean really can't stand it, and you still need to get storyboards and an animatic done for your film, then pre-vis is the way to go!

■ ■ ■

So, with the culmination of pre-visualization, you know your *story* is something worthy of your dedication, time, and effort.

With the solidification of *technology solutions*, you know of what you and your equipment are capable, and you know the pathways and workarounds that you'll be using to do what you'll need to do.

You've got all your pieces lined up and ready to go. This is where things get exciting!

Also bear in mind that there is no way to plan for *every* contingency. So, you've got to have confidence in the creativity and problem-solving abilities that you used to explore your *technology solutions*. Remember the quote from *The Art of War* at the beginning of Part 2? To paraphrase, your greatest strength is in your ability to adapt to changing conditions and to know from the start that you will need to do so, no matter how "clever" your preparation and planning.

This point in production is a little like bungee jumping. You've done your best to prepare as best you can. Then you take the leap! All that potential energy that you've built up by climbing to this point grabs hold of you, and you're in for one heck of a ride!

Chapter 15

Animation

Wow! Animation. The bestowing of life (or at least the *illusion* of it). *Animation* is the magic that lets us fall in love with characters again and again, every time we see their performance. Animation is the gateway to another dimension where tigers and foxes and wolves really do speak and think and act as we do.

Do I still get "spirited away" into the magic of an animated film? Oh, heck yeah! I mean, what's the point of being in love with this medium so much that you want to be a part of it if you try to pretend that you're "too grown up" for that kind of stuff? I tell ya, I'm right there along with the "kids of all ages," wowing and aawwwing and tearing and cheering at all the right places. When I'm *watching* animation, the "director," or "critic," or any other part of me that focuses on analyzing things gets to go on a field trip to Nepal, so *it* can enjoy the "deep spiritual essences" of life, and *I* can sit back and enjoy myself silly.

This is a distinction I have to make if I'm going to enjoy both my work and my life here on this little blue-green planet. The harder I *work*, the harder I've got to *play*. As an animator or director of animated films, I've got to allow myself to *play!* I've got to let myself be a member of "my" audience, swept away into the magic and beauty of the stories that come through the medium. I've *got* to do this if I am going to know what I want out of my own dream/film!

When it comes time to create again on my own films, the "director" in me returns from points continental, refreshed and ready to sift the "excited talk" of inspiration that my "play-self" felt while *enjoying* films. It is *then* that as a whole being my "work" and "play" selves work as one, analyzing the films that were so inspirational. Only then do I begin sifting the tools used to create the magic of the other films into the *next logical steps* that I will need to create similar effects in my own work.

When I sit down to work, I still *remember* the "wow" of films that have inspired me, and I activate the analytical part of me that knows how to do what needs to be done.

To be honest, sitting in a theatre, I might not have the first inkling as to how to create the effects I see before me (to do so would dampen my enjoyment of them). But, sitting down in front of my tools, the part of my mind that knows that *everything* is a *solution* waiting for its path to be found, I find that the first step, which leads to the second and then to the third, is clearly visible and well within my range of ability.

Animation, for all its magic, for all the "wows" and wonderment it embodies, is a *skill*. Like any skill (like typing, for instance), it can be learned by any and all who dedicate themselves to finding and following the ways that *they, personally*, need to learn that skill.

In my studios, I've had people who thought of themselves "only" as modelers, who we needed to become animators, look at me with overflowing wonder and excitement as they watched their first feature-quality animations play out on their monitors.

Learning animation isn't "hard," but it does take a certain kind of teaching method to allow the student to teach himself (which is all any good teacher does). We, as "teachers," do nothing; it is the student that provides the fire. We simply bring the kindling.

LightWave 3D Character Animation and *Fundamentals of Character Animation* dedicate half their length to teaching animation and characterization in the way that I taught "young-at-heart" artists within my studios. The text is important to read and understand but the real "magic" of the methods is in the *exercises*. If you follow the exercises, working with the material from the CD as instructed, you too will "wow" yourself with seeing your animations quickly gain the life and magic you've seen in the animations that have inspired you.

NOTE

A friend told me of a time when he was young and his mother first took him ice skating. He clung unsteadily to the rails surrounding the rink, while they both watched a man skating with effortless grace some distance away. "I wish I could skate like that," my friend told his mother. "Well, how does he skate? Show me," she replied. My friend skated away, a picture of the utmost grace and skill, returning shortly to the rails. "And how do you skate?" his mother asked. My friend wobbled unsteadily from the rails, returning just before falling. "You realize you skated just like that man over there, only a moment ago," his mother said.

In general, we are all operating here with the same "bio-machinery" (two hands, ten fingers, two feet, etc.). For the most part, the only difference among humans is in what has been *allowed* into the *mind*. As we can all *choose* what goes in there, we are *all* capable of becoming all that we wish to become.

Just as the above story and my own experience with training animators illustrates, the socially accepted time requirements for attaining a skill need not apply if you *choose* to simply *do!*

NOTE

A little something I stumbled across about art, being a musician, sculptor, actor, dancer, painter, animator, etc., is that all the arts I explore seem to pull from the *exact same source*.

The same *feeling* I got when I was "in the groove" with a painting or drawing is the same feeling I got when I was flowing through a well-choreographed series of modern dance moves. This is the same feeling I got when I was jamming with some other good musicians, lost in the music itself.

So, a theory evolved: Let yourself experience that feeling you feel when you're in the groove with an art form that you know when you're doing an art form you're learning, and the same level of proficiency should result in the new art form.

For myself, and the other artists I've suggested this to, the results were astounding.

Once you've seen that you are capable of doing this caliber of work, that knowledge itself becomes your "magic feather," giving you the confidence to do the kinds of animation that (in my understanding) you were capable of all along.

Beautiful, emotional, spirit-touching animation requires only time and effort. That's all. As an artist's skill increases, the amount of time required to produce quality work decreases, but the balance is upheld as the effort that the artist puts into the piece *increases proportionally*. (I voice this primarily for those who find themselves directly influencing the work of animators, directors, and producers.)

In order for an animator to create his best work, he has to put the entirety of his soul into the piece while it is being created. The kind of "art-zone" I drop into while animating is far more intense than anything I've ever felt while doing any other art form. Some would even say that a successful animator *channels* the spirit of the character, and the *character* directs the creation of the animation.

Because this is where the magic happens, when the animated scene is the result of the spiritual union between the artist and the story, when the resultant scene is for all intents and purposes the *child* of that union, care *must* be taken to ensure that this child is not sacrificed. If the person directing the show doesn't have a clear idea of what he wants to begin with, if the animator is asked to make changes to his work simply because it isn't exactly what the director had in mind, the animator will not feel *safe* extending himself into the embrace of that or any future scene for the run of the picture. If this happens, what results is animation that may be technically proficient but hits the audience with all the inner fire and life of earwax.

So, just like in *storycrafting*, if you're watching a scene and it isn't playing out *exactly* the way you thought it might, take a closer look at it. Perhaps it's telling you something. Perhaps you're being shown an insight into something that is a bit of genius that couldn't have occurred otherwise. Things like this happened constantly while animating with both Kaze and Itsua.

With Kaze, these "insights" were usually a gesture or a facial expression I had no idea I was working into the scene. I'd just go on "autopilot" and pretty much blank out while I was working. Then, while watching the work play out, I'd be floored at something perfectly "Kaze-like" that would never have occurred to me.

With Itsua, he showed me an entirely new characterization that was very different from what I had first envisioned. Right from the first scene of his that I animated, his personality took hold of my tools and said, "I am supposed to be represented *this* way."

At first, I had pictured him more like Leon in *The Professional*, if he had lived to open up a little restaurant, or like DeNiro's character in *Ronin*. But right from that first scene, I noticed strong influences of Milt Kahl's Robin Hood. I had no idea that kind of undertone to his character would be so effective, but now, I can't imagine Itsua being any other way!

Where to Start

So where do you start when you are presented with a sizable blank "canvas" that stretches through time? Do you, as the Mad Hatter suggests, "Start at the beginning, go on until you get to the end, and then stop"?

A lot of filmmakers take the approach that by the end of the film, the actors, artists, animators, and whatnot know their characters so well by the end of production that they "blow away" any kind of understanding that they had at the beginning.

Like the old saying goes, "You don't get a second chance to make a first impression." So a lot of films start by doing scenes closer to the middle of the story, scenes that aren't supposed to have a lot of "wow" or "punch" to them. Then, as the artists become more comfortable with their characters, scenes are worked closer and closer to the beginning *and* the end of the film. So finally, the last scenes to be completed are the climax at the end of the film and the introductory parts where the characters have to grab and hold the audience's interest for the rest of the film.

Since I'm confident in my own ability to do action scenes, my own choice with *Ghost Warrior* was to begin with the fight scenes in Sequence 2, the Tavern. After doing that volume of work, I felt totally comfortable with the characters and their controls, having done more writing, directing, and producing than animation over the past few years, and then started working my way "outward" toward the beginning and the end of the film from there.

How to Start

Once you have a scene on which to begin working, there are things you should do before you even open your 3D package.

First, take a wander through the storyboards. Study closely how the artist thought this scene should play and *feel*.

Second, sit through a few passes of that section of your animatic. Watch footage that's at least a minute before your scene all the way through footage that extends well after your scene ends. You want to get a good *feel* for what has brought the characters to the point that they are in your scene, how they feel about that, and where they hope to go afterward.

Third, if you have a director, schedule some time to talk with him to figure out his feelings as to what is *moving* the scene forward. You want to find out why the director feels the character couldn't just say, "Hey, I'm not buying this — see ya" and walk off the set.

Fourth, *sketch* (even if you don't feel you can draw worth a hill of beans). Take three to five minutes before you open up your 3D package to just "think out loud." Get ideas on paper. Remember that the ideas "on top" of your mind usually get "dried out" and that the really "juicy" ones are most often under that little bit of "crust" that forms there (like the crud on a squeeze bottle of mustard).

Fifth, after you've logged your first ten to 15 minutes working on a scene, save your work as a revision (just in case this "trick" doesn't work). Reload the setup version of your scene (the version of the scene without any posing, positioning, or motion), and *start over from scratch*. This has *always* resulted in me getting better-quality work, faster than if I had kept at it with that first attempt.

Sixth, when you start to get something that looks like animation, begin checking your work by sandwiching your preview animation between the previous and post scenes (whether they be in animatic or animated form) in your editing package. (Every well-animated character has a *past*, *present*, and *future* and *opinions* and *feelings* about each one of these stages of its life.) Even a beautifully animated scene that has sparkle, jazz, and magic may lose these qualities when seen in its place amid the pre- and post-scenes. Since a film is a single, contiguous whole (not a disconnected grouping of individual thoughts), your scene's functioning within this flow is what truly matters.

Seventh, keep at it until the scene is done!

Rhythm

I like to look at everything artistic as a kind of dance. Everything has a *rhythm* to it. Linework's balance of straight, curved, short, and long lines has a distinct rhythm. The *pacing* and *timing* of words in dialogue, their pitch, and tonality are like the music that drives the movements of a character through the scene.

I suppose as an artist I would classify myself as *empathic* or *kinesthetic*, rather than *visual*. To know if something that I've done is "right," I need to translate it into something that makes sense to me emotionally or physically. Then, to make changes to, say, a drawing or painting, I need to translate those feelings back into the artistic terms that govern that particular art form — lines and brush strokes in the case of drawings and paintings.

So, I'm saying that if you, personally, don't "see" things in motion but rather "hear" them as music or "feel" them as sculpture, don't worry about it. Just figure out whatever it is you need to do to *translate* to and then from your own ways of "seeing" things.

When I first found out about holography in ninth grade, it was like a whole new way of thinking that made a lot of this world suddenly make sense. (Forget the "light-in-the-attic" analogy; it was like finding a Rosetta stone for art, math, science, dance, theater, writing, and just about everything else that seemed like something cool to explore.)

A simplified explanation of holography is that it uses light made up of exactly the same wavelength (*coherent* light produced by a laser — an acronym for light amplified by stimulated electron radiation) and a series of partially transmissive mirrors to split the beam in two and expose an ordinary plate of photographic film from both the "front" and from the "back" by light bouncing off the object to be made into a hologram.

The result of developing the film exposed in the manner described above is an *interference pattern* that looks like absolutely nothing at all under diffused light (like fluorescent tubes), but when lit with a point light source (like the sun or a smallish, bright lightbulb), that interference pattern suddenly becomes a completely 3D representation of the subject object.

NOTE

Described above is a *reflective hologram*. There are many kinds of holography. If you'd like to explore making your own holograms, Edmond Scientific (http://www.scientificsonline.com) has some inexpensive "sandbox" holography kits where you can make your own holograms using a standard laser pointer.)

An interesting look into the actual hows of holographic interference patterns, William J. Beaty has a very interesting short paper online about hand-drawn, "abrasion" holograms at http://www.amasci.com/amateur/holo1.html.

There are many fascinating aspects of holography, but the one that is pertinent here is that when you break a hologram in half, you don't get one piece showing only the left half of the subject and the other piece showing only the right half. *You get two complete representations of the subject* but as seen from either right or left *points of view* (depending on which half of the broken hologram you're looking at).

Break a hologram into a thousand pieces, and you have a thousand complete visions of the subject object but from a thousand points of view!

So, this gave me an impression that we, like the different bits of a hologram, are perfect representations of a greater whole (call that whole by whatever name feels right to you). Like little holographic bits, we all represent slightly different points of view. While some things are visible from some angles, some aren't. That's perfectly as it should be!

So, while some of my other artist friends *see* their art in a very *visual* manner and I can't, it doesn't mean that I am any less of an artist. For me to try to *see* as they do is like trying to view something that was hidden from my own holographic point of view. From my own point of view, I don't *see* art; I *feel* it, *emotionally* and *rhythmically*.

The moment I stopped trying to force myself into a point of view that wasn't my own (the moment I learned to say, "Oh, when you say 'X', I can *translate* it into meaning 'Y' *in my own way of experiencing things*"), I quickly became a much better artist.

So, because I don't "see" things as much as I *feel* them, I equate almost everything artistic, including animation, to *choreography*: the combination of music and dance. So, as I'm working out a scene, I am watching very carefully for the rhythms as everything in motion relates with everything else.

A person's eyes come up first and then the head. A punch begins from the twisting of the waist, snaking whiplike through the body. These are balances of rhythm that are more like the elements of *dance* than of a single, still image.

- No two elements on screen move at exactly the same time at exactly the same pace.
- All motions flow like waves from an initial source
- All impacts radiate outward from their impetuous, like ripples in a pond.
- Smooth motions that unfurl like a whip need to be accentuated by other motions that are quick and percussive.
- For every action, there is an equal and opposite reaction.
- For every action, there is an equal and *appropriate pre-action*.

These are the core essentials to good motion, and all of them have to do with the *relationship* of one element's motion to another —

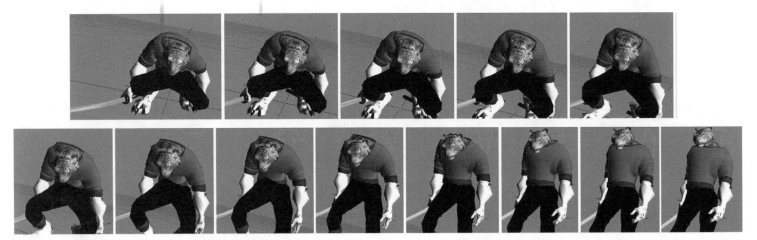

Figure 15-1: His motion leading from his torso, Kaze rolls upward in what is actually a dancer's exercise. I treat every scene I work as if I am choreographing to an almost undetectable rhythm that moves from one scene into the next.

their *rhythm*. (You can learn a lot more about the *rhythmic* tools and effects of animation in *LightWave 3D Character Animation* and *Fundamentals of Character Animation*.)

Rhythm is not just the domain of things that move through time. Rhythm plays an equally important role in *still images* as well.

Dichotomy

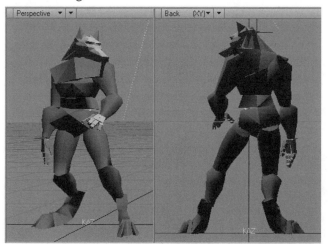

Figure 15-2: A simple "ready" pose. Though it is simple, there is a complexity to its rhythms in that no two body parts fall on exactly the same horizontal or vertical line with the same degree of angle.

In Figure 15-2, the character's right side creates more of a "straight-up-and-down" *silhouette*, while the character's left side has more "bumps" and angles. The character's left side reads with a tenseness and readiness to it, while the character's right side reads as more relaxed. (Hold your hand over half of the illustration to see the vast difference between the two halves of the character.) This dichotomy itself sets up a rhythm that, like *constructive*

interference in wave propagation, increases the impact that this pose has on the audience.

Twinning

Even though we're working in 3D, what we do can easily look "flat" if we have both halves of the character mirroring each other.

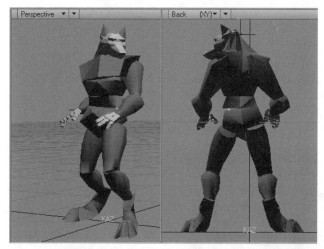

Figure 15-3: Notice how much more *weakly* this pose reads, even though it is very similar to the one in Figure 15-2. By shifting the character's weight so both legs are supporting him equally and moving his right hand so it is in the same relative position as his left, the *feel* and power of the image is reduced to a constrained caricature of the original pose.

The *symmetry* of Figure 15-3 (even though not exact symmetry) is an example of the emasculation that *twinning* can do to a pose. So always keep your eyes out for this. With the wonders of 3D animation, it is *extremely* easy to fix. Through the manipulation of a control or two (with my riggings, as described in *LightWave 3D*

Character Animation and *Fundamentals of Character Animation*), twinning in a pose can be *eliminated in five to ten seconds!*

Contraposto

Contraposto is another simple thing to watch for in your poses that will instantly add "oompf" to them. It is something that you learn about when studying ancient Greek and Roman statuary in art history. Quite simply, it means that if your character's right hip is up, your character's right shoulder is down.

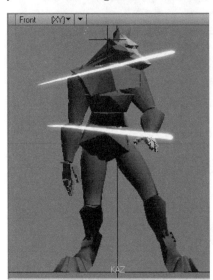

Figure 15-4: It doesn't take much; a little contraposto goes a long way toward making any pose look a whole lot better. (Like cologne, don't think that if a little contraposto is good, then a lot must be really good. Too much contraposto just looks goofy.)

Compound Curves

A *compound curve* is a curve that bends in two directions at once.
FREEZE!
Without moving, mentally inspect the angles and relations of your own "carriage." Take note of the angles of your pelvis, midsection, and torso and how they relate to one another. Chances are, you're bending in more than one direction at once. Chances are, you're both twisting around your y axis, while "canting" around your z axis, and probably even "slouching" along your x axis.

Things in "real life" are seldom ever just rotated along one axis. They're almost always rotated in a combination of at least two axes, if not all three. So another quick-and-easy way to add a bit of realism to your work is to just make sure that your character's spine, and other parts not directly in contact with a floor or other flat surface, are *subtly* rotated on at least two axes! (Neat, huh?)

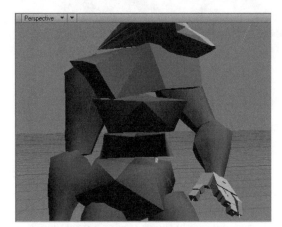

Figure 15-5: The character's chest is pointing off-screen right, while his pelvis is angled off-screen left. This is a bit more pronounced since the character is in a martial arts "ready" pose (with most "normal" poses, this *compound curvature* is more *subtle*).

All these rhythmic devices must be thought of in *three-dimensional space* because that's the world in which we're working (both with our characters and within our own personal, "real" worlds). But because that space will eventually be displayed as a *flat, two-dimensional image* (projected on a screen large or small), you've always got to do your final evaluation from the point of view of the final camera position(s).

For me (through my *translations* of understanding), art is all about rhythms, having enough variety within these rhythms to grab and *hold* the audience's attention. It's all about setting up patterns and then breaking them. Rhythms are mythic. Rhythms are ancient tools that have the same effect on us today as they did thousands of years ago. They are tools that, for me, translate into every aspect of art, every aspect of life.

Breaking these "rules" down into rhythmic devices is my way of making them understandable to me; it's easier for me to get a handle on their relationships and interrelationships that way. If you experience things from a different *holographic point of view*, you've got to find out what translations work for you. Doing so will give you a "Batman decoder ring" through which you can understand anything!

Character Animation

All the magic of *character animation* boils down to just two things: *posing* and *timing*.

If a character's poses are strong and appropriate, and the timing between them is fitting, you've got good animation. All the acting, all the action, all the incredible performances you've ever seen stem from these two simple things.

Broken down this way, most anybody can say, "Heck, I can do that!"

There's a fair amount that goes into the learning of seeing the subtle silhouettes that make up a good pose and feeling the subtle rhythms that make up good timing. But, taken one step at a time, these are skills that any dedicated person can master.

Acting

Character animation is *acting*. If you haven't yet read *To the Actor* by Michael Chekhov and *Audition* by Michael Shurtleff, please put them high on your list. The exercises in both these books were pivotal to my own skills as an actor. Both authors break complex concepts into easily understood pieces that just click into place.

To the Actor teaches you ways of actually *becoming* the character. The experience is nothing short of magic. Going through the exercises, actually feeling myself as Kaze, walking around in that world, I didn't have to wonder how Kaze would do something; the answer was right there — simply paying attention to what *I* did.

This is something that all method actors experience — *becoming the character*. This made it very difficult and very unnerving working on the scenes with Soshi. I think the reason why his scenes are difficult to watch is that all of us have something of him deep inside us. It is by *conscious choice* that we don't let that thrill-at-domination out when we could bully someone, human or animal. Playing Soshi brought me face to face with many buried feelings and thoughts that I had to stand toe-to-toe against while animating his scenes. Through method acting, I was forced to confront those similarities within my own personality.

Upon finishing the scenes with Soshi, I found that for having been so "front and center" with the factors that motivate *him*, almost like therapy, I noticed marked points of personal evolution within myself. It was almost as if the medium of animation had created a safe environment to unleash and battle those "demons" that Soshi represents in us all.

NOTE

C.S. Lewis, author of the *Chronicles of Narnia* series, also wrote *The Screwtape Letters*, a story told through letters from one of Satan's minions, Screwtape, to a "junior tempter," Wormwood, concerning Wormwood's mission to corrupt a human. Lewis reportedly had a very difficult time working on the book, saying that through writing as Screwtape, he found himself actually thinking and feeling as Screwtape.

Empathic Record-and-Playback

I'll let you in on my one main "secret" of character animation here (not that it's much of a secret, but it'll do). This secret is what I use for creating all my performances. Every bit of acting that goes on in any scene of mine was created through the use of this little secret. It's really just a way of "tapping into" the archetypal influences for the character. I call it *empathic record-and-playback*.

I find an existing performance in another film that *feels* like the inner core of the character with which I'm working, digitize it so I can "scrub" back and forth through that *reference performance*, and then exactly recreate that reference performance with the character in 3D. While I'm doing this, I pay very close attention to *how recreating this reference performance makes me feel inside as I'm doing the recreation*. I'm not talking about any kind of stress or elation about the labor of moving the controls themselves; I'm talking about sensing the almost inexplicable feelings that "click" with

your creativity itself that hold the inner core of that character's existence. This is what happens when you're doing a (believable) impression of someone: You actually *feel* what it feels like to make the kinds of decisions that result in the sounds and gestures the rest of the world sees.

Then, when creating a performance of that character's own, I simply "replay" the feelings I had from recreating the reference performance, and it almost seems that the character himself takes hold of the controls and *he* shapes the scene before me.

Now, the empathic record-and-playback technique works best if you're at a technical level of skill where you can forget about all the details that go into the mechanics of making the art. Like jazz, if you've got the riffs, scales, and arpeggios down, they just seem to fly out of you at the right moment when you're lost in the act of *listening to the art that's being created through you*!

NOTE

This idea of empathic record-and-playback happened in my first year of college. I had been working on a piano piece by Beethoven, having memorized it, and was focusing on honing the performance. I thought I sounded pretty good — that is, until I recorded myself playing it. I needed a *lot* of work.

Strangely enough, that same Beethoven work was played later that afternoon on the local public radio station. Now, granted, the pianist was a professional, but he sounded incredible; it was almost as if he were playing a completely different piece of music. I noticed how powerfully moving the piece was, stirring emotions within me from joy to tears.

Since I knew the piece by heart, I started focusing on *remembering* how each passage made me feel inside while listening to it.

When I got back to a piano, I set a tape recorder running and started playing the piece again, but this time, while doing so, I *let myself feel inside* how I had felt while listening to the public radio performance.

Listening to the tape recording I had made of this performance, I was dumbstruck. I could tell the areas where my technical skills weren't quite up to snuff, but for almost all intents and purposes, *the sounds coming from my little tape recorder were almost exactly the ones I had heard over the radio earlier in the day!*

Over the years, I found this little trick worked with everything, from learning how to animate, draw, and paint better to becoming much better at cooking. (Yes, it even works with the Zen of archery and motorcycle repair.) The great thing about it is that everyone I've mentioned this empathic record-and-playback technique to and who has tried it has had *exactly the same results.*

Pretty cool, huh!

Action

The films that most influenced the action in *Ghost Warrior* were *Drunken Master II*; *Crouching Tiger, Hidden Dragon*; and *The Crow*. Now, not all these films' action revolves around martial arts, but the timing, the pacing, the "Holy cats!" factor of them was what I wanted with *Ghost Warrior*.

I wanted the action in *Ghost Warrior* to match these films in emotional depth, breadth, and complexity. This is not action simply for the sake of action. This is action that furthers the story and helps define Kaze and his views on life. Kaze is not interested in hurting people who don't *need* to be hurt (evidenced in both the tavern and glade scenes when he allows combatants the opportunity to *choose* not to fight). The only time this is not the case is when he is enraged by the carelessness of the chain-weapon troublemaker who almost hits a bystander. This is the only place in the film where his reason is submerged into rage, and because of this, that rage is all the more unnerving.

Kaze's style of martial arts is a "do-what-needs-to-be-done," "hit-someone-only-hard-enough-so-they-can't-cause-immediate-problems" kind of style. It's hard to pin down a specific style to Kaze's arts, rationalizing by saying that he has traveled far and wide and assimilated what has fit with his philosophies. Kaze not only knows what he's doing with the speed, senses, and reflexes of a cat, he is huge and uses his mass to his advantage. So, when Kaze does make "martial contact" with someone, I wanted it to be businesslike and with the unmistakable read of effectiveness.

With that kind of power, speed, and skill, I wanted to really have the audience "take a step back" from the more traditional martial arts film fare, where people hit each other hundreds of times and come right back. I wanted this to have a kind of "serious" feel to it, right from the first throw. People see the name of the film, *Ghost Warrior*, and (correctly) assume that it is going to have martial arts fight scenes in it, but when Kaze starts to do his thing, I wanted the audience to say, "Oh, maybe this is going to be a little different than what I'd expected."

One of the "rules" that Kaze has is that while he does have three-inch-long talons, he reserves them for special use only. Someone has to *earn* the "privilege" of having Kaze's claws within them. This "privilege" is reserved for those people who go out of their way to make other people's lives hell. It follows on the philosophy that one's departure from this life will influence one's entrance into another. Kaze, in using his claws on Yashin (the lead troublemaker), whispers a prayer to the other's departing soul that future lives may be free from the hatred that Yashin has chosen to perpetuate in his current life. Through events that will be revealed in future stories of Kaze, he has come to take this "cleansing" as his *penance*, his job.

"...which is a kind of integrity, if you look on every exit, as an entrance, somewhere else."

— The Player, *Rosencrantz and Guildenstern Are Dead*

"It's what you don't say that matters."

— Old rule for negotiations

Dialogue

I've always liked doing dialogue scenes. Because you have certain things that have to happen at certain times, I find them a lot easier to do than silent scenes. Even so, there is very little dialogue in *Ghost Warrior*. This was done on purpose to get as much of the story told in *pantomime* as possible.

Silence is more powerful than sound.

This goes back to the concept of *throwaway lines*. You watch the performances of Robert DeNiro, Jean Renault, Harrison Ford, and Gregory Peck, and you see so much carried by just a look on their face or the way they carry themselves. This is a way of communicating that doesn't need words to make itself understood, and therefore it is understood regardless of language. Because these looks represent what's going on inside the mind of the character (the things "real people" try to keep hidden), they come across as being more truthful than any line of dialogue.

So, I tried to tell as much of the story through silence as possible, knowing that if I was able to carry the scene *without* dialogue that it was a scene that did so through the quality of its acting. Of the scenes that did feature dialogue, I went through them and highlighted every line that could qualify as a throwaway. In the recording of the dialogue, I made sure to either just "think" those lines silently, *subvocalize*, or otherwise downplay those throwaway lines. The result was dialogue that itself relied heavily on acting to convey the point of the scene.

Doing this was a challenge. It required me to have the characters actually *act*, rather than simply mouth their lines. The process of animating the body first to make sure the story-point within each scene was clear *first* before doing the dialogue helped establish a solid base. The tools provided within Lip Service, letting me easily craft a beautifully complex and yet subtle flow of visible thoughts playing across the characters' faces, only served to enhance what was already there.

Live-Action Reference

I didn't use *live-action reference* in *Ghost Warrior*, but I feel I should mention it because it can be a huge time-saver.

Live-action reference is when you videotape yourself (or a helpful subject or cast) doing something that you'll be animating. You use this videotape for *suggestions* as to important points, cues, and subtleties about the action. (You don't directly copy it, which is known as *rotoscoping* and almost always ends up looking stiff.)

Using live-action reference can help you figure out the exact *timing* of the individual body parts as a character descends a ladder. It can help you figure out *balance* as a character runs, swinging a heavy firearm. It can be every bit as useful as motion capture but at a fraction of the cost.

But, like when using motion capture, when shooting live-action reference footage, make sure your subjects have props of appropriate proportionate weight, if they are using props. If you have a character swinging a big, double-handed broadsword, make sure the subject has something of comparable *mass* and *balance* with which to work. Just swinging a stick around won't do you any good if your character is supposed to be wielding a battle-ax — the balance and weight of the motions will scream, "Hi! I'm swinging something around that weighs next to nothing!"

Where can you find folks that may be able to help you out with your live-action reference? If you're near a college or university, start with some of the clubs and groups there. From martial arts clubs and Civil War re-enactors to "live-action role-playing groups," you can usually find lots of help from people who would love to see things done "the right way" in a film. My own personal favorite whenever dealing with things of a "medieval" touch is the Society for Creative Anachronism (or SCA for short).

"I can't see a thing in this helmet!"
— Luke Skywalker, *Star Wars: A New Hope*

NOTE

The SCA is usually made up of people with very high levels of creativity and intelligence. Some "shires" are much more historically accurate, while some "recreate the Middle Ages the way they wish they would have been" (leaving out things like smallpox and starvation and the like). With *guilds* that focus on everything from armor-crafting, brewing, and vinting to spinning, illumination, and costume design (and many, many more), there is a wealth of information and enjoyment to be had by dropping by an event or meeting.

Perhaps what the SCA is most popularly known for is its fighting. Armorers recreate suits of armor from various materials, and then the fighters battle it out with rattan swords, axes, and whatnot, trading blows that will most definitely clear the sinuses (speaking from experience). At these battles and practices, you can see real people using weapons in ways that will most definitely inspire a sense of "you are there" that is important in good filmcraft. In a practice, you will probably be more than welcome to don a helm and armor yourself and see first-hand how it really looks and feels to be facing down an opponent. The experience of actually "living it" gives you, the artist, a much broader palette from which to work.

Effects Animation

There wasn't really that much in the way of *effects animation* in *Ghost Warrior*. Effects animation in traditionally animated films usually takes care of things like fire, sparks, water, ripples, smoke, lightning, and so on. The only thing that would really qualify as effects animation in *Ghost Warrior* is the sometimes almost imperceptible levels of fog that swirl amid the backgrounds.

Fog

I found out while doing the piece *Daybreak Denali* that trying to find the right balance of settings to get fog to render "properly" along with all the other elements in a 3D scene takes a lot of time adjusting the controls. With a scene full of elements, those renders sometimes took upwards of three minutes per frame — far too long for my production schedule.

Figure 15-6: The "before" and "after" of the mist in sq01sc04. When comparing the two, the mist is quite noticeable. However, as the scene plays out in the film without the comparison, the mist is a subtle lightening of the scene, barely registering but to the viewers that really look for it. ("Real life" is full of things that are noticeable only when you really look for them.)

Figure 15-7: *Daybreak Denali*, a parody of Max Parrish's famous painting *Daybreak*, was my first *proof-of-concept* to see if what I was planning on doing with *Ghost Warrior* was actually possible.

By using the tools, controls, and compositing methods in Digital Fusion, I was able to adjust the fog to be *exactly* what I wanted it to be, *all in real time!* Squashing, stretching, masking, flipping, rotating, and compositing using screen, overlay, dodge, and luminosity are all completely viable options when assembling your layers in a compositing program.

After a few scenes of prerendering a fog plate, I began to use Digital Fusion's Fast Noise to create a softly roiling fog for my backgrounds. This was much quicker, and combining a *stretched* Fast Noise with a gradient background and some blur, using a soft-edged, polygonal mask to place the noise where I needed, I found that I had much more control in producing the result I wanted, *quickly.*

Almost 100 percent of the time, I used depth fog to combine this fog layer with the other layers based on each pixel's "position" on the z-plane. The result was an *atmospheric perspective* that greatly heightened the sense of space and production value and took almost no time at all to render.

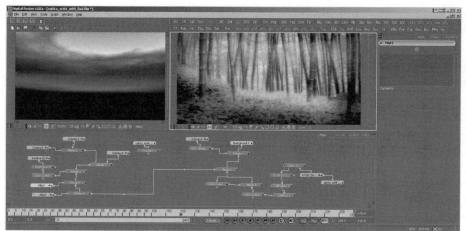

Figure 15-8: Sq01sc04, in the opening "glory shots," was the first scene in which I composited a separate, pre-rendered "fog plate." (The fog plate, seen on the left view, was rendered using the ultra-fast *fake volumetric ground fog* explained in *Essential LightWave*. Render time for each HD720p frame was 20 seconds!)

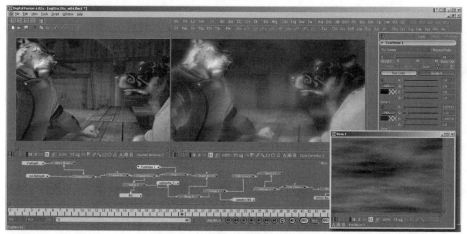

Figure 15-9: On the left view, you see the pre-depth-fog, depth-blur, and glow version of the scene. On the floating view (labeled View 1), you see the Fast Noise plate used to fog the background based on z-buffer (depth) information. Between these views is the final composite.

Multiplane Camerawork

I used the "trick" of compositing my foreground elements onto a single, static background plate a lot in *Ghost Warrior*. I estimate that it saved about *three weeks* total rendering time (on my two machines). Doing this was no different than layering animated cells on top of a hand-painted background in traditional animation (see Figure 15-10).

Even in many of the shots where the camera was moving in perspective or "dollying" slightly around a character in the foreground, I was able to use a single background image thanks to the motion tracking and de-/stabilization tools in Digital Fusion (see Figures 15-11 and 15-12).

When using tracking guides (Figure 15-13), I found that it is best to have each of the four present a different shape for the trackers to lock onto. This is why in the surrounding illustrations that each of the tracking guides has been rotated along its z-axis by 90 degrees.

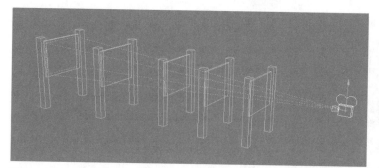

Figure 15-10: The basic concept for the real-world multiplane camera allows artwork to be suspended at different levels from the camera. This enables real-world camera effects within traditional animation like depth-of-field and multi-layered parallax movement.

Figure 15-12: When compositing a single-frame element/layer into a scene in Digital Fusion, in addition to rendering the other layers, I'd render a pass of the scene with only the four *tracking guides*. These guides are placed in the same z position relative to the camera as the single-frame element were it actually in the scene. The resulting image sequence provided me with the exact changes based on perspective and movement that the camera would "force" onto the element over the course of the animation.

Figure 15-11: This is an obvious *multiplane* shot; each of the levels was rendered separately and then composited in Digital Fusion. (The trees are combinations of hypervoxel sprites, the bumpy, leafy stuff being distributed with particles emitted from the branches. The mountain silhouettes were hand-drawn in Macromedia's Flash MX.)

Figure 15-13: A closeup of one of my tracking guides.

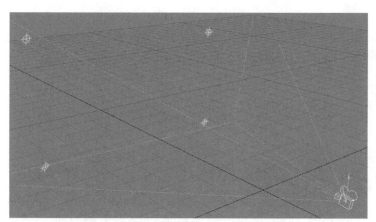

Figure 15-14: In order for the compositor to be able to *distort* a layer in proper perspective, in the 3D package the tracking guides have to be placed where the object(s) being substituted by the single, prerendered plate would be.

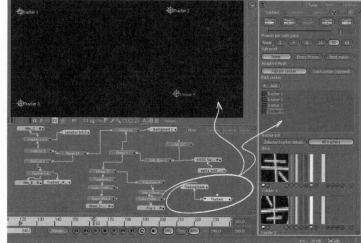

Figure 15-15: Then, in Digital Fusion, a *tracker* is assigned to each tracking guide, working from a rendered series of frames that has *only* the tracking guides. The trackers follow the pattern of their own unique tracking guide through the length of the scene. (There is an art to motion tracking. It's best to play with it a bit *before* you need to depend on it so you know how and what to target as a viable pattern and how to best use the settings so your trackers don't jump around on you and yet still track quickly.)

Even though *Ghost Warrior* is 3D CGI, I made use of tools both old and new to get the effects that I needed *fast!* Using this high-tech, digital take on the multiplane camera to use a single image for what would have been another render pass through a scene saved an immense amount of time. I could then dedicate that time saved to other important things!

History is a toolbox, my friend. Just because something may have been developed 50 or 100 years ago (or more) doesn't mean that it can't hold "secrets" that can make your life much easier if you're able to see that tool from just the right angle! Creativity and *problem-solving ability* are your greatest assets! Through your ability to "think outside the box," that which was thought of as being improbable yesterday will be your status quo tomorrow!

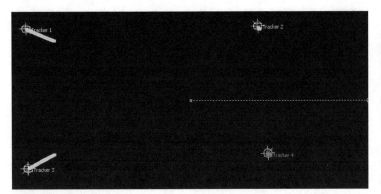

Figure 15-16: As the trackers follow their specific target patterns throughout the length of the scene, paths are generated, marking each tracking guide's position at every frame.

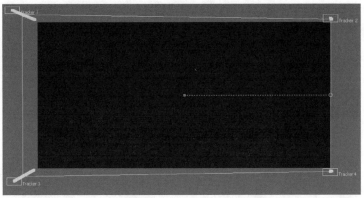

Figure 15-17: I then selected each *set* of the *tracker*-generated path points and moved them so one end of their path would be just outside their respective corner of the *renderable area* (otherwise the edge of the static plate would show during the scene as the image was warped into the renderable area). When using the corner positioning function of Digital Fusion's tracker function, the single-frame background plate is warped in an exact replica as the relationship among the four tracking guides. The end result is that the static plates appear to move in perfect perspective with respect to the camera's motion!

Chapter 16

Production Management

Half of life is showing up. The other half is following through.

Management… Filmmaking all boils down to management. You educate yourself as to what is needed in order to complete a goal, make fair assessments of the ability you have to complete the requisite steps for completion of the goal, and then keep on keeping on until that goal is finished. Of course, the real art to business and management is in *problem solving* when things don't quite work out as your *educated guess* had foreseen.

With good management, you can achieve anything.

- Management isn't managing *things*; it's managing *people*.
- Always hire people better than you.
- As a manager, your job is to make yourself obsolete.
- Making the people "below" you look good makes *you* look *great!*
- Always be as truthful as you can be, especially about the things you cannot discuss.
- To lie is to allow into yourself a poison that will eventually lead to your demise.
- Overtime happens when *management* fails in *its* job.
- Hire the best people you can afford, and then *let them do their jobs!*

The Art of Business

There is an entire industry that caters to *training* abilities in management (and yes, it is a *training* anyone can learn, even an "arr-teest"). Books, tapes, seminars, courses — there's a plethora to choose from. But I find that the best in western schools of management are only beginning to barely touch the wisdom and understanding of one of the earliest known treatises on

"management," Sun Tzu's *The Art of War*. (It was written in China, circa 500 B.C., though there was and remains debate as to its age and the identity/existence of Sun Tzu himself.)

The book *The Art of War* is standard issue for intelligent, business-oriented individuals. In my opinion, it should be standard issue for anyone who plans on interacting with other humans over the course of their lives. It is packed with short bits of wisdom that apply to everything from negotiating a deal with an agent or company to keeping spirits high and focused over a long sojourn such as filmmaking.

> "In good order, they await a disorderly enemy; in serenity, a clamorous one. This is control of the mental factor.... Do not gobble proffered baits."
>
> — Sun Tzu, *The Art of War*

However, it must be realized that the *ultimate* success in business is *not* as war, in which one side must be victorious and one side is overcome. *Ultimate* success comes from doing what's best for the project *and* the others involved. Like in a theatre troupe where each of the actors is focusing on "making the other guy look good," everyone looks a hell of a lot better than if one person is trying to steal the show.

This could be a wonderful change to the "big-studio" mentality of scheduling film releases to try to draw business from another studio's release. This kind of thinking is *infantile!* Another's success *does not* negate your own!

A change in many ways in which this world is run could be fused by people realizing, truly realizing, and imprinting into their every thought, word, and deed that, as John Nash said, the ultimate success comes from members of a group doing what's best for themselves *and the group*. If enough companies adapt the "theatre troupe" method of making the other guy look good (in a genuine fashion), the old, "voracious combatant" methods of today's high-powered business world of taking advantage where advantage is to be had *will cease to have power.*

Someone working *with* you is ten times more powerful than someone working *for* you; it seems like it should be common sense. But every single place I have been hired to work, I have been hired to work *for* and have been constricted to the point of loss of artistic consciousness.

Yet, in the work environments I created within Exile Films and started in Studio Mythos, we were all working *with* one another. The final products were things in which we *all* had ownership. The people working with me on the projects I oversaw created work of a caliber that astounded themselves (and made for very happy clients). Working in this manner is the only way 12 minutes of better-than-TV-quality, full-character animation were able to be created in five weeks for Mattel by a team of three people.

In managing any gig, I acknowledge that I know what I know and am excited by what I don't! I make this crystal clear to the people who need to believe in my leadership. The people working with me are giving me part of their *lives. I owe them this respect.* In your own experiences of working with others, I strongly urge you to do the same.

Production Tracking

Right from the start, you need to have a solid way of tracking your progress. If you don't know how far you've come, you have no way of knowing how much there is yet to do. Poor production tracking is why things begin to feel overwhelming and the reason why some projects end only partially completed.

Because of my keeping precise track of how much progress has been made on *Ghost Warrior*, I know how intense the work will be over the course of the next three months.

Databases Are Cool

A sign of one of the biggest problems with the handling of the production tracking on *Dinosaur* was that quite often, we'd have three or four production assistants (PAs) coming around asking the same questions about our progress on our scenes. When Exile Films expanded into Studio Mythos, and I finally had a budget to "do things right," I made sure all the management got PDAs (personal digital assistants) for production tracking.

DDH Software (http://www.ddhsoftware.com) makes a great, inexpensive forms-based database solution called HanDBase. It runs on both Palm and PocketPC. It comes with a desktop PC version and allows data synchronization with other hand-held devices, desktop PC, and/or a centralized data server. (Prices vary from $29 for entry-level, which is still quite powerful, to $99 for the Enterprise version. All versions can run the hundreds-if-not-thousands of free databases that cover everything from production management to the periodic table.)

So, with production tracking using a PDA database program like HanDBase, everyone who needs to know the status of animations, director walk-through requests, questions, comments, or problems can know *instantly*, just by looking at their up-to-date synch of the production database.

The database I set up in HanDBase also has a field for showing on which take the scene is. I don't expect that there will be many "take twos" or "take threes" of scenes, simply because I'm the director, and if I don't know what I'm envisioning for a scene to work with its surrounding scenes, I've got larger problems that I need to address.

There is also a field in the database labeled Cut for postmortem tracking where in production a scene is found to be unnecessary. Hopefully there won't be any entries with the Cut box checked, but

if there are, I need to know where I found my mistake, so I can make better decisions on my next film — hopefully.

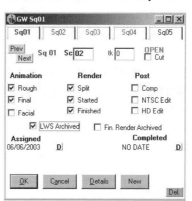

Figure 16-1: With the database I worked out for *Ghost Warrior*, every scene's number is a database entry, with checkbox fields for Rough, Facial, and Final (animation), compositing, NTSC editorial, HD editorial, archival, Assigned and Completed dates, and a "referential" field that tells me at a glance whether the scene is open or finished.

For the Good of All, and According to Free Will

When I was being trained for my first "real" assistant directing job, I was told by a friend who was an accomplished producer/director that part of an assistant director's job (and part of a producer's job as well) is to not quite say that a shot is taking too much time or will cost too much. Instead, a producer's or AD's job is to ask the director if the time/money spent on this shot will be worth the requisite trimming of shots scheduled later ("Sure we can do *this*, but it will mean we won't be able to do *that* later. It's your call.")

So, aside from actually keeping track of production, part of production management is to *adapt to the constantly changing needs of the film itself*. Will you spend an extra day getting the motion of a move perfect? If so, from where will that extra day's time come?

- Will you cut a scene entirely?

- Will you push in closer on a character to reduce the amount of animation required?

- Will you shift from a frontal dialogue shot to a reverse angle that will only show the listener's face as he silently nods his head, drastically reducing the need for facial animation for that shot?

- Will you shift the planned camera angle to reduce the number of characters in the shot?

All of these are ways in which a director can choose to *adapt* to the flowing nature of making a CGI animated film. Yet, all of these decisions must be made with the mind and heart clearly on the focus of the finished product. Every decision to extend work on a scene or reduce work on another must be made *for the betterment of the final product*.

NOTE

> The "spotlight" doesn't shine on us; we simply reflect the brilliance of the art that comes *through* us.

Changes

Everything you do needs to be for the betterment of the film. No matter how "foresightful" we hope to be in our storyboarding or animatic and all other areas of pre-production and planning, there are times that we look at what we've done and cringe (in varying degrees). Sometimes what we thought was going to be really cool falls totally flat. While I like to try to learn from my mistakes (so I can make *new* ones next time), I admit that as a living being, the "unforeseen combinations of events requesting a re-evaluation of the currently accepted interpretation of 'reality'" are a fact of life.

> "Okay.... So?... She's a dog."
> — Dr. Peter Venkman, *Ghostbusters*

As you evaluate each piece that gets cut into your animatic, watching its flow from the previous scene to the scene that comes after it, don't be afraid to accept that what you once thought was going to work simply isn't working. As you begin each week, watching your production reel in full, make a note to change a scene if it isn't working out the way you *need* it to.

A scene that may read beautifully on its own may lose its sparkle of magic when shown amid its pre- and post-scenes or storyboards. If you find this happening with a scene, you *must* find out the reason for this before you can solve the problem.

> "If a king is plagued by bandits, he must find out where their camp is before he can attack them."
> — The teachings of Buddha

Rethink the single, key story point that particular scene exists in the movie to tell. Is that point coming across *clearly*? Is that point *absolutely necessary to the telling of the story*? Is the acting up to par? Are the composition and camerawork working with the pre- and post-scenes?

You've got to be tough on this labor of love. All audiences that see your work are, in general, extremely well cinematically educated. There is no such thing as a "lay audience" anymore. If you're spending any amount of your life doing anything, you may as well dedicate yourself to doing the best job you can.

NOTE

One of the "N" points of animation is: "Would anyone but your mother want to see that scene?" This applies to all arts.

To this, I add, "Is the work you did today better than the work you did yesterday?"

(Every animator has his personal take on the famous points of animation, with numbers of entries ranging from ten on up.)

When you revisit a scene, all of your 3D and compositing scene files should reflect the *current take* (revision). The new 3D scene files and renders that you create from that point should *all* be suffixed with "_tk02" at some point in their name (increasing the numbers as needed for the different takes). This helps you to track the progress of the scene as it moves through your *asset management*. By not deleting previous working revisions, it lets you go back and work again from a point that you found more promising than your current work if you find yourself painted into a corner.

Your project management database gets updated with the current take of the scene and its status, and you cut your new work into your animatic at your earliest possible convenience to make sure that you are heading in a better direction than you were before. (I like to cut a version of my scenes into the animatic right out of the OpenGL shaded preview animation to see if I've got my thoughts in the correct places.)

Beginning animators will probably find that after doing a few scenes, their work drastically improves. Please rework your production schedule to give yourself time to redo those early scenes.

(Chances are, you'll get them done much better much more quickly than your first time through. If you have fantastic work and really crummy work in the same film, the fantastic work will really make the not-so-good stuff all the more noticeable.)

"Do not consider your painting finished unless it is exactly what you want to see. If you feel that you are not skilled enough to do that, take the time and trouble to learn what it is you need to know to do it."

— Richard Schmid, *Alla Prima, Everything I Know About Painting*

However, *don't go out of your way to find things to change.* (Trying to prove the validity of one's position of power by issuing changes is a paper-thin façade seen through by those above and below with dreadful clarity.) Ask yourself if your proposed changes are *really* making things better or just making things *different*. Having a clear vision of what it is that you are looking for *before you begin work* is key to producing great work on time.

"...it often takes two to do a good painting — one to paint it and another to rap the painter smartly with a hammer before he or she can ruin it."

— Richard Schmid, *Alla Prima*

Production Reel

The *production reel* is the current, up-to-date version of your film as it evolves with storyboards slowly being replaced, first with OpenGL shaded preview animations and then with final scenes as they come out of compositing. It is a constantly changing beast that, like *the force*, both controls your actions and obeys your commands.

Dailies

Every morning, before work begins in earnest, *dailies* (a collection of the work that was done the previous day) are shown to *everyone* working locally on a project. Animations at various stages of evolution from where they were the previous day are discussed aloud with the director. People with "extra" time on their hands slip in joke-versions of scenes, as is often required as part of the hiring contract (just kidding).

Dailies, first and foremost, give people a feeling of what it will be like to see their work with an audience. (It can be scary the first time, having your work seen with the hundred or so people working on a big production, but if you feel embarrassed by what you've done, I swear you will never let sub-par work come from your desktop ever again.) Each scene is, of course, shown "sandwiched" between its pre- and post-scenes so a sense of *flow* can be gathered from the work. The public discussion between director and animator almost always provides pertinent information to the other animators present on how to solve their *own* issues that they may (or will) be encountering.

> "Never feel like you're the only one in a class who has a question. More than likely, there's quite a few who are wondering the same thing and are just too scared to ask."
>
> — Richard Albee

Dailies also really help to strengthen the feeling of *camaraderie* and *companionship* among the members of a team putting together a film. I like to see everyone there, regardless of their position within the company. (A secretary who feels he is part of something that he can believe in will give that much more because he feels that what he is doing actually means something as it *contributes* to the greater whole.) You have to build and maintain a sense of *pack* that each person is contributing what their *job* is for the *current production*. *Everyone's* job is vital to the completion of a film, and so *everyone is respected equally*.

> "A genuine, heartfelt gesture of thanks and acknowledgment can sometimes mean more to a person than a raise."
>
> — Richard Albee

NOTE

I noticed a strange thing when, while "making ends meet" here in Alaska, I found I was doing almost as much (if not more) *direct trade* (bartering) for goods and services as I was exchanging currency. What I noticed was that I was feeling a heck of a lot better about myself as a person and as an artist than I had in ages.

Upon examining the experience, as barter has remained a vital part of my very survival, I've come to understand it this way: When I pour my heart, time, and effort into something like a painting for someone, and they are pouring their heart, time, and effort into something I will receive in exchange (like a dogsled, rent, or food) the exchange *means something dear to both parties.* They get a painting they will cherish and will be cherished by their children and children's children. *I* get something I either dearly need or will dearly cherish, something that I couldn't easily afford otherwise.

Barter is an exchange that actually means something. You can *feel* it in the exchange itself. There is a gratefulness to the entire transaction that has never existed (for me) when it concerns the movements of paper, almost worthless except for the mutually accepted belief that they somehow have value.

In a way, I do not yet have the ability to understand that there is a *realness* and a *thankfulness* to bartered exchanges. You walk away from an exchange feeling that you, and what you do, is worth something in the eyes of another.

"...which is odd because it wasn't the small green pieces of paper that were unhappy."
— *The Hitchhiker's Guide to the Galaxy*

Weeklies

On the first of the week, it's a good idea to show everyone working on the film the really good-looking stuff that was completed the previous week ("sandwiched," of course, with their pre- and post-scenes). Scenes in *weeklies* are usually only the *director-approved* scenes from final animation and compositing.

Weeklies are great ways of "jogging" people's memories as to what they were thinking about the week before, having some fun, and making people feel really good about their part on the project. There's nothing that feels quite as good as seeing a final composite, in all its glory play out before all your friends and coworkers and knowing that you helped to bring that bit of magic to life!

Director's Weeklies

As director, it's *your* job to start your week with a refresher on how the film has shaped up over the course of the previous week. *Your* weeklies are watching the *whole* production reel, making notes as to what strikes you as good and what needs some closer attention.

You need to watch these runnings of your film as if you are seeing it for the very first time. You need to be moved to tears where you would like the audience to cry, and you need to belly-laugh where you want the audience to laugh.

You'll refresh your memories as to the directions that you were heading toward the previous week. You'll find yourself having refined your thinking process over the weekend. You'll be more prepared to guide those who are trusting you to lead them to a good place. Director's weeklies are a key tool to knowing exactly where you are in a production and exactly where you and your pack need to go from there.

Chapter 17

Soundtrack, the "Invisible Actor"

"There are far greater things on Heaven and Earth than are dreamt of in our philosophy..."

— Hamlet

There are things that we *know*, and there are things that we *feel*. Regardless of how much we may feel we *know* something, that *knowledge* will always affect us less powerfully than that which we *feel* with equal certainty.

Feelings are powerful tools; they were used by storytellers throughout the ages to draw audiences into the worlds they created. Perhaps it is that our hearing is not as focused as our sense of sight or that wherever we are we are surrounded by an envelope of sound (or lack thereof), but we define our places within our environments subconsciously more through *sound* than anything else.

In LA, there were always sounds, the constant rush of "The Ten" freeway a few blocks over and the dull, pervasive thump of passing "gangsta rides." There was a *soundtrack* to everything within the different elements that made up the constant, enveloping "white noise" of the city.

My first night in this cabin in Alaska, I almost couldn't sleep for the deafening roar of silence. It was almost oppressive. Like scientists working in soundless chambers, I had lost all the little acoustical points of reference that placed me in a subconscious relationship to the world I knew.

The "reality" that our brain registers to sounds that are "really, really real" (not the overused, "canned" sounds from sound effects CDs) is enough to almost produce vertigo. Twice, I have been surrounded by wolves — once while winter camping alone in the Yukon Territories and once sitting in the dark on the front porch of my little cabin here. Both times, the sounds of howling coming from all around me, bouncing off the nearby trees, created a reality to the sounds that, though I had never heard exactly that sound before, stirred memories that are best explained by the phrase "soul-deep." When you hear those real sounds, ringing with a clarity that Dolby and DTS have yet to approach, you are *electrified*, almost overwhelmed by the feelings flooding through your mind/soul.

A film's audio track has often been called the "invisible actor." A good soundtrack, through score, Foley (sounds like footsteps, swords "swishing" and clanging, etc.), and effects added to the different tracks, creates an immersive environment that surrounds the audience members within the reality of the story.

Just as all arts pull from the same artistic centers, the same *sensitivity*, *subtlety*, and *attention to detail* found in every other aspect of filmmaking must also be applied here. "Real life" is *subtle and complex* (only films that are themselves caricatures of reality step into the melodramatic stylization of having each and every acoustic accent clearly stated).

The Instruments

As much as I am fascinated with electronics and computers, I am passionately in love with *acoustic* instruments. The most beautifully reproduced digital sounds don't even come close to the magic of the way a harp's sound is directed through the soundboard straight into your heart, the way a bamboo flute leaps and vibrates in your hands as if alive while you're playing it or the feeling of a real, professional, tuned hand-drum that rings clear and deep straight through your body and into your bones.

Bamboo Flutes

Bamboo flutes produce such incredible, vibrant tones. The sound waves reverberate through the fibers of the plant, letting it ring like a chime in perfect sympathetic resonance with the tones being

Figure 17-1: The rightmost instruments are *transverse* flutes, played like a classical flute or the Irish fife. The leftmost flute is a *shakuhachi*, a Japanese, pentatonic flute based on a five-note scale. All but the lighter flute were made by the flutemaster who instructed me, Master Rob Yard. (The lighter flute was one I made during my apprenticeship.)

produced (when it is held with just enough pressure to close the finger holes that need to be closed to produce the desired note). The scorching of the bamboo not only adds to the look of the flute, but it puts extra *tension* in certain areas (when done properly), subtly but dramatically altering the individual *sound print* of each handmade instrument.

NOTE

After college, I apprenticed to North America's most renowned maker of bamboo flutes, Master Rob Yard, secluded in the quiet hills of West Virginia. I have played bamboo flutes from all over the world, and with the exception of one shakuhachi from Japan that retailed for $7,000, I have never heard their equal.

The instruments that Master Yard makes are precision works of art. He would walk through stands of bamboo in Florida searching for hours for perhaps one or two perfect, aged stalks that Nature herself had offered him. A special curing and aging process that lasted over two years would finally present him with a stalk worthy of becoming a flute.

There is an artistry to Master Yard's techniques of tempering the bamboo through precision scorching of the reed that I am not at liberty to describe. But the result is that holding the flute "blank" exactly at the right spot and tapping it lightly produces a chime-like ringing that was absolutely unearthly.

Master Yard would then create a mouth hole and finger holes based on a system of mathematics, which I've never seen duplicated, that produces the most clear, ringing tone that I've heard from any flute, ever. The precision tuning process that he uses yields an instrument of concert quality (I've actually used them in performances across the U.S. and fielded many questions as to their origin).

I found it amazing that even at the end of my apprenticeship, it still took me five to ten times longer to make a flute than Master Yard. While the tones of my flutes' lower register were perfectly in tune, both the pitch and the overtones of their upper registers were a shadow of the quality of his. Whereas most other bamboo flutes I've played have seemed more like toys than instruments, Master Yard's flutes are works of art in and of themselves. In the hands of an accomplished flautist, they are nothing short of the touch of the gods here on Earth.

I still have the first flute I purchased from Master Yard in 1984, and it somehow seems to play even more beautifully today than it did when I bought it. However, visiting him several years after my apprenticeship concluded, I was amazed at his progression of technique in flute making. As perfect as his earlier works may be, his more recent techniques yield a sound more vibrant and bright than I would ever have thought possible.

Master Yard and his family still quietly make flutes in their humble, beautiful West Virginia retreat, making flutes for those who have found out about his work through many and varied ways.

There is much of Master Yard in the stories of Kaze, much of his teachings that have imprinted upon me and will never leave. He puts into practice with every flute he makes, with the very life he lives, the focus and belief in the magic of dreaming aloud. He lives his beliefs of music connecting us all, of perfection through continual mental, spiritual, and physical evolution.

The main distributor of flutes by Master Robert Yard is Seeds of Light in Blacksburg, West Virginia. Visit http://www.seedsoflight.com/rob_yard.html or call (540) 552-4886.

Figure 17-2: Native American flutes are a whole other breed of instrument than the transverse flutes shown in the previous section. It is played in alignment with the body, like a shakuhachi (or a clarinet) and has a pentatonic (five-note) scale (as opposed to our diatonic — eight-note — "western" scale). But that's where its similarities end.

Native American Flute

The little "hook-like" thing tied on with a thin leather cord is called a *fetish* and focuses air over a small hole on the outside of the flute to produce a sound that sounds vaguely reminiscent of a recorder. Many of the haunting passages within *Ghost Warrior* were played on this beautiful, custom-crafted work of art.

NOTE

You don't just walk into a store and buy a Native American flute (well, you could, but I wouldn't really recommend it). More than any other instrument, the *Native American flute* is meant to represent the *soul* of the player through the music that is created by the union between Great Creator, human, and flute. In some tribes, it is how a woman could know the soul quality of a potential mate.

In coming together with this flute, I spent *years* looking for a native flutemaster whose heart, mind, and spirit were in alignment with what I know of my own. The flute in Figure 17-2 was custom-built by him based on what he felt inside me, after it was known that our own spirits were similar. It is not meant to have another like it in the world.

Harps

There are some things that you just know you were supposed to do. For as long as you can remember, you've known these things as if they were physical parts of your own body. Playing the Celtic harp was one of those things for me.

Made of walnut and mahogany, Soinnach taught me the first revisions of the song today known as *Maiden*, the base for the music of *Ghost Warrior*. I have many wonderful memories of nights relaxing after work with sandpaper and carving tools, the television droning in the background (I was in the process of weening myself away from television as a way to fill an evening's hours), slowly watching her beauty take shape. She was the first proof to a "young me" as to what can be accomplished by combining the hours normally spent gazing in partial trance at a phosphorescent box with a more worthwhile pursuit.

Figure 17-3: I built *Soinnach* (pronounced "shoo-nach" where the "ach" is Germanic sounding — the name means "fox" in Gaelic) in 1990 from a library copy of *Better Homes and Gardens: Wood* magazine. Though she isn't a performance-quality harp, she did teach me much of what I needed to know to become a professional *harper* (one who plays "folk" harps) and *harpist* (one who plays classical, pedal harps) a few years later.

NOTE

I was thrilled when, later that year, Soinnach took first place at Phringe-Con, a Phoenix, Arizona-based SF convention. I was even more thrilled to meet and talk with Tom Baker (my favorite of the doctors from *Doctor WHO*), who had played Soinnach and was thrilled that she was a real musical instrument, not just a prop.

Figure 17-4: I've never been able to find a name that fits my "big harp." She is 38 strings and is based roughly on a James Rydecki design. I built her in the evenings over the course of about three months from 1992 to 1993. Over the course of the long and jarring journeys that she and I have traveled together, she has broken twice, most recently the day after making the final recording of the music for the *Ghost Warrior* trailer in late June of 2003.

I make mention of the fact that she has broken to point out that nothing we do is perfect. We do the best we can at each stage of our lives. When something beyond our control, like the intense dryness of the Alaskan winters and the intense wetness of the Alaskan springs, makes evident things we could have done better had we known then what we know now, you do not "beat yourself up," as painful as a situation might be. All you can do is what needs to be done again and keep on keeping on.

The time-out from working on *Ghost Warrior* to complete the text of this book allowed her new glue joints to be properly set and strings to restretch. When it came time to record the final music for *Ghost Warrior*, she was in better shape than she had been when recording the music for the trailer.

Dumbec

There are only two rules I've found with hand-drumming: When you're playing a specific rhythm, know it *perfectly* and *play it perfectly*; when you're just "jamming," never lose the *feel* of the beat in whatever you do. All is driven by the beat. The beat drives all.

My particular dumbec is cast aluminum with a synthetic head. I love the sound of more traditional dumbecs, but this one is never affected by the humidity, always producing a clear, deep, resonant tone to its "dooms" (when hitting the head's center) and crisp, bright "tacks" (when hitting the edges of the drum head).

Figure 17-5: The dumbec is a Middle Eastern drum that I learned to love while working a short gig as a drummer for a belly-dancing troupe in southern California. I'd had experience with this and other hand-drums with various Gypsy groups and Renaissance fairs. But in the hands of the experienced drummers of the small troupe I was working with in San Diego, I was mesmerized.

Electronic Wind Instrument

The Yamaha WX-5 (electronic wind instrument) and VL70-m (acoustic tone generator) provided the sounds of the cello, double bass, oboe, clarinet, French horn, and bassoon for *Ghost Warrior's* soundtrack. The WX-5 is played like a clarinet and measures wind and reed pressure in conjunction with traditional flute, clarinet, and saxophone fingerings, feeding the information into either a standard MIDI-in or the VL70-m's WX-in.

With the WX-5 reading lip and breath pressure and the VL70-m actually *shaping* the *timbre* of the sound accordingly, you get sounds that have the *feel* of the real, acoustic instruments. (I don't know how Yamaha did it, but just like playing a real saxophone, you really have to tighten your embrasure and focus your breath to get those high notes.)

One of the nice things about the WX-5/VL70-m combination (other than keeping the cost of one's musical instrument habit within reason) is that you can plug the stereo-out directly into the line-in of your computer when you record. This means that you can record those delicate sounds of the cello without worrying about a sound booth to silence the whirring of computers, the howling of dogs, or "Harleying" of distant motorcycles.

Didgerieedoo

I'm not showing a picture of the "didge" I used on *Ghost Warrior* because it is nothing more than a four-foot section of two-inch diameter PVC pipe with a PVC pipe adapter that brings the two-inch diameter to a hole of one-and-one-quarter inch wide for the "mouthpiece." While not photogenic, it produces a fantastic tone that I think only a "didge" aficionado could tell doesn't come from the real thing. This didgerieedoo cost about $2.16 to make.

Score

Music is the language that transcends all barriers. It reaches to the core of our being, carries us away, moves us to tears and joy, and brings back memories long faded. Using the tools of sound and rhythm, music is a sculpture created by the musicians out of the emotions of the listener.

The sound vibrations within music are like the carrier frequency that holds the information within a radio transmission. It tunes our mind to the same mental, emotional, and spiritual frequencies of the musicians. It lets the listener live within the world for a momentary eternity.

Every film score is specifically tailored to be the best, most perfect acoustic representation of the film's *emotional, inner dialogue.* The bits and pieces of temporary score laid in for the animatic (in Chapter 14, "Pre-Visualization") only serve to guide the process for composing the unique musical fingerprint that defines the film empathically. I'll talk about my own way of scoring, which is how many other classically trained musicians write their own music. However, programs like Sonic Foundry's Acid Pro and Syntrillium's Cool Edit Pro have opened up musical composition to the masses in ways I never would have thought possible.

Looping

Looping is about using little snippets of music that can fit in Lego-like perfection with one another. In the *looping program,* pitch is shifted, tempo is altered, and the pieces somehow stay locked to one another, each beat "sticking" perfectly with the beats of the other loops in the project. I'm not quite sure how the programs do it, having never worked in this manner before, but the results are astounding.

In the old days, you could go into a music store and buy CDs of sampled sounds for *sampling keyboards* that would play a different sampled sound for every key pressed, blending different versions of recorded sounds based on how quickly the key was struck, how much pressure was being applied as it was held down, etc. The effect was like having a full-sized grand piano right there in your tiny studio. But load in a different set of samples and you can change your keyboard into a sitar, harp, or hammered dulcimer.

Today, these sample CDs have been greatly replaced with recordings of professional musicians and groups of musicians large and small playing tiny bits and pieces of songs. One *loop* may be an ascending *arpeggio,* another may be a trill, and another may be chord riffs or a repeating bass line. Instrumentation and style range from acid jazz to zydeco, classical, heavy metal, and everything in between. When a loop artist (DJ) layers these pieces together, the program somehow produces something that sounds like a perfect, live performance. With the work of an accomplished loop artist, you'd never know by listening that his music was put together from small, bite-sized, Lego-like pieces.

I used to associate looping with the repetitive, mesmeric beats of techno/rave music. It wasn't until a few years ago when working on a spec project with Jeff Connor of Pressman Films (*The Crow*) that I got an eye-opening experience as to what programs like Acid Pro and Cool Edit Pro could do.

Hearing the loop artist's work for our project floored me. Over a weekend, using Acid Pro, he cut together seven, three-minute tracks that each sounded really good in their own right. My initial fear was that *looping* would be the musical equivalent of "paint by numbers." The complexity of the music that the loop artist created was as good as anything I could have hoped for in a session band.

Though I, myself, don't know the first thing about looping, I have seen (heard) enough to realize how powerful a tool it can be. In short, it allows non-musicians to craft performances as varied and sensitive as any professional at a recording session. With a looping program like Acid Pro or Cool Edit Pro, you don't need to know how to read music, write music, or even play an instrument. All you need to know is how to find your way around the program's interface and what kind of loop CDs to buy. You also need a good idea of what kind of music you're looking for when you hear it come out of your speakers.

Composition

Musical composition is also something that has seen much in the way of benefits from computers. It used to be that a composer would have to write notes by hand on staff paper (paper that has been ruled with the staff lines for notating music) as he went through sections of his piece again, and again, and again, slowly fleshing out the musical themes.

Today, with MIDI instruments, you just set your computer to record the notes you've played, and with a few minor adjustments here and there to make all the notes fit properly inside their measures, click a few commands and you've got a complete, notated musical score. Play through your piece a few more times, recording different instruments on your MIDI device. Cut, paste, and shift things about where needed, and the notation program can have sheet music for each instrument in a fraction of the time it would take to write by hand (and look as good as any commercially available sheet music, as shown in Figure 17-6).

Since I was going to be the only musician on this piece, I opted out of the rather time-consuming process of actually writing down the music. I had written a piece of music called *Maiden* some years ago that fit perfectly with the themes of Kaze and decided to use

Figure 17-6: A little musical "sketch" done while working on music for *Ghost Warrior*.

the different parts of that song for the different situations and characters in the film.

Musical Themes

It is an old operatic tradition to have each character have their own *theme*, a bit of easily recognizable music. This lets you build tension and expectancy in the audience subconsciously when the music takes on faint overtones of a character's theme prior to his or her entrance or over a section of film that is heavily influenced by that character. (Think about the wonderfully recognizable themes for Darth Vader and Princess Leia in *Star Wars*.)

Sometimes, you'll want a certain place to be associated with a theme, shifting it through minor and major modes to color the way the place feels to the audience as the story progresses.

Sometimes, *silence* is the best "music" for a section of film. "Music is the space *between* the notes." There is much emotional power in leaving music conspicuously absent from a place where the audience expects it.

For so short a film as *Ghost Warrior*, I didn't go into much detail with developing the musical themes for any character but Kaze himself. (In the lyrics to *Maiden*, Kaze's theme is associated with the line "I've walked deep blue wastes of foreign sky.") The other themes within *Maiden* were just sprinkled in wherever they seemed to fit best, recording my harping while I watched the animatic on VCD (video CD) playing on a DVD player that was quiet enough to not be picked up by the microphone I was using to record the harp.

NOTE

> Why do I compose on a harp (as opposed to composing on a keyboard)? There's no other reason than it fits most closely with my spirit. On a harp, my fingers just seem to know what to do, even before I'm aware I'll be doing it. More than on any other instrument, I can sit back and be an "amazed observer," listening to the music that is created *through* me.

There really wasn't much "science" to the scoring of *Ghost Warrior.* I'd try different theme parts from *Maiden* while watching the production reel (animatic) play out. When a theme seemed to fit well with a section, I'd make a mental note for the next time through the piece. Where themes didn't fit, I usually got a gut feeling as to which theme would be better in that section and gave it a try next time I ran the production reel.

Each time I'd play through watching the production reel from VCD, I would record the session on minidisc (see "Performance/ Recording"). I found that just the simple act of recording my playing makes it easier to remember my thoughts as to what pieces of music should go where. When I'd come back to the composition after a night's rest, I could play the disc in sync with the production reel and pick up right where I left off but from a fresh, fully rested perspective!

Were I actually *notating* a score (writing it on sheet music so others could follow my direction later), this is the point where I'd start marking up the staff paper. But since this part of the scoring

took place over the course of a few days and everything was fresh in my mind and held securely on minidisc, I opted out of writing down the notes of the score.

Having a *take* of my harping where all the pieces and parts fit with the action going on in the production reel, I dumped the MD data into the computer and laid it into an audio track in ToasterEdit. I then made another VCD of the production reel with that first layer of music in place.

Using that layer as the foundation for my score, I listened through headphones to the music playing along with the VCD, recording another harp track. I repeated the process for the flutes, electronic wind instrument, and percussion. In a matter of days, I had a score that did everything I wanted it to (one of the benefits of being your own client — you get better quality work much more quickly than when your focus is on pleasing someone else).

Performance/Recording

There are two ends of the spectrum in the process of creating any work of art, regardless of medium. One end of the process is trying to nail exactly what you've got in your head, without giving an inch either way (micromanaging). On the other end is preparing as best you can and then letting the universe create the piece through you (expansive-managing). There are "different strokes for different folks," and each artist has to find out where he is on that sliding scale. So, as I'm talking about my way of doing things here, you've got to balance that with the knowledge of how *you* prefer to work.

I'm a "one-take" kinda guy. I suppose it comes from my passion for jazz, but I love to work out the score, hone the musical ideas, themes, and "riffs" beforehand, let the visuals play out, and just let the music happen. I know full well that there will be things that I hadn't planned in the performance, and for me, that's great!

If I try to nail things down (in any art form) to being *exactly* what I have in my head, I'll be nailing things down to my own limited, human perspective. I can do this, I have the training to, but to do so emasculates the piece when compared with letting the universe play its part in the creation of the piece!

Saying that I "let the universe play its part" doesn't mean that I slack off in preparing my skills or practicing the music beforehand. What I mean is that I don't get all worked up about something that may happen that I'm not expecting. I know that those "unexpected" things often have the most magic within them. I may find myself *improving* for a bit as I work my way back to the way I had planned the music, and rather than stopping and starting over, I am *listening* to the sounds created by this *improvisation*. Almost 100 percent of the time, those sections are the most passionate, most powerful parts of the score.

I find that if I narrow my mind, constrict my mental focus, and only accept what I already know, I'm limiting my creativity and doing a disservice to the power that the piece can become.

Proficiency

This kind of interplay between creative, universe, instrument, and artist can only happen when the artist knows his instrument/tools so well that he doesn't have to worry about the physical mechanics of creating the art. So, you *have to be proficient* at whatever you're doing *first*, then you can let the art breathe life of its own.

How do you attain this proficiency? You first learn how to produce every note that instrument has within its range (in visual art terms, this would be color and value theory) in quick and *easy* succession with any other note (scales and arpeggios — in visual art terms, this would be exploring silhouette). Then, you learn how to make all the different kinds of sounds (*timbre*) that you've heard others produce through different hand/mouth shapes, positions, and whatnot and how to get them whenever and wherever you need (in

visual art terms, this is exploring surface texturing). Being able to do all this well and on demand gives you a level of proficiency from which you can begin to explore the *fun* stuff of the artistic tools.

Once you've attained proficiency, you can then let the same force that moves your art in an area you already know do the same for this area that you are learning. What you do now is beg, borrow, or buy as many CDs that have as many different kinds of music featuring that instrument as you can (slow tunes and fast), covering the entire emotional spectrum. You play your instrument along with listening to these pieces. You can roughly copy the performances to learn what those particular artists were thinking when that particular performance moved through them. However, I find that simply *playing with* the recordings is much more enlightening to the creation of my own music (the empathic play-and-record described earlier in the book).

Layering

With the harp track providing the anchor for the musical themes for the score, I begin to record the other instruments, adding each to an audio layer of its own within ToasterEdit and burning another VCD.

NOTE

When working with audio layering, you want to keep all your tracks separate for as long as possible. This lets you tweak their *track-specific* audio effects (like volume, pan, and reverb) right up to the last minute.

Doing each instrument in one take and layering that take into the ToasterEdit project as a complete *layer* lets me hear the whole score take shape at the same time. Listening to the project play, I get a good feeling of what I'd like to hear next added to the rough mix. Whatever it is that "asks" to be put in next, I obey and pick up that instrument for the next pass!

Simply because ToasterEdit lets you layer an unlimited number of tracks, time permitting, it is tempting to just go crazy and have layer upon layer upon layer. True, this does add a kind of Eñya or Trent Resnor-like richness, but you need to ask yourself if that kind of sound is correct for the story you are telling.

For *Ghost Warrior*, I wanted the same "clean," "open" feeling of the music of *Crouching Tiger, Hidden Dragon* that inspired me musically. So, I kept myself from going wild with the number of layers, trying to keep the same *feel* of the inspirational music that I used in my temporary score.

It's easy to get carried away with adding layers when there are no limits to what you can do. So it is vital that you have a clear idea of what it is you are looking for in your score *before* you start recording. (Your temporary score of inspirational music can help you narrow in on what it is you want.) You don't want to constrict creativity by not letting the unexpected shape your music, but you should be able to say "Aha!" when you know that you've hit your *empathic* mark for that piece of music. When you hit that mark, leave it alone. Most artists are guilty of falling into "Tweaksville" where you spend endless hours noodling some small part that can sometimes disrupt the whole piece when heard as a whole again (taking more hours getting the work back to where it was, if you haven't been saving revisions).

ADR (Additional Dialogue Recording)

There was only one part where I found I needed to do ADR (additional dialogue recording). That was where Kaze is whispering his prayer to Yashin as he eases him into death. As filmmaking went on, I found I really didn't like my original takes of those lines, so I had to redo them.

Having the animation of that section of the movie already done was a huge help in honing my vocal performance of that section. To do the recording, I rendered a small section that "sandwiched" that performance as an MPEG file and transferred it to my iPAQ. Taking that small, *silent* computer into my "sound booth" (the cab of my truck), I ran the minidisc recorder as I let the MPEG file play. On the fifth take, I had a performance that fit exactly with what I was looking for.

> **NOTE**
>
> Quite often nowadays, a lot of a live-action film's dialogue is rerecorded after *principal photography*. There are many reasons for directors wanting actors to rerecord lines for scenes that have already been filmed, from problems with ambient noise to fine-tuning performance and/or dialogue of characters whose mouths aren't seen in a particular shot.
>
> Knowing full well that it is hard for any actor to match the exact timing of an earlier performance, audio engineers often trim, shift, and stretch this additional dialogue to expertly match the newly recorded dialogue to the preshot footage.

Foley

We've already talked about Foley once before in pre-production, while working on the scratch audio track. This is the time, after having lived with your movie for quite a while, where you take a good, hard listen to those sounds and honestly decide whether they are working for you or not.

Specifically placed, ambient sounds really help to place us within our environment. We don't even think about it, but when you close your eyes, you can almost tell what kind of place you are in simply by the sounds around you — the buzz of fluorescent lights, the whir of a refrigerator, the distant rushing sound of a freeway, the buzz of insects, chirping of birds, the whisper of wind through the trees.

If you watch the movie *Alien*, by Ridley Scott, you find some absolutely brilliant sound design. Almost everything has a very *subtle*, almost *subliminal* sound. The camera pans past a fluorescent light fixture, and you hear the soft buzzing we associate with fluorescent tubes. The sound of the ship itself is like that of a heartbeat, deep and alive. These things are handled with subtlety so that like in real life, they are only discernable for those who are really listening for them. For those just enjoying the ride, they serve to define the space, just as the sounds around you are doing right now.

There are times when you will want no sounds at all. It is a wonderful *stylistic* approach to have scenes that you would normally expect to be filled with layers of sounds to be eerily quiet or the sounds muffled as if coming through wet cotton. Using a *lack* of sounds creates a very uneasy detachment for the viewer, like the silence after the hollow *whump* of a car accident. I used this in the trailer to hone a kind of *otherworldly* feel to the dance-like ballet of its fight scene. It is a *stylistic choice*, and only the director can say whether those kinds of choices elicit the emotional/mental/spiritual spaces into which he is seeking to draw the viewer.

NOTE

In the film *The Hudsucker Proxy*, there is another great example of using Foley to create an impression for the audience that differs slightly from what was "real" on set. When Sidney J. Mussburger asks Norville Barnes, fresh from the mailroom, to sit in his executive chair, the *near-dead* silence of that section is punctuated by the soft sounds of an *extremely plush* and expensive leather seat cushion being sat upon. While Mussburger's leather chair looks to be of the highest quality, from what I can tell, the seat cushion isn't the kind that makes the sound overlaid into that section.

NOTE

Concerning my own experience with sound effect CDs, I have only found them helpful once, when I was looking for the sound of an old military tank for a commercial I was doing. I found that I expended tons of time and was disappointed and frustrated, thumbing through the discs at the studio, and almost always these sounds are so overused that people who know their stuff can almost tell them by name. On those occasions where I was looking for sounds like gunshots, car engines, doors, and whatnot, I would have had a lot more fun and found better, *more topical* sounds had I just gone out and recorded them myself.

People know what things *really* sound like. In *Saving Private Ryan*, the storming of the beach was made that much more powerful by the *real* sounds of the bullets whizzing overhead and impacting water, sand, and metal. Even if you've never been shot at yourself,

269

there is a *power* to the reality of those sounds that a viewer's mind just somehow knows is *real!*

Regardless of what is the "popular" trend in audio styling, I will always recommend going out and recording reasonably close to the real thing when it comes to sounds. (How dated are films that use that slapstick "smack" sound when people punch each other? Did we ever really think that was cool?) One of the things that made the fights in *Fight Club* so unnerving was the sounds of the fists actually hitting flesh (with a little sub-frequency to add a bit of that which is *felt* and not heard).

So, unless you want to go out and buy the specific sounds from a Hanna-Barbera sound library, my recommendation is to save yourself the disappointment of having sounds that are not quite what you need and take a field trip to get the sounds you want! You want a lion roaring? Go to the local zoo! You want a sword clang? Find a good-sized piece of iron and hit it with another! You need gloppy-sloppy sounds? Spoon out some cat food. How about gurgley-bubbly sounds? Play in your toilet with a plunger for a bit.

(Always use your mind and common sense and take proper safety precautions, of course. Creativity is rewarded and foolishness is punished.)

There are sounds all around us all the time, from common objects that are indeed the real thing to sounds from "found objects" that are cooler than the real thing. Most "project-specific" sounds will always sound much better than "canned" effects. (Remember how cool the *Star Wars'* blasters sounded in Episodes 4 through 6? From what I understand, that was the tapping of a telephone pole's guy [support] cable.) Get creative! Know that while there are indeed good sound libraries around, their sounds may one day become trite to the educated audience.

Now, just as important as the sounds themselves is how the sounds *sound*. This bridges into the next section on *sweetening* the sounds. More than just making voices over public address speakers and telephones sound "tinny," audio post-processing works well with my own little theory that more than just bats, dolphins, and whales use a kind of "sonar" to tell where they are in their worlds.

"Sweetening" Audio Post-Processing

Just having a sound recorded is only the beginning of *sound work*. Sweetening the sound and adding audio post-processing brings the sketch of the rough audio track almost to its final form.

I evaluated two audio programs while working on *Ghost Warrior*; these were Sound Forge 6.0 by Sonic Foundry and Cool Edit Pro by Syntrillium. I was very pleased to find that each program offered a slightly different point of view on the art of audio manipulation, and yet both were equal in terms of the quality of 98 percent of their effects and tools. Since both are available for demo downloads, you can give them a spin to find out which package best wraps itself around the way you like to think!

There were, however, three main things that separated the programs from each other. Sound Forge came with Acoustic Mirror (there's a whole subsection dedicated to Acoustic Mirror in just a moment). Cool Edit Pro came with a very nifty spline-enabled surround sound encoder (discussed in the section on surround sound later) and an entire section of Cool Edit Pro is dedicated to multitracking and looping (Like Sonic Foundry's Acid Pro). (Having limited time for exploration of Cool Edit, I didn't get into the multitrack section, but it appears quite robust and worth the mention.)

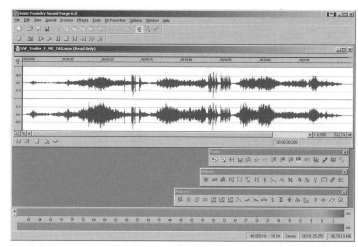

Figure 17-7: Sound Forge 6.0 by Sonic Foundry

Figure 17-9: Cool Edit Pro 2.1 by Syntrillium, showing Cool Edit's multitrack view (showing the default session that plays the Cool Edit theme music)

Figure 17-8: Cool Edit Pro 2.1 by Syntrillium, showing Cool Edit's waveform view

Acoustic Mirror

There was one tool in Sound Forge that blew away anything I'd ever seen or imagined before in audio mastering: Acoustic Mirror. Acoustic Mirror uses impulses derived from recordings of a test tone within real-world environments to *exactly recreate the effects of those real-world environments on your audio files!* Sound Forge comes with well over a hundred of these impulses, recorded in famous theatres, halls, stairwells, parking garages, and other ambient places. It also includes impulses recorded with current and "antique" microphones so if, like me, you're recording with an "el-cheapo" microphone, you can feed your .wav file through Acoustic Mirror and have an output that sounds like you recorded your voiceover on a several-thousand-dollar mic!

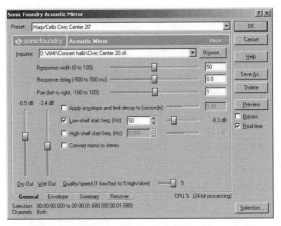

Figure 17-10: A simple interface, breathtaking results: Sonic Foundry's Acoustic Mirror

NOTE

Acoustic Mirror also comes with the test tones you'll need to create your own impulses. So, if you have a specific audio environment in which you want your dialogue to appear, make an impulse from that space, run your recordings through Acoustic Mirror using the impulse you generated, and your recordings will sound like they took place in that real-world environment! (A great thing for live-action filmmakers too is that recording a test tone on location will let you create an impulse from that space, so using Acoustic Mirror, you can have ADR *exactly match* what was filmed on the set!)

Playing around with Acoustic Mirror at first was pretty impressive to me, as it got the voices recorded using my cheap mic elements sounding like they had been recorded on a high-end microphone. But what really knocked me out was running my harp recording through the impulse generated from recording a test tone in the

Chicago Theatre, about 25 feet from the stage. The before and after ("dry" and "wet" mixes) were absolutely night and day. I could close my eyes and listen to the music on my surround-sound system, and it felt like I was listening to a recording that was actually taped right there at the Chicago Theatre! Suddenly, the (perceived) *production value* of my piece went up a few million dollars!

It's that subtle thing of *subconscious* audio cues. Our minds know what it sounds like to hear something *real*. As nice as electronic reverb may be, it doesn't come anywhere near the sound of "the real thing." I don't impress easily, and Sound Forge's Acoustic Mirror impressed the heck out of me. For making a low-low-low-budget film sound like a million bucks, I've never seen its equal.

Audio Tools

When I first tried my hand at sound engineering, these tools came only as rack-mounted devices that filled the walls of a recording studio. Now, computer programs can recreate the effects of these tools in real time on recorded audio.

Equalizer (EQ): "Leveling" the Audio Spectrum

Decent speaker systems have a *range* between 12,000 and 20,000 Hz. Every moment of sound that issues from a good speaker can span any collection of *frequencies* within that range. But, in order for sounds to be most clearly perceived by the audience, each *kind* of sound has to be given its own little "slot" within that spectrum of frequencies.

It's easy to think of different musical instruments as having different "turfs," which they claim as their own. A rich musical score makes sure each frequency range is thoughtfully occupied. But when a character is speaking, it is important to "clear a path" for the frequency range associated with the human voice.

The most important sounds to separate out from the mix are the voices. It's easy for human voices to get lost, submerged, or otherwise rendered unintelligible by "running over" their frequency "slot." It may be surprising if you haven't paid attention to it before, but the acceptable range for voices falls within the easily producible range of the little speakers inside non-hi-fi television sets. If you listen to a radio announcer (even the commentators on NPR), you'll hear deep bass coming from your stereo hi-fi. Play a movie over your hi-fi, and you'll hear that even the most deep-voiced characters never touch the rumble of a sub-woofer's frequency.

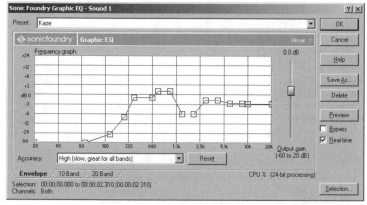

Figure 17-11: For the "cleanest" handling of the characters' voices, I found that I needed to use an *equalizer* to completely eliminate frequencies below 80 Hz and, depending on the character, "ramp up" to 0 dB change for frequencies between 80 and 500 Hz. It was a bit of a fight to get a bit of bassy *rumble* to Kaze's voice without having it become unintelligible amid other sounds and music, and I found that 350 Hz was the lowest frequency I could have remaining at 0 dB change without Kaze's words getting "muddy."

There are other "notches" that you need to clear in the frequency spectrum for voices, and as I'm not really an audio producer, I can only say that I played around with mixes until I found one that

sounded like the movies I regarded as high-end in my genre. If you look at Figure 17-11, you'll also see that I lowered a section of frequencies between 1.3 and 2.5 KHz; this cut out a bit of the remaining "tinnyness" from my cheap microphone. Then, you can see that the levels are brought back up for frequencies above 2.5 KHz; this kept the "brightness" of higher frequency sounds like the letters "f," "s," "z," and "th" while lowering their intensity to cut their interference with the less sibilant sounds of speech.

Mic Rumble

I had a problem with *mic rumble* with all my recordings. This is a low-frequency sound picked up by the microphone that rumbles through your sub-woofer even when you thought you recorded silence. Mic rumble is just one of the many reasons why you want to have a good sound system when you're doing your audio work. If you are mixing on a system that doesn't reach those low frequencies and you have a case of mic rumble, you may never know it until you release your film to be played on high-end sound systems that *do* reach those low, low frequencies.

The EQ settings used on Kaze's voice shown in the previous section also eliminated the mic rumble. But I had to be a little more careful when removing the rumble from low-voiced acoustic instruments to keep their bass frequencies and still do away with the unwanted rumble.

Noise Gate

Noise gates are good when you want to get rid of a bit of background noise that isn't noticeable when the talent is speaking but can be heard in the surrounding silence.

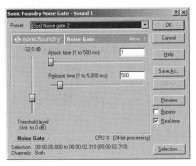

Figure 17-12: A *noise gate* is like the VOX circuitry on cell phones, requiring the incoming sound level to reach a certain *threshold* value before letting sound pass through the "gate." More complex noise gates let you set the *attack* and *release* time so the "rise" and "fall" from complete silence is not abrupt.

De-Esser

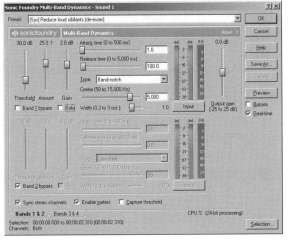

Compressor/Limiter

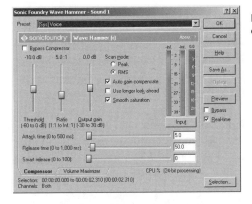

Figure 17-13: A compressor/limiter

Figure 17-14: A de-esser is used to remove loud "s" sounds (and other sibilant, "hissing" sounds). It blends the functionality of an EQ with that of a compressor/limiter. It "waits" for levels at a certain frequency range to get above a certain volume and then *limits* just that frequency range and only while those *dry* levels are above its threshold value.

Much better than just lowering a whole range of frequencies in an EQ, a *de-esser* preserves the *brightness* of speech and singing without letting sibilants overpower the recorded voice.

Using a *popper-stopper* did a lot to help cut down on sibilants, but I still needed to use this really ingenious tool with *all* of my dialogue recordings.

Timbre

Timbre (having little to do with trees falling in a forest, regardless of whether or not there is someone around to hear) is about the *distinctive qualities of complex sounds*. *Overtones* mix with *undertones*, creating a very identifiable acoustical pattern to each and

Compressor/limiters take sounds that span a wide range of volumes and boost the quiet and "bring down" the loud so everything is closer to the same volume level. With a compressor/limiter, you can set how quickly the effect starts to act upon the incoming sound (*attack time*) and how slowly it will let the volume level return to "normal" afterward (*release time*). They are rather ingenious bits of equipment (or computer code) that can be very helpful in eliminating your need to be constantly adjusting the levels of your voice talent in your editing software.

every sound. It's because of timbre that you can tell the difference between a violin and a viola playing the same note.

We also subconsciously use timbre to tell us more about our environment. If you know the dry sound when you snap your fingers, and you are blindfolded and put into a place that *absorbs* much of the high frequencies of the reflected sound of your snapping, it's easy to imagine yourself in a place of shag carpeting and other sound-absorbent material. But, should you hear the sound of your snap returned "bright" and clear to your ears, you'll know that you are in an area of hard, "polished" surfaces.

So, if you really want to get deep into creating a believable acoustical environment for your audience, you can use an *EQ* to affect the timbre of your voice tracks and sound effect files based upon the audience's point of view of the scene taking place. This, coupled with a good *surround sound mix*, will do wonders for creating a truly *immersive* acoustical environment. (This is why my vote went with using Sensaura in doing the surround mix for *Ghost Warrior* — see below.)

Final Mix

When you have all your tracks "layered" in place, all the music, dialogue, and Foley properly processed, and everything sounds pretty good, you need to put yourself into the "average, ideal presentation environment" to fine-tune your audio mix into its final form. For feature film folks, this means working with a mixing board right in a theatre itself! For myself, since this first *Ghost Warrior* story will most likely be seen primarily in home venues, I do my final mix in the comfort of my own home/studio.

In doing your final mix, if you'll be working with surround sound, you have to make sure the environment that you're working in has the surround system properly set up according to the manufacturer's instructions. You have to make sure you're sitting in the *right spot* (again, according to the manufacturer's instructions), usually where the volume of all the speakers is at the same level.

Levels

A lot of getting the final mix right is in adjusting the levels of the different tracks. You want the things that need to be understood by the audience (like dialogue) to be clearly heard and understood. Music and sound effects both need to settle in, appropriately around the "mid-range volume level" of the dialogue. Sometimes you need to "fade" levels around a character's dialogue so the words aren't lost (though sometimes you *do* want the dialogue to be lost).

I find *audio mixing* to be pretty subjective, the domain of the personal vision of the filmmaker as to how the audio layers should *blend* and the emotional states that blending elicits. I usually go on "gut instinct" more than on any set of rules that I've memorized, always comparing what I'm hearing in my film's audio track with what I've heard in the best of my film's particular genre.

A rule of thumb I've found to be a good place to start is that dialogue is only about half as loud as things ever get in a film. That way, when listeners set a comfortable level for the voices, the *occasional* deep, "bassy" impacts can really knock their socks off.

Surround Sound

Here's something I don't get. Why is it that a $20 sound card can decode surround sound in real time, but it's difficult to find a way to *encode* surround sound for under $3,000?

If you want to know *why Ghost Warrior* was made for $5,000, it is in great part to not overspending. Part of the pre- and pre-pre-production process is about finding solutions that will work, and *work reliably* under pressure and within a *reasonable* budget.

There are several different kinds of surround mixes. There's the "good ol' fashioned" Dolby Pro Logic (common on video tapes) where left, center, right, surround, and sub-woofer information are encoded into a "standard" stereo, two-channel mix. Most high-end DVD players support home versions of the theatrical formats of Dolby Digital and DTS digital surround formats, where each channel is completely separated from the anothers (whereas sounds "bleed" a bit from channel to channel in Pro Logic Surround). The digital surround formats also allow for more sound channels, and in home versions that means that the rear channels are completely separate from one another. (The terms associated with these formats are often "5.1" and "6.1," where the ".1" stands for the sub-woofer channel and the "5" or "6" is the number of *discrete*, "normal" speakers.)

Knowing that this first episode of *Ghost Warrior* was not likely to hit the local cineplex, I decided to do a Dolby Pro Logic mix, which sounds equally good on two-channel stereo systems and multichannel surround systems. Pro Logic offers (mostly) separate channels for left, center, right, and rear, plus the ".1" of "sub-woofage."

Pan Handler is shareware, so you can get a tiny taste of how it works for free, but using it as shareware means that every two seconds it inserts two seconds of silence in your output audio file. I found it very difficult to get a feeling of whether this program was going to work for me or not.

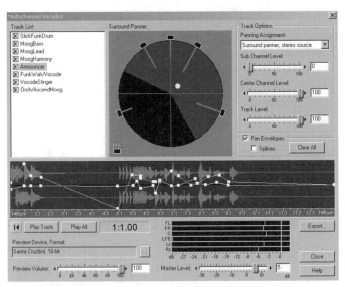

Figure 17-15: One of the best (affordable) surround encoders that I found was actually a part of the Cool Edit Pro suite. With graphical representations of the effect that a specific positioning would have on the various 5.1 surround speakers and a fantastically powerful set of spline controls to place the surround sound, I was most impressed with this little addition to Cool Edit Pro.

So, I explored some more and found something that worked beautifully, producing both a surround encoding and adjusting the timbre of the sound based on research of how *positional audio* is decoded by our minds. This was a free tool that came with the Turtle Beach sound card that I favor over other, more expensive sound cards that don't do nearly as much, nearly as well (http://www.turtlebeach.com). The tool I found was Sensaura's demo program of what their proprietary code can do for creating 3D positional audio (3DPA).

Sensaura is a company that makes technology for real-time 3DPA that works incredibly well even through two-speaker

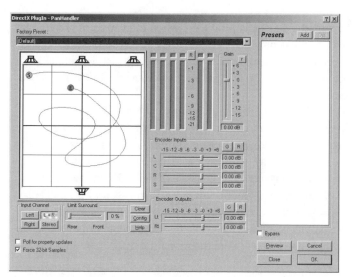

Figure 17-16: Another surround encoder that I came across is Pan Handler, a plug-in made by Sonic Engineering (priced between $75 for the DirectX interfacable plug-in to $199 for the version for Nuendo; http://www.sonicengineering.com).

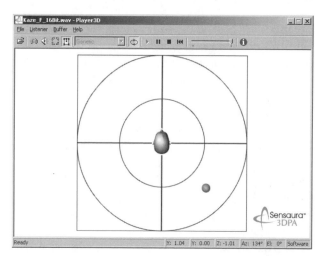

Figure 17-17: This demo program that shows off Sensaura's 3DPA lets you load in a .wav file and then control its 3D positioning as it plays the .wav file back. You control the positioning of the sound in 3D space represented by the quadrants around the iconic, top-down head by moving a small, red dot around the window (or by letting the program move it for you).

systems and headphones. They use what seems to be a combination of adjusting a sound's timbre and working out the *audio holography* that comes from sounds bouncing around in the unique shapes of our ears before reaching our brains. (Their white papers on sound and hearing can be found at http://www.sensaura.com/whitepapers/template1.php?article=list.htm.)

By using the Listener/Software 3D/HTRF full setting, I was able to get perfect 4.1 surround results from my Pro Logic stereo system that my computer's audio runs through. The "bonus" from using the Sensaura 3DPA was that as sounds moved further and further into the rear channel, their timbre became less and less "bright." The closer a sound was moved into the front channels, the more "brilliant" its timbre became. While it is true that the

center and rear channels of Pro Logic don't handle the full dynamic range of the left and right channels, this manipulation of a sound's timbre is *exactly* what Sensaura's 3DPA technology does to help a listener position a sound as being at a *specific distance from the head*, rather than simply "in front" or "behind."

Multiple Mixes

Sound is *waves*, and as such, it follows *wave dynamics*. While we all know that we're supposed to hook up our speaker systems so the red wire goes in the red terminal and the black wire goes in the black terminal, it's a little more elusive as to why.

The *why* of this is all about *phase*. With your speakers hooked up correctly, "normal" sounds coming from the speakers will be *in-phase*, which means that both speakers are producing the peaks and troughs of their waves in unison. When one speaker is hooked up with its connections reversed with respect to the other speaker, the speakers are *out-of-phase*, and when one is producing a peak, the other may be producing a trough.

This matters because of wave dynamics. When two waves meet, their values are *added* to one another. When two equal wave peaks meet, the resultant wave peak is *twice* the value of one of those wave peaks alone. The same thing holds true for two equal wave troughs meeting. But, when you have a peak with a value of +10 meeting with a trough with a value of –10, the two "cancel each other out." The resultant wave value is *zero*. This is what happens when audio is *out-of-phase*.

This matters to audio producers when their work is played over a device that has only one speaker. You can have beautiful left and right channels (let alone multiple, discrete surround channels) that reduce each other to nothing when played over a TV with a single speaker.

So, for the sake of those not quite so "home-theatrically-hip," you'll want to test your audio mix over your TV set's single speaker to make sure that voices, sounds, and music are reading as they should. You may even want to make a mono-mix that addresses these issues and the issue of the reduced frequency range of "low-fi" equipment. Whereas it's no secret that DVD players support multiple audio formats/tracks, it might surprise you to know that videotape does as well. The *hi-fi* left and right tracks on a videotape are *separate* from the monaural track.

Chapter 18

Final Visuals

In skilled hands, the output of a good compositing program is to the output of a 3D package as a painting is to its sketch.

The *final look* of your film is what *you* want to see and has nothing to do with what anyone else thinks is "good," "cool," or anything else. *You* decide how *you* want your work to look. Making educated decisions from exploring as much cinema, painting, music, dance, and theatre as you can, you blend what has powerfully moved you with what you feel best enhances and aligns with the story you are telling.

With the tools within reach of CGI filmmakers today, every single style imaginable is achievable, from *South Park* to *What Dreams May Come* and beyond! 3D CGI, as output from your 3D package, is only the *start* of the look of your film. With the tools available in even the most plebeian of compositing packages, you can completely rework the look of your rendered frames *without needing the hours required to re-render the scene in 3D!*

Compositing packages are like Photoshop for movies. They do a heck of a lot more than just stick layers together. They let you shift coloring and lighting, add depth effects, and change the quality of your edges. In short, they allow you to be an artist with the "raw material" that comes out of your 3D package in *real time!*

Compositing packages let the final visuals of your film be nothing short of *exactly* what you want to see.

Compositing

A good *compositing* program lets me simply sketch with the 3D package, getting my ideas out "on paper." It is in the compositing program that these ideas take on their finished forms. Compositing is more than just layering elements and shadows, shifting colors, and softening edges, though these are all a part of what *good* compositing programs allow you to do.

A good compositing program is difficult for the layperson to identify; "they all do pretty much the same thing, don't they?" Yes, for the most part. But where they really begin to separate is in how they let you work, how they task your microprocessor(s), and how *forward thinking* the designers are *at integrating the findings and wishes of those who have gone before you.*

Digital Fusion

Figure 18-1: Eyeon's Digital Fusion — the "final third" of the reason why *Ghost Warrior* looks the way it does.

I can't say that my own experience with compositing software is extremely extensive, though I have used some. Digital Fusion (from Eyeon Software, http://www.eyeonline.com) is the fourth compositing package I've tried, and I've been *most impressed* with how it works. It is a *completely* different mindset than using a program like Adobe AfterFX, and it took about three days before I actually understood how to work efficiently within it. But, once I went through the courseware for Digital Fusion (where you go through examples you'd actually encounter on a production), I was working about 500 percent faster than I ever had in AfterFX.

It's not the streamlined methods for working in Digital Fusion that made it so much faster; it was the fact that Digital Fusion is so well programmed and lets you still work even while it's "deep in thought." If you have multiple processors, you'll see multiple *branches* of your *flow* rendering at once, and you can set its

preferences so that while you're thinking about what to do next, DF will be quietly rendering the frames surrounding the current one in the background.

The quality and ease of use of DF's tools are what you'd expect from a program designed to work in the feature film environment. Things like color correcting (which can be numbingly pedantic in other packages) are a breeze in DF.

Quite simply, while LightWave gets much credit for letting me complete *Ghost Warrior* in six months, Digital Fusion gets much credit for *Ghost Warrior* looking the way it does, and taking only six months.

Layers

Most scenes in *Ghost Warrior* were split apart before final rendering, so separate layers containing the background, foreground characters, and foreground elements, each with another image file containing the shadows, specular "hot-spots," z-buffer, and "Tim's special buffer" were saved for each layer. (I chose to save the "extra buffers" as a separate image because, quite frankly, I don't know enough about the extended image formats that can allow for some extra buffers to really *trust* that things are working well under *all* circumstances.)

Figure 18-2: Here you see the grass layer, with its *depth channel*, Kaze and Yashin, with their *multichannel* image (more on that in a bit), and the final composite.

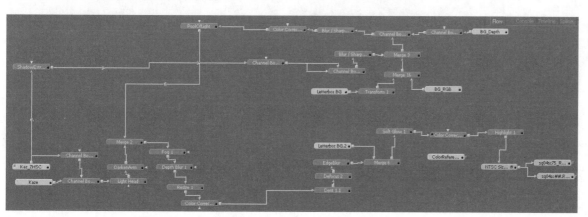

Figure 18-3: Here is the flow that generated the final composite.

Common Tools

There are so many tools in Digital Fusion that there are some I've never even explored. But here is a short list of the tools that I *do* use on *almost every single composite.*

Color Corrector

The following image looks pretty convincing; only a trained compositer would notice that the grass around the polygonal mask is also affected by the color gain. However, the real brilliance of rendering to *separate layers* is that you could apply this *color corrector* before the layers get composited, so the effect is *only* applied to Kaze's head and not the background!

NOTE

Since I planned on doing so much color-correcting on the work that came out of my 3D package, I knew that I had to save my renders in a high-dynamic-range image format. Normal 24-bit images (like JPGs) are *only 8 bits per channel.* This looks pretty good for TV and VGA but breaks down on film, especially when you start to push and pull the brightness, contrast, gamma, and gain too much. 24-bit image formats can look "gritty" or get banding in areas that are supposed to be smooth gradations or have parts of the images disappear altogether.

There are 16- and 32-bit image formats that have 16- and 32-bits per channel, logarithmic image formats (like *Cineon*), and *floating-point* images that store channel information as a percentage (that can go above 100 percent and below 0 percent).

For *Ghost Warrior,* I chose the flexible image format (.flx) to save images since both Digital Fusion and LightWave read and wrote the floating-point files with ease. However, knowing now what I know about ILM's new and *open-sourced* Open-EXR format, that's the format I will most likely choose for my next project (http://www.openexr.com).

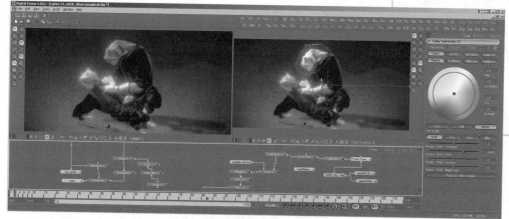

Figure 18-4: One of the most *intuitive* tools in Digital Fusion is the *color corrector.* I just love how its color "bull's-eye" lets you quickly add exactly the right tint to an image, without mucking about with R, G, and B values. Here you see it being applied (via a soft-edged polygon mask) so Kaze's head looks like it's hit with the same bright light that is shining on Yashin's (left: no effect, right: with effect).

Channel Booleans

Channel booleans perform mathematical operations based on the content within each individual *channel* (red, green, blue, alpha, etc.). I most often use them to combine an RGB image with the grayscale image that represents its *depth channel.*

Figure 18-5: In the upper left, you can see the multi-buffer image of Kaze, Itsua, and the plane that "grows" the grass for the shot. In the upper right, is the blue channel (*extracted* from the multi-buffer image with a channel boolean), which I've used to store shadow density. In the lower left is the "Tim's Special Buffer" channel (also extracted from the multi-buffer image with a channel boolean) I've used to produce a silhouette of just the ground plane. In the lower right is the result of a simple divide operation performed by the channel boolean that creates an image that can be multiplied (just like in Photoshop) over the grass "plate" to give me shadows of any density I want!

Remember that a depth buffer ("z-buffer") is a separate channel within an image that assigns a grayscale value to every pixel in the image. Depth channels are much like alpha channels, except that where an alpha channel uses this *grayscale* information to determine transparency of the RGB pixel that shares the same X/Y position, a depth channel uses its grayscale information to assign a distance from the image's "camera."

This depth information can be used in compositing two images together, *automatically* letting each pixel that has a lighter depth channel value be seen *in front of* pixels with darker depth channel values (as we explored in the chapter on technology solutions).

But the cool factor of depth buffers doesn't end there. Higher-end compositing programs can provide you with tools that use an image's depth buffer to *instantly* create the effects of fogging and depth-of-field "lens effects" (and more). Whereas these effects

could take an extremely long time to render (and re-render) in a 3D package, with Digital Fusion's instant updates, the iterative process for achieving a particular look was only minutes per tool, per scene.

Figure 18-6: Depth buffer

Depth Fog

Figure 18-7: Depth fog

Once you have a z-buffer (depth buffer) attached to an image, you can quickly adjust its color/hue/etc., based on how far each pixel is from the "camera." You drag an eyedropper to the area of an image that is at the appropriate "distance" from the camera for both near and far planes, and you get real-time updates (in DF) showing the results! In Figure 18-7, you see my grass that was rendered about 2.5 "stops" too bright has been quickly toned down to a nice, "night-like" feel by "fogging" with black.

Depth Blur

Anyone who has ever rendered depth-of-field "lens effects" knows how bloody long they take. Yet, having DOF in a scene makes it look so luscious. Almost every "real world" camera will have at least some *blurring* based on how far away items in the scene are from the camera.

NOTE

When working with depth effects (like depth fog, depth blur, and depth-based compositing), I found I needed to render my scenes out *twice as big* as I would eventually need them and render them *without antialiasing*.

If you soften the edge of a depth buffer, the composite can't accurately know the z-position of those "softened" edge pixels. Likewise, if you have a nice, "sharp-edged" z-buffer trying to work on the soft, "sub-pixel" antialiased edges of the RGB portion of the image, those pixels that are partly one item and partly another item will not be blurred, fogged, or composited correctly. (The result is a strange "gritty halo" that just looks bad.)

Figure 18-8: These two images have exactly the same depth blur tools added to them. The left has had its focal point "eye-dropped" on the "rear" pixels, and the right has had its focal point "eye-dropped" on the "front" pixels (approximate render time per final, HD frame is ten seconds).

Soft Glow

Figure 18-9: Soft Glow increases the *gain* of some parts of an image, so, before I add that tool into the flow, I add a color corrector to "bump down" the gain accordingly. The results of Soft Glow is a gentle, "fuzzy," "atmospheric" feel that takes the harshness off the edges of a piece.

For me, regardless of whether I'm painting or drawing or working in 3D, art is all about *edges*. One of my biggest beefs with 3D has been how nice and crisp and sharp every single edge is, even when you're using depth-of-field lens effects.

With paintings, you have some of your painting rendered nice and tightly, and other areas are only *suggested*. This lets the viewer's eye be *drawn to the areas of most definition*. It's a painter's tool that has been used throughout the ages. With DF's Soft Glow tool, it's now a part of a 3D CGI artist's palette too!

I've used *masks* a lot in *Ghost Warrior* to isolate my *centers of interest* in a scene, protecting them from the effect of the Soft Glow so their edges are more crisp, more defined. Using masks to isolate areas where the edges need to be *soft* and where they need to be *sharp* makes my 3D work much more *painterly*. The audience's eyes are drawn to the key focal points (faces, hands, and important props) *first*, and then as the scene plays out, they begin to see and explore the "supporting" areas of the scene.

It is through this control of edges, sharp and soft, that *Ghost Warrior* looks more like a painting come to life than it does a work of CGI filmmaking.

The Process

After I've rendered all of a scene's layers (background "plates," mid and foreground "levels," shadow "buffers," etc.), I start bringing them together in Digital Fusion (although DF does let you work on a project when all the frames haven't yet been rendered; I've found this to be most helpful).

NOTE

After the highlight in Figure 18-15, you see a Resize tool to bring the video down to NTSC resolution and the savers used to export to Video Toaster format for editing and an image sequence for me to pick a frame to post on the *Ghost Warrior* web site (http://www.wordware.com/ghostwarrior/).

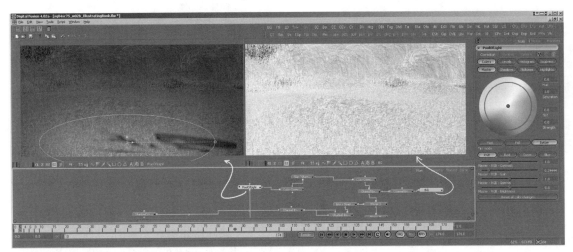

Figure 18-10: I usually start with the background, layering in shadows and correcting any "sloppiness" in my lighting. On the right, you see the "raw" background. On the left are the shadows that have been *multiplied* onto the grass and the mask I am using to protect an oval from being darkened by the currently active tool, a color corrector I am using to give the effect of a nice "pool of light" seen in well-painted backgrounds of traditional animation. (On the far right-hand side of the image, you see the controls for the currently active tool, the Color Corrector, that is reducing the gain for all areas *outside* of its elliptical mask.)

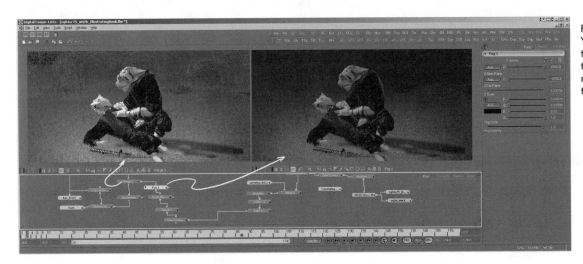

Figure 18-11: Bringing in Kaze and Yashin (using *depth merge* to get them to sit *into* the grass layer), I then add a depth fog (shown on the right view) to separate them from the "busyness" of the background.

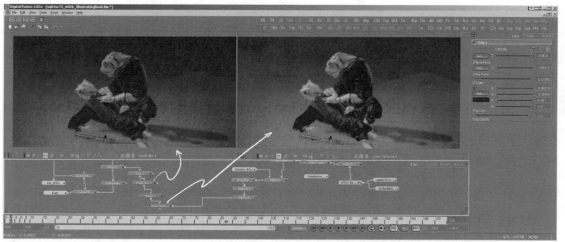

Figure 18-12: I then add a depth blur. Then, since my work with depth channels is done, the tool just downstream of the depth blur resizes the image from twice-screen-resolution to its actual, projected screen size. (I've rendered my layers at "twice-size" because I am working with depth buffers. See the NOTE just prior to the "Soft Glow" section in this chapter. Reducing them by 50 percent gives me my *antialiasing*.) On the right view, you see a color corrector that I'm using to fine-tune the image.

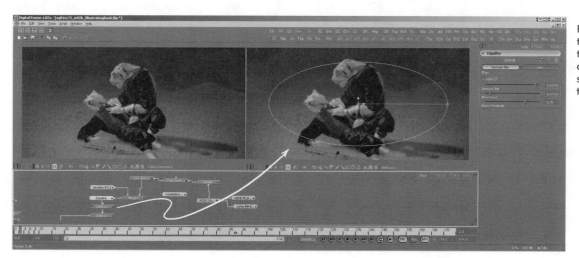

Figure 18-13: I then added a Dent tool and a bit of *defocus* to simulate the effects of "real-world" camera optics. (On the left view, you can see the effect of the Color Corrector tool from the previous illustration.)

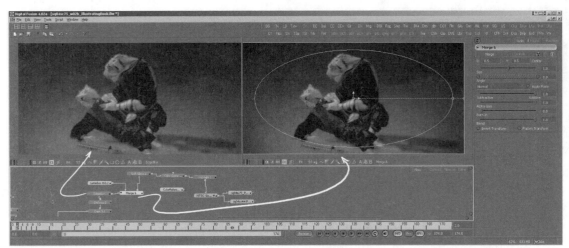

Figure 18-14: Then, I found that I wanted to darken the edges of the frame even more to heighten the "spotlight" effect on the characters and their "pool of light." But I didn't like the way that the color corrector I used looked, so I *merged* a black background over the image, protecting the center areas with a soft-edged ellipse mask.

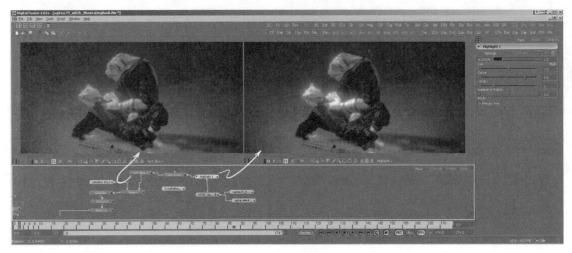

Figure 18-15: Adding a soft glow (seen on the left view) looked nice, but I wanted something more. After adding another color corrector to match a reference frame from a previously completed scene from Sequence 4 (the *detached* "loader," seen just below the color corrector in the flow), I added a highlight that punches up the brightest "brights," adding nice little "star" effects to them.

"We'll fix it in 'Post...'"

> "All successful techniques are the end result of a clear vision of the work to be created."
> — Richard Schmid, *Alla Prima*

> "Honey, we are 'post.'"
> — overheard comment from unknown compositer

What's that old saying? "Misjudgment on *your* part does not constitute an emergency on *my* part." Far too often (today, with all the digital effects possible in *post*-processing more than ever), the people in *post*, the compositors and digital paint artists, are left to be a catch-all for the shortcomings and shortsightedness of directors and/or others within the production pipeline. In live action, misplaced microphones are digitally painted out, as are entire people, "flags," and other production equipment that was supposed to be hidden from view.

What some people high in the chain of production don't seem to understand is that for every frame that has an inappropriate shadow of something that needs to be painted out, the talent of a highly skilled artist, a human being, is being squandered by the saprophytic nature of having to fix *someone else's mistake*. It's hard for a director to really see the effect that kind of menial labor has on the creative soul. (All the workers are so "chipper and happy" when the director is around, right?) I can tell you from seeing the effect it has after having watched some very fine artists, wonderful people, become wax shells over the course of a production. All that can be avoided by a simple series of checks, of people *simply doing their job*, before the camera starts to roll.

As *director*, it is *your* job to make sure that you have a clear vision of what you want ahead of time! "I don't know what I want, but I'll know it when I see it" is the mark of someone who shouldn't be sitting in a director's chair. "Right" or "wrong," as director, you should *know your vision* and feel strongly enough about it to commit your life and dreams to it — especially when you are responsible for other people's creative lives and dreams as well.

So, yes, you *can* do a lot in "post." Compositing tools are powerful tools to let you bring your 3D render into the realm of honest-to-goodness *artwork*. But make sure that you have a *clear vision* of what you are doing and how you'll be making it happen *before you start production!*

Remember the chapter on technology solutions? *That* is where all the exploration and experimentation take place. That is where you can say things like, "Dang, Bill, can we actually *do* that?" When you're finally *in* post, there should be no surprises. Like walking through a supermarket that you've known for years, you should know exactly which aisle has the Post Toasties and on which shelf you can find the freshest gallon of milk. Neither you *nor the people working for/with you* should have to hunt for things. You should know exactly what each and every scene needs, and "wham-bam" get that scene done so you can move on to the next one.

That is just part of the one main "secret" to getting *Ghost Warrior* done and looking the way it does in the time it took to produce. *Have a clear focus of what will be done before each and every task comes due*. When the work before reflects what you've envisioned beforehand, you know your work is done, *and you move on!*

Chapter 19

Editorial: The Final Polish

If you've done your job well in writing, editing the storyboards into an animatic, and replacing the storyboards with finished work as you've updated your production reel, there should be very little left to do in editorial.

The *editing* of your work at this point should be little more than fine-tuning, polishing the timing of the elements, and honing the way the scenes flow together to tell the narrative.

At this point, the process of filmmaking is very much like the process of a poet, working within the structure of the words he has already laid out, shifting their order, and making subliminal changes through almost imperceptible changes to the rhythmic devices and implied meanings. At this point, you have all the polished pieces laid out in front of you — you know they go together one way —

the way they've been in your production reel. Now see if, by making slight changes in length and order, you can increase the power of the performances.

For instance, I've never heard a satisfactory explanation as to where the *cut* should be when starting from someone turning his head to cutting to the object that he is turning to see. A common convention is to cut on the frame where the motion blur is greatest. But I've found that you can totally alter the *subtext* of the person's looking by cutting either before or after the "standard" way of "cutting on the blur." I doubt there is a hard-and-fast way of explaining how any editorial decision will affect an audience's feelings about what they are seeing. *Every situation is different*, and you must trust your gut instincts as to the approaches that are best.

"Offline" Edit

Offline editing is editing that is done at a lower resolution than your final target resolution. This lets you work much faster than you could if you were trying to move all the pixels in, say, a series of 4K film-resolution frames.

NTSC and PAL resolutions are often used as an offline for film because it is so much easier to work nowadays in *non-linear* editing suites than by cutting and splicing actual film stock. However, if

your final target medium is NTSC or PAL (or lower "Internet" resolutions), and you've got a good editing system, you may not need to do an offline at all; you may find your system quite fast enough to handle all your needs in real time.

With my own desired resolution of HDTV 720p, I have no way of editing at that resolution in real time, so even though I worked entirely digitally, I still needed my edits in NTSC as offline so I could get all the *real-time* benefits of the VT[3]'s ToasterEdit system (which includes real-time *lossless* NTSC editing, color correcting, compositing, "slip-sliding," "ripple-editing," and "relational in/outs"). It makes the editing process so much easier when all I need to do to see my changes *the instant I make them* is to just press Play. (Some other digital video editing suites still require you to wait while the machine *renders* the edits that you've just made.)

The "insta-feedback" of working in real time is vital because it lets you have the thought process that suggests the changes still fresh in your mind as you see the results. Just as in painting, this is the point where everything looks pretty darn good, and you make a small change, step back at "viewer distance" from it, and think about what that change did.

Every change you make at this stage of the game should only be a *minor* change to make the story read with more of the impact and clarity that you need. *If you've done your job well up to this point, minor changes are all that is needed.*

Elements, Order, and Rhythm

All the magic we have woven to this point was done for the sole purpose of telling a story. Editing hones the *storycraft* of a piece by rearranging, inserting, and removing scenes, but also, powerful changes in how the story *feels* can be made by slightly shortening or lengthening the existing scenes, altering their *rhythm*.

Every story element interrelates with every other story element. Changing their order can completely change the interpretive meaning within the mind of the audience. Changing the relationship of their lengths can change how the audience *feels* about the story they are seeing.

As you watch your work in editorial (seeing each pass as if for the very first time), ask yourself if everything is clear that *needs* to be clear. (If you're telling a *mystery*, there need to be many things

that are slightly unclear that fall into place as the story goes along.) Are things and/or knowledge *assumed* that need explanation? Are there elements disclosed that give away too much of the punchline?

Only *you*, as director, can make the decisions about these elements. Only *you*, seeing your work as if for the very first time, can answer these questions. No "focus group," no hodgepodge of people (some for whom this film was never intended) can tell you what you know deep inside.

Usually, having done your work well at the outset, with strong writing, good storyboarding, and intelligent cutting together of your animatic, honing your story at this point is a matter of either realizing that you're giving too much away (not giving the audience enough credit) or finding a character having jumped to a conclusion without adequate explanation as to how that conclusion was derived.

You may find that you need to insert a bit of footage earlier in the film to show a character "overhearing" something important to make an epiphany later on be *believable*. You may even need to add another sequence of scenes to delve into backstory.

You may find a scene that doesn't really contribute to the one main goal of the story. It may be a scene that is beautifully animated, but if it "just sits there" (storywise) or leads the audience into thinking something other than what you want them to think, that scene needs to be cut.

Everything needs to be for the betterment of the story — the one, main reason for the film having been made in the first place.

Often, you'll find yourself cutting little bits and pieces off the ends of scenes to keep the film moving. You might find a sequence dragging and need to pick things up a bit. Here, the real work is in honing the intended *feel* of the story while altering its rhythm.

So you watch the film, again and again, in bits and in whole. You make mental notes and implement the subtle changes in timing until the rhythm of the piece tells the story in *exactly* the way that would make you leave the theatre cheering (or swooning, or jumpy, or however the film should make you feel).

Every story has its own rhythm, as does every genre. The rhythms of a pastoral piece, with the smoothness of a late-summer's evening, are vastly different from the Gen-X, MTV quick-cut, skate-punk, thrasher movie.

You watch your work, again and again, making smaller and smaller revisions, until the piece fills you with the exact feelings you want it to at *exactly* the correct moments in the film. Once you've done this, you need to get a fresh pair of eyes. It's time for *test screenings*.

NOTE

> If you've done a good job with your *writing*, with creating your animatic, then most of your editing should be already done. All the big changes should have already happened when your movie was just a collection of storyboard frames edited together with temporary music. *Thinking ahead* and working so that you don't have to go "backward" is the mark of a well-trained artist — regardless of medium.

Test Screenings

If you can watch your film and honestly say to yourself, "Holy cats! That's the movie I've always wanted to see," you've done your job! But, since you've sat very closely to it for who knows how long, it's easy to overlook important things. So, as you draw near to putting the final polish on your final edits, plan on showing a screening or two of the *work print* of your film.

While I think it is wrong to try to cater to all walks of life in such a personal expression of vision, such as film, I do think it is important to get as many different kinds of opinions as possible (taken with a grain or a gram of salt). So, friends and family are okay to invite along, but they already have somewhat of an alignment to your way of seeing things. If you can get "friends-of-friends," or coworkers, this is even better. (In Hollywood, the big distributors hand out flier tickets on popular pedestrian thoroughfares throughout LA, signing up people who have no connection with the industry to see work prints of films.)

Where can you hold your test screenings? I recommend contacting some of the local community organizations around you. Regardless of where you are in the U.S., there should be any number of lodges belonging to community-minded people who would be more than willing to help out another fellow member of the community, especially for the chance of seeing a locally made film before its "official" release!

More important than interviewing test audiences, I think, is sitting behind them and watching them as they sit through your movie. Offer free soda and keep a close eye on the "bathroom brigade." People usually save having to go to the bathroom for the boring parts. Watch how restless they are. Do they shift in their seats and cough or stay transfixed, riveted to the screen? Do they laugh or jump at the right spots? As you watch the people watching your work, do you feel embarrassed about anything you feel you could/should have done better?

As you talk with the test audiences, try to get a feel for the type of person to whom you are talking. Make an honest assessment of whether or not this person represents what you feel is your audience. If not, then you can take those comments as a pretty good assessment of how the general public may see your work. If the person *does* seem to be your target audience, pay close attention to his thoughts and concerns, and if possible, arrange time to talk with him again a few days after the screening. The best stories sometimes take a while to sink in to make their full impact.

NOTE

If I had been in the test audience for *Fight Club*, I'd have given them a rant about violence and glorifying it in films the likes of which would have made their heads spin. But... given a few days for the initial knee-jerk reaction to fade and for the real "meat" of the story to sink in, I realized that *Fight Club* wasn't about fighting. The violence in *Fight Club* is a *device* to wear down the mental and emotional barriers of the audience so the real meanings can mesh deeply within the psyche of the viewer. A week after my first viewing, which left me repulsed, I couldn't wait to see *Fight Club* again.

The real meaning of *Fight Club* is, "If you were to die in the next minute, what is the one thing that you wish you would have done before dying?"

(This is a very large part of why my home is now Alaska.)

Changes/Additions

So what do you do when you find, even with the best planning and work all throughout your production and pre-production process, that you need to make changes or additions to your film? You archive your old work and sit down and start redoing the scenes that need changing! It's as simple as that. No muss, no fuss; you just get to it and do it!

It's well known that the act of thinking about something is often as strenuous as doing that something (like holiday thank-you cards). So I really want to say to you, if you know you need to change something or add something to your film, dude, just get to it! Slap on a "Tk02" or a "b" or "c" to your scene work and start doing what needs to be done!

That's all.

"Online" Edit

When you have your offline edit to the point where it's as good as you can make it, if your "final" medium is something other than what your editing software can manage, you export an edit list (*EDL*) and start hacking away at the "real" footage.

So, in doing the online edit, you need something that can do the same sorts of things on your higher-resolution images that your editing software did on your lower-resolution ones. My compositing tool, Digital Fusion, came to the rescue.

In my initial tests, I found that Digital Fusion can read EDLs. So, it was a relatively easy task to replicate the work done on the NTSC offline edit on the HDTV frames. Other than the time and physical RAM required (about 2 GB to not have issues with the HDTV frames rendering on both processors), the process pretty much took care of itself.

However, in my researching film festivals for Chapter 21, "Let It Shine," on getting your film shown, I found that most film festivals are quite amenable to showing work in NTSC format. As time goes on and the HD format is more and more accepted and accessible, more and more festivals will support it. NTSC is about half the resolution of HD720p, so there is a loss in the *beauty* of the images, but with the original data archived, I know I can recreate an HD version if it is ever needed.

So, as much as HD was the focus of my early tests and work, in the end I opted for the VT[3]'s uncompressed NTSC edit of *Ghost Warrior* as my online edit.

Chapter 20

Media Output

At one time, the only format that filmmakers could use to get their work seen by others was, well, film. Now, in addition to film, there's videotape (from professional to consumer, analog, and digital), DVD, VCD, and a plethora of *streaming* ("webcast") and *downloadable* computer movie formats. For the computer-based formats, there seem to be new forms of compression and improvements on old ones coming out several times a year, so it's best to do current research on what's new and what will work for you.

The main thing is to get the work seen by those who want to see it. (It seems strange that there may be hundreds of thousands of people wanting to see your film, and it might take some work to get it out to them.) The second main thing is to be able to make enough money doing this so that you can make another film, even better than the one you just finished.

Film

If you have "beaucoup bucks," a rich benefactor, a *distributor,* or some other source for a lot of cash, you can get your CGI film printed to film itself!

I was prepared for printing to film to be pricey, but with the increased number of people working digitally, I imagined the supply and demand figures to have spawned more houses that could do film printing and the prices to have gone down accordingly. I wasn't quite prepared for the just-over-$10,000 average price tag attached to printing *Ghost Warrior* to 35mm with an optical, two-channel audio track. "Ouch, baby!"

What a bummer! It would have been wonderful to actually hold a can of film that had "Ghost Warrior" stenciled on the side and watch the ultra-crisp resolution of Kaze in 35mm, but hey, whatever.

It was a great relief to find out that most film festivals accept entrants submitting work on "reasonably priced" formats. (I even found out that some film festivals accept *screening* copies on VHS, which is actually a very low-quality format.) So, with a deferential nod to Cirrus (the god of money, whose shrines you can see scattered all over the U.S.), I bowed quietly out of the whole "printing-to-film" thing ... for now.

Professional Videotape

Betacam, BetacamSP, Digi-Beta, D1, "Umatic," et al., are the videotape formats that the "professionals" use with decks costing many thousands of dollars (and sometimes much, much more!). DV (not to be confused with MiniDV) is a professional videotape format where you can get cameras and player/recorders for as little as a few thousand dollars.

If you send "director reel" work out to production studios, many like to receive work on Betacam. (This phenomenon seems more prevalent on the east coast. West Coast studios I've talked with are fine with VHS.) Other than the fact that the image quality of Betacam is true *broadcast quality*, the tapes themselves start out at around $30 for a 15-minute tape. I've never received a straight answer as to why they *insisted* on Betacam as a "Hi, pleased to meet you" format, so I can only assume that it is one of those things where if you can *afford* the $30 per tape that you send out to all sorts of studios, you must be worth something.

Now, in my experience, there are two main reasons for "Joe Average CGI filmmaker" recording to a professional tape format. One is for archival purposes. Their image quality is second to none, and these tapes are made to last much longer than even the best consumer-grade tape ever dreamed of remaining viable. The other reason is to use it as a master for tape duplication.

Since most people can't afford to *buy* one of the Betacam decks, you should know that in most places, you *can* rent them. Prices vary by location but should be within the reach of most people if you really want to drop your work to these formats (just be *very* careful with the equipment — it's expensive). If you're not into *professional* video, it should be noted that many professional decks have only *component* (YUC) inputs. So before you go making all the arrangements, make sure that your NTSC (or PAL) broadcast video card can interface with what you're renting. (All the *professional* NTSC/PAL cards that I've worked with, the VT[3] and DPS perception/reality/Hollywood systems, all have *component* out, and the VT[3], I know for a fact, can accept a separate, serial-digital "daughter" card to output to Digi-Beta.)

So, when you get all the cables correctly hooked up, you just play your output from your NTSC/PAL *online* final edit right into the deck, and you're good to go! (In the old days, we had to use a *single-frame VTR*, controlled via serial interface, to get our animations to tape. DPS' Personal Animation Recorder on the Amiga was the first affordable way to play animations real time right onto tape.)

Consumer Videotape

We all have our good ol' trusty VHS videocassette recorder. We can all make tapes of our film on these consumer-end machines for friends and family, but haven't you ever noticed that the tapes you buy at the local video store are of such higher quality than what you can record from your NTSC (or PAL) video-out card at home?

The inner workings of *professional grade* "consumer videotape" machines is much better *on purpose!* This is so even if someone does practice VHS piracy, the tapes they buy/rent are still better than the ones they could make through piracy. (This isn't counting the signal-strength "tricks" that current VCRs do when they sense an incoming "protected" video signal.)

If you want to make VHS tapes for sale or demo purposes, it really is the best idea to go to a professional duplication house (which most larger communities have) and have them take care of things. Using their professional VHS decks, the image quality is much better, and generally, they can do about 20 tapes at once.

When you factor in the fact that these professional duplication houses have "pre-wound" tapes from T-5 (five minutes in standard play) in five-minute increments up to T-"really-huge," you only pay for the tape you use. You really do get a much better deal when doing things this way. Besides, if you are selling or otherwise distributing your tapes to the public, it looks so much more *professional* when you don't use a T-120 to hold a two-minute short film (or demo reel).

Now if you're wondering if it is worth archiving your film on your Hi8, Digital8, or MiniDV, the answer is a hearty "absolutely!"

These media were developed as "acquisition" media, suitable for "in-the-field" gathering of video to be edited on a "more robust" form later on. (Actually editing with these media isn't so great because the tape is so thin and "stretchy" that even when you are working with *timecode* on these media, the edits can still slip up to 12 frames, from my own experience.)

There is a difference between *professional* grade equipment, *pro-sumer* equipment, and *consumer* equipment in these formats, but for the most part, even the consumer grade equipment and media (Hi8, Digital8, and MiniDV) will be just fine for archiving your work and transporting it to a tape duplication house that supports mastering from those formats. The adage "you get what you pay for" *mostly* applies with video equipment, so do your research well, both researching online and quizzing those who've used the stuff, before making any kind of purchase.

"Computer Movie" Distribution Formats

There are umpteen different kinds of video/audio formats for *compressing* digital movies that you can use for letting your work be *downloaded* onto another's computer for infinite reviewing or *streamed* so that the end user must be connected to a site in order to view it (like "on-demand" television). So, I'll only hit the major ones, as they've applied to my own working with them in getting *Ghost Warrior* out there.

MPEG

MPEG (Motion Picture Experts Group) is an old format (reaching back to 1988) that in my experience produces the best-looking picture quality at the smallest file sizes.

The *Ghost Warrior* trailer is an MPEG-1, running at 15 FPS (frames per second), at a size of 368x152 *compressed* down to 4.7 MB. While the image quality isn't stellar, its motion is smooth and fluid, and the sound is rich and vibrant.

MPEG currently has three "flavors," MPEG-1, 2, and 4, each successive one offering better compression, which means better quality while requiring less bandwidth. Most computer operating systems in use today offer direct support for playing MPEG-1 and MPEG-2 files.

Out of all the file formats that I experimented with in encoding the *Ghost Warrior* trailer for access over the Internet, I was most happy with MPEG.

NOTE

One of the best resources for MPEG information on the web for players, encoders, history, and FAQs is http://www.mpeg.org.

QuickTime

Apple's QuickTime gave the best-looking still images and the ability to "scrub" quickly forward *and backward* through the movie file, but the playback on my high-consumer-end graphics card was not as smooth as the other formats, and even using QuickTime 6's MPEG-4 encoding, the file size was outrageous (28 MB at the same 15 FPS and resolution of the much smaller MPEG-1 mentioned above!).

The biggest benefit of QuickTime, that I can see, is that when you encode using QuickTime, all users of that revision of the QuickTime player will be able to download and view your movie without having to get extra plug-ins (as with the DivX *CODEC* — "COder-DECoder" — for .avi files). If you want a movie format that end users won't have to think about to use, this is the one.

NOTE

Information about QuickTime and QuickTime players can be found at http://www.apple.com/quicktime.

Windows Media

Windows Media is a relatively newer compression format that plays its own .wmv (audio and video) and .wma (audio only) files as well as "older" Windows .avi files. Windows Media also appears to automatically stream its content, buffering it in accordance with how much data you are able to fit over your Internet connection. This means that the file will begin playing very shortly after clicking on it, not waiting for the full file to download, even on a 28.8Kbps connection.

What amazed me most about the Windows Media format is its file size. The full *Ghost Warrior* trailer (the one that takes 28 MB on QuickTime and 4.7 MB on MPEG-1) was only 1.6 MB as a .wmv, with identical frame sizes and frame rates as the other two aforementioned compression formats. The quality of this 1.6 MB .wmv file was about halfway between that of QuickTime and MPEG-1.

The only problem with Windows Media files is that many laypeople have never heard of Windows Media and don't know if they can play a .wmv or .wma and don't even bother to try downloading the movie. (Or so I gathered from e-mailed comments about the soundtrack to the trailer of *Ghost Warrior*, which was provided on the site as a .wmv.) So, as a "secondary" format to have available for the technologically inclined, Windows Media is a very good thing.

NOTE

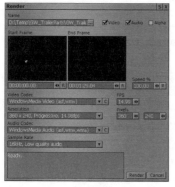

Encoding to Windows Media is usually built in as a part of your editing suite. With the VT[3], you simply select Windows Media as the desired output codec, choose video and audio options, and press Render.

Standalone Windows Media encoders and capture utilities can be found by selecting Windows Media Encoder from the Select Download section of http://www.microsoft.com/windows/windowsmedia/download/default.asp.

Windows Media players for Windows and Macintosh operating systems can be downloaded from www.windowsmedia.com.

.AVI/DivX

The good ol' .avi movie file is still the most popular video format on Windows-based computers. Other companies have released codecs that work with the .avi format, enabling better and better compression. The most popular of these third-party codecs is the DivX codec (available for Linux and Mac in addition to Windows formats).

DivX is an MPEG-4 based format (with at least one "next-generation" home DVD player supporting DivX, MPEG-4 format) that allows for high-quality audio and video at relatively small file sizes. Comparing the DivX (MPEG-4) encoded .avi for the *Ghost Warrior* trailer (21 MB) with the QuickTime MPEG-4 encoded .mov (28 MB) using the same frame size and frame rate, the DivX version looked every bit as good, played more smoothly, and was about 7 MB smaller.

NOTE

> Windows, Linux, and Macintosh encoders for DivX, "adware," consumer, and professional versions are available from http://www.divx.com.

Real Player

A long-time player in the *streaming media* scene has been RealNetworks. They offer players and encoders for Windows, Macintosh, and Linux and real-media servers (Helix) for "webcasting."

NOTE

> More information about RealNetworks and their suites of programs can be found at http://www.real.com.

Publicity / Stills

There's another type of media output that you'll need to consider, and that is posters, prints, stills, etc. If you're planning on sending out packets to distributors and screening notices, putting up "one-sheets" (movie posters, for all intents and purposes), or generally getting other people to be aware of the fact that you've got something they want to see, you'll need to think about print output. (While the Internet is great, there's just something that says "solidity" about being able to hold something in your hand.)

Design

We're all artists, and that's good. But *design* is a full, four-year degree in and of itself. There's a lot going on in design that, unless you're practiced at it, you might miss. So, if you're planning on doing your own design and aren't a *designer* by trade, it will do you much good to swing by your local (high-end) bookseller and thumb through the current edition of the *Design Annual* by Graphis Press and see what the current measurements of *good design* are. (Other books in the design/typography section include advertising annuals and poster, logo, and typography annuals.)

Just as in learning an existing animation style, you're not looking to copy what you see (aside from being illegal, that's also stiff, static, and generally boring). You're looking for bits and pieces that *inspire* you and fit the general look and feel of your own film. Knowing what others consider *good design*, either for packaging, presentation, or whatever, will always help you make *better decisions* as to your own design (or at least "more educated" ones).

Inkjet Printers (Home/Office)

I do a fair amount of my own printing, running an Epson Stylus Color 3000. It doesn't quite live up to its advertising, but it does an okay job. In getting into doing one's own printing, the inkjet printers, whatever the brand, offer the most "bang for the buck," in terms of print quality and cost — both cost of the actual printer itself and the cost of the media you'll be using up every time you print something.

What I wasn't prepared for in deciding to do a lot of my own printing was how frustrating it was going to be just trying to match the output that comes from the printer with what I see on my screen. Even the calibration programs that let you get a "color-correct" output on your monitor still leave a huge gap between what is on screen and what is on paper. Not to mention that every type of paper (substrate) you print on will take the ink differently, resulting in different color balances.

The "color-matching" capabilities of printer drivers (that control the distribution of the inks) have gotten better, but they still leave a lot to be desired when I've worked darn hard to get just the right blend of hues in my render and see even a slight shift toward green or violet in my printout. So, be aware of the fact that you're going to probably have to do a lot of "massaging" to get your color prints looking the way you want them. It should be noted that the better you get at this process, the pickier you get as well.

Another drawback to printing using inkjet printers is that the inks and dyes are water soluble, meaning that if someone is holding a print and sneezes on it, you've got problems. There are *resin-coated* papers (like Epson's professional-grade "photographic" papers) that protect to a great degree against this and help to increase print longevity, but I've still noticed some smudging in my own tests.

Local Printshops (Black and White)

For doing one-color prints, like the kind you see plastered on construction sites about local rock concerts, local quick-and-cheap printshops are fantastic. Even here in Fairbanks, they offer their own software so you can "print" over your modem to their printers and zip in town later that day and pick up the couple hundred black-and-white "posters" you sent.

I say that these places are good for black and white only because doing color is such a tricky process. Even in going with professional, "high-end" offset lithography places, I've always had my work cut out for me in making sure the prints I get look like the artwork I created.

Offset Litho

Doing prints and posters for myself and local organizations has brought me in close contact with the *offset lithography* process. "Lifesize" plates are burned of each color to be used (usually the "standard" printer's inks — cyan, magenta, yellow, and black — but can also include specific premixed colors for that extra, added "pop"). A big press then imprints the paper with the colors of each plate.

Just as it's a challenge for the home user to get the colors exactly right, it is a challenge even for the professionals who do it every day. Some places are better than others at working out the balance of lights and darks required in the separate photographic plates (and others are downright awful). I've yet to be really thrilled with what I've received from offset lithography (even when I've provided an "approved" Epson print for them from which to work). The only saving grace has been that the end recipients of the prints and posters don't know what the artwork "should" look like and are happy with what they've got — if you can call that a "saving grace."

Now the strange thing is that when I've had my artwork used as cover art for magazines and books, the printers that the publishers seem to have found reproduce the artwork *perfectly*, even when working from RGB images. (Most offset litho places that I've worked with whine or make excuses about color shifts unless they are given CMYK image files.) So, this hangs a huge flag over the importance of shopping around and making sure in the contract you sign with an offset litho place that they will not charge you extra as they figure out how to do their jobs right.

Online Proof Internet-Only Printing Services

In theory, thes places are neat. In practice, I wouldn't touch them again with a ten-foot pole. I'm talking about the places that *don't* send a proof in the mail for you to approve. These places give you web access to a .pdf file, which you look at on your own monitor and approve for printing. If you're working with black and white, this would probably be fine (you can't go too wrong when you're only using one ink color). But as I hope you've seen from my earlier paragraphs about color printing, this is just bad news in a can *waiting* to be opened.

Yes, I do speak from experience. I had a very simple gig for The Yukon Quest International Sled Dog Race for a couple thousand posters. The line-based artwork was very "cartoonish," and the colors could shift quite a distance, and both I and the client would be fine. So, together we decided to try one of those online printing companies. We got treated well, right up until we received the actual prints — what was supposed to be blue turned out *brown*. When I called to ask if these were the colors that they saw on their own monitors, I was very rudely told no. They saw blue on their monitors where it should be, but it was *my* problem that *they* printed brown where it was supposed to be blue.

I'd not recommend trusting anything important to any company that does not let you see an actual sample of the finished work before printing the run.

I'd also recommend checking through any print runs that you order to make sure that the "good ones" aren't placed on top while less-than-excellent prints hide at the bottom, *before* handing over any form of payment.

Chapter 21

Let It Shine!

Right! So you have your work wrapped, and it's everything you've wanted to see in a film since you don't know when! How do you show it off?

This was the most challenging section of the whole book to write, the most challenging and most educational. My first thought when I wanted to get *Ghost Warrior* out into the public's eye was to give my agents a call and let them do what they do and await their calls of, "go see so-and-so at such-and-such; your appointment is for blah-de-blah."

But I had to put on serious brakes here because most people don't have agents yet. Most people hope to use their first films to land representation or distribution or otherwise let the world see that they can do what it is they say they can do. (Agents are tricky creatures. The best way to land one is to be referred by one.)

So, halfway through dialing my agency's number, I hung up the phone and dedicated myself to "hoofing" it along with the rest of the "great but as-yet unknown filmmakers of the next generation!"

Local Showings

If you've never directed a play, screened a film, or had to take a deep breath held through the entire performance as you let your "baby" take its first steps where it would live or die of its own accord, you have no idea how incredible an experience it is. (If "they" could bottle that experience and put a label on it... wow.) When you see *your* actors come back for a third curtain call on opening night to a standing ovation, even the most stoic person will find himself with tears streaming down his face. It's an experience that can't be topped, anywhere. It's an experience that you don't have to leave your hometown to know!

You too can get that confidence-bolstering feeling that you've just done the best thing you can do with six months (or a year or more). It's these *local screenings* that carry the filmmaker through the times of doubt that seem to haunt artists no matter how "good" they are perceived to be. It's these warm receptions where people clap you on your back and praise you for believing in your dream that help you get those few more applications out the door to film festivals. It's knowing that other people *believe in you* that really makes the dream worth living.

Press Releases

The first step in getting people to come to your screenings is to *let them know about it!* A simple way to reach a huge local audience is to give your local newspaper(s) press releases.

I've always handled local press releases as writing a short, interesting article about a local person who's done something that can make the community proud to claim him or her as one of their own. (The article just happens to be written by and about the same person. What's important in these articles is that the focus is not on myself but on *how the work that's been done benefits the community*). These are easily placed within the "community" section of the local paper and reach far more people than a lot of paid advertising does.

As the time of your screening draws near, you can approach local public radio and television stations to run information about your "shindig" in their "community calendar" sections. You could even think about making it a bit of an event by showcasing production artwork and providing hors d'oeuvres before the show.

Playback

It probably isn't the best idea to cart your online editing computer out and about to play back your film at local screenings. Thankfully, there are many other high-quality options open in the burgeoning era of digital video.

DVD

If the place that you'll be showing your work has a DVD player, you can burn your film to DVD. Or, if you'll be bringing your own projector and have either a laptop with DVD capabilities or one of those "slimline" portable DVD players, you can feed the signal to your projector directly from the player.

DV/MiniDV Player

There are several DV and MiniDV players designed for "video professionals" to review their work in the field. These offer great solutions for playback but tend to be pricey.

Hi8/Digital8/MiniDV Camcorder

In my own research, the "bang for the buck" equation was best solved in the area of playback by the high-consumer-end camcorders (encompassing the Hi8, Digital8, and MiniDV formats.) If you have one of these format camcorders that supports video/audio in *and* out, you've already got a great high-quality solution for feeding your film into a digital projector wherever you go. (If you've been thinking about getting a camcorder, for whatever reason, this can be a great excuse for getting one.)

Projection

I found it well worth my interest to look into getting my own digital projector. It made a lot of screenings possible in places where I wouldn't have been able to show my film before. (Only one local venue here in Fairbanks had plans to purchase their own digital projector.)

Digital projectors have come a long way in a few short years, and the prices have come down from their beginning highs to what I consider very reasonable for the quality they produce. I did a lot of searching online and finally refined my searching via the web site Projector Central (http://www.projectorcentral.com).

At the time of publication, the two projectors whose ability, clarity, quality, and resolution caught my eye were the Epson PowerLite S1, which uses LCD technology, and the InFocus X1, which uses DLP technology. Both systems now sell for under $1,000 (U.S.).

LCD technology is similar to the technology that is used in "flat-panel" LCD computer monitors. It produces a nice, crisp image, though sometimes you can see the individual pixels.

DLP uses a digital micromirror device (*DMD*, developed in 1987 by Dr. Larry Hornbeck of Texas Instruments), which has a single, hinged, microscopic mirror (about one-fifth the width of a human hair) for each and every pixel represented in an image. Based on digital information sent to the DMD, each micromirror can be tilted *toward* the light source inside the projector (resulting in a white, "on," pixel) or *away* from the light source (resulting in a black, "off," pixel). These micromirrors can be switched on and off thousands of times per second. The more often per second that a micromirror is set to "on," the brighter the corresponding pixel appears on the screen. Color is added to the home/business DLP systems by passing the light that strikes the DMD through a constantly moving color wheel that filters the light into red, green, and blue. Coordinating the micromirrors with the spinning of the color wheel, home and business DLP projector systems can produce up to 16.7 million colors. Theatrical DLP projection systems use three DMDs, using a prism to separate white light into red, green, and blue, feeding that light to a specific DMD dedicated to that color alone. Theatrical DLP systems can produce "no fewer than 35 trillion colors." (Information gathered from http://www.dlp.com.)

These digital projectors are small and lightweight (under 7 pounds and, as such, are probably best locked up when not in use). Both the Epson S1 and InFocus X1 support HD as well as NTSC and computer inputs. Neither supports digital inputs.

One thing to keep in mind about digital projectors is that their bulbs don't last forever. The Epson S1's bulb is rated at 2,000 hours of life, and the InFocus' X1's bulb life is rated at 3,000 hours. (Replacement bulbs range between $200 and $400.) But when you figure that an average movie lasts two hours, that's at least a

thousand feature films before having to replace the bulb. When you figure in that both projectors give you a display size of *at least* 260 inches across (provided you have enough space to display such an image) and a brightness rating of at least 1100 ANSI lumens, my own "bang for the buck" ratio of being able to waltz into a coffeeshop and ask if they'd like to feature a screening of a really cool martial arts CGI movie is most well and truly satisfied with either of these projectors.

Local Theatres

If you've got a *local* theatre (one that hasn't been bought by the "cineplex" mega-corps), these are usually a great place to start. If they're locally owned and operated, you'll probably find a warm reception for "one of their own" having "done the dream."

You'll need to be almost *completely done* with your film before approaching anyone, however. Many places know how much work goes into filmmaking, and what a challenge it is to get a film to finish on time. So don't be taken aback if they raise their eyebrows at you and ask if your film is finished yet, with a knowing look in their eye.

You'll need to provide them with publicity material (prints, posters, and whatnot). Once you have a date lined up, you can then approach the community section of your paper with a "local artist does good" kind of press release/story, directing people to when and where your film will be screening.

One thing that a local theatre might *not* have is a way to play your film directly from its digital source. So you'll probably need to pick up one of those digital projectors mentioned earlier and work with the local theatre owner to patch your playback device into his auditorium's audio system.

Art Associations

A call to the local Fairbanks Arts Association was a very positive thing. They were more than happy to schedule a screening and suggested arranging a talk to their members of how the film was made. Wherever you happen to be, there is bound to be something like a local arts association that you can contact. Even if they do not have building space for you to screen your film, they will probably be very happy to help "one of their own" find places to do so.

Local arts associations exist to help local artists! For artists of any art form, they are great places to find kindred spirits and help of many kinds!

Coffeehouses

I can't think of a *local* coffeehouse that *wouldn't* want to help out a local "arr-teest" in screening his film. Coffeeshops that I've visited from New York to San Diego have all had the feeling of resonating with the "bohemian" lifestyle. Poetry jams and slams, impromptu jazz, performance art, and all sorts of explorations of the arts find second homes at coffeehouses across the world.

Libraries

Libraries? Oh yeah! (Most public libraries require all events that happen there to be free to anyone who shows up.) Public libraries are great centers of community outreach. You'll more than likely find a very warm reception for screening your G/PG film at the local public library.

"Special Interest" Groups/Alternate Venues

In Fairbanks, there's one cineplex, and there's one "everything else." The Blue Loon is part restaurant, part bar, part art house theatre, and part concert venue. From featuring the best jazz musicians in town (and from out of town) to the most recent art and foreign films, The Blue Loon is the place to go.

It's not exactly what you would call a "theatre"; it's more of a "special interest" venue. But every town has something like this. (In my tiny hometown of Cass City, Michigan, the local bowling alley was a place like this.) It doesn't hurt to approach places like this and ask if they're interested in holding a screening.

If your film appeals to a special interest group, such as martial arts crowds in the case of *Ghost Warrior*, a screening at a local dojo is a possibility. If you are near a university or college, there are *always* groups of like-minded individuals who would *love* to see their own dreams echoed in your labor of love.

Of course, there are *conventions!* Science-fiction, fantasy, and speculative fiction conventions are wonderful places to have your work seen by others of similar mindsets. (There are also conventions for nearly every other kind of group imaginable as well!) Usually, getting screening time is a matter of contacting the convention board at least eight months prior to the date of the convention and mentioning that you have a film that fits with their particular genre. As more and more people begin to create these CGI films, conventions themselves may become film festivals in their own right.

No matter how "unique" your film is, should you do what you have always wanted to see, there will *always* be an audience for your film. The more true to your own centers you make it, the more strongly people will want to see it a second time.

Film Festivals

Above all else, *film festivals* are the manifestations of the community of filmmakers. Just as getting out and helping in your local community gets you noticed locally, getting your films into film festivals is how you get noticed in the cinematic community. Festivals are where people who really *know* and *live* cinema get together to share energies. The feelings you get at a local screening are multiplied exponentially when you participate in a film festival.

Festivals are also where you can attract the attention of the people with the money who can make your next, "even bigger and better" filmic dreams come true. They are also the "haunts" where distributors go to find the products they would like to invest in bringing to "mainstream cinema" and DVD/home video distribution.

There are the well-known festivals, like Cannes and Sundance. There are also smaller, regional festivals. *Both* have equal importance in the life of an up-and-coming filmmaker!

You may really want to screen at Sundance but are only able to get into the smaller regional festivals. Don't fret! The people who *run* the bigger festivals usually are out and attending the smaller ones. You may find yourself with an e-mail *inviting* you to participate in the film festival of your dreams shortly after screening at one of the smaller fests!

But how do you start sifting through the thousands of film festivals worldwide to find ones that match your genre and accept screening submissions on the media you can afford to send out? How do you find the ones that have entry fees that you can swing?

Some festivals only accept material to screen on film (while accepting material for *review* on a variety of media). Some require steep, nonrefundable entry fees. Some are animation only.

A simple Google search will return an overwhelming number of festivals. How do you go about sifting through this deluge of information?

Without a Box

A fellow independent filmmaker directed me to Without a Box (http://www.withoutabox.com), having successfully used it to submit his short film to over 12 festivals in a single evening.

Without a Box maintains an indexed, searchable listing of over 150 film festivals in over 80 countries. You can freely use their services indefinitely for researching festivals, finding ones that fit your film and your resources. You can submit your film to two festivals for free during a 60-day trial period. (After that, you must pay a $79-per-year fee to submit to an unlimited number of festivals in that year's time.)

Internet

The Internet is a wonderful place. It is responsible for the distribution of more knowledge and the interconnection of more like-minded souls than any other semi-physical construct in humankind's history of this planet. I am more thankful for (and owe more to) the Internet's existence than nearly any other single bit of technology I know.

The Internet was originally designed for military purposes. Then it was turned over as a domain for scientists and intellectuals. It quickly became a storehouse beyond imagination for *freely available* information about anything and everything. On VMS and Unix consoles one can search through Usenet newsgroups, use text-based search engines with names like Archie and Veronica, and immerse one's mind within ASCII-based multi-user-shared-hallucinations, always on the lookout for the Greased Mjölnir that would make your NetHack dreams come true.

Above all else, the Internet was freedom, and it was free.

I personally think it's a big mistake for anyone to try to leash anything that has *freedom* (freedom of thoughts, freedom of ideas, freely disseminated and interpreted at the sole discretion of the user himself) at its core into being even remotely commercial. I hope the Internet will always be a place for this kind of freedom, passion for knowledge, and the spreading of information to all those who wish to know such things. I think that trying to commercialize the Internet is like trying to license the wind.

As much as I'd *love* to live the shamanic, tribal lifestyle, where the needs of the visionaries and seers are met by the communities that they benefit so their works can be shared freely with all who may benefit, we all have to eat!

So let me just say it in plain English: The Internet may be a great place for exhibiting your film to a worldwide audience, but one should not *expect* any monetary return for doing so.

There are some downsides to Internet exhibition. If you're hoping to sell to television markets, cable, overseas, or otherwise, they usually require you to exhibit *on their network* before exhibiting on the Internet. Some film festivals are even making this a mandate to submitting to their festival. Of course, the Academy of Motion Picture Arts and Sciences says that you must complete your qualification for award nomination (taking best in class at one of the film festivals on their "short list" *or* running for three consecutive nights for paid admission in a theatre in Los Angeles County) *before* having the film shown on TV *or* over the Internet.

Personal Hosting

If you do decide to screen your film on the Internet, you need to decide whether to host it on your own web site or as a part of a compendium of other works, such as I-Film or AtomFilms.

If you host your film locally on your own web site, you may have trouble driving people there to see it. You'll also probably have to deal with any technical issues yourself. (If your film *does* become popular from your own site, you may incur the wrath of your web-hosting service for the huge amounts of data downloaded by your fans throughout the world.)

Submitting for exhibition on a place like IFilm.com or AtomFilms.com takes care of bandwidth, encoding, streaming, and technical issues, but in such places, you are "one of many."

IFilm.com

If you are going to go the Internet route for exhibiting your film, IFilm.com is my top choice. However, like a film festival, of the 20 to 30 films they receive a week, they only accept five to ten.

In part, acceptance has to do with the quality of the film itself (mostly focusing on the writing). Another larger and more legally imperative part has to do with the *clearing* of the film — making sure no copyrights are being infringed upon, like using unlicensed music (if you were to *not* replace your temp score, this would be considered bad, very bad) and trademarked items (in the case of the world of live action, even *wallpaper patterns* can be registered trademarks of companies — it's evil, but it is the way of "big business"). Of course, illegally using copyrighted characters, stories, scripts, and intellectual property of all sorts will keep your work out of most every professional venue you can imagine, so just don't do it! You must prove to these companies that, yes, these things came entirely from your own head.

One of the best things about IFilm, at the time of publication, is that *you*, the filmmaker, retain all rights. IFilm is *nonexclusive*, which means you can have your film up on a dozen other web sites, in film festivals, showing at your Aunt Edna's, and in your local video store, and at least IFilm is quite content with things.

You won't make any money directly from IFilm (they make their own operating costs by running a less-than-20-second commercial before your film), but they do offer places to house your contact information. I've heard that agents and distributors do browse the annals of IFilm, and it might add a bit of "coolness" to your resume for you to be able to let your contact know that while your tape is in the mail to him, he can see a *bandwidth-specific* version of your film on a well-known Internet film site.

As far as security goes, IFilm *only* allows for streaming of your film, which isn't good for 28.8 dial-up viewing, but it does mean that Joe Average won't be burning your film and handing it out at parties. (Only honor can direct the actions of anyone who truly knows their way around a computer.)

In talking with John Halecky of IFilm, he gave me some good news to pass along. *Animation* always goes over well on Internet film places like IFilm. He said that pieces *under ten minutes in length* work best online (they actually stay away from pieces over 40 minutes). Though he strongly agrees that the best films are the films that the filmmaker has always wanted to see, he said that *funny* always "out-downloads" more serious material. (To quote John directly, "…sex and *Star Wars* always sell over drama.")

AtomFilms.com

(AtomFilms didn't get back in touch with me in time for my deadline, so this information is gathered from the public sections of AtomFilms' and AtomShockwave's web sites.)

AtomFilms appears to actually *purchase* licensing rights to your film if they accept it. I couldn't tell how much that rights assignment covers from searching through their site. The rights could pertain to just the one short you've created, but it could be more. Because there is a purchasing of rights going on, money can be expected to change hands, but how much (is it a percentage of views or a lump sum?) is unknown.

They went into very heavy detail about *clearing* your film, making sure that everything from concept and script to props, sets, locations, and, of course, music were all legally licensed for you to use in your work. So, for the "newbie" filmmaker, their section on clearing should be an eye-opening required read.

The one thing that stopped me in my tracks while reading their submission form was this (excerpted from a public section of their web site, AtomFilms' submission form, paragraph 3, browsed on September 10, 2003 — my areas of surprise printed in italics):

> **You believe the material and its features are unique and novel. You acknowledge, however, that because of AtomShockwave's position in the interactive online entertainment industry, other persons, including Atom-Shockwave's employees, may have submitted to AtomShockwave or to others, or may have made public,**

or may hereafter create, submit to AtomShockwave or make public, similar or identical material that AtomShockwave may have the right to use.

What this boils down to in "legalese" is that you might submit a film to them, they might turn it down, and then a few months later, you could see something *identical* to your work, having been made in-house by the *employees* of AtomFilms/AtomShockwave. *And,* because this is part of an *agreement* you make when you *submit* work to them, which you would have to have signed in order to have your work viewed by them, *you will have signed away your right to do anything about it.*

Ethical? Well, let's put it this way… Kaze would have some fun "chatting" with people who believe that treating others in this manner is acceptable.

This brings us to the "big game," the essence of "big-business gone wild": *Hollywood*.

Hollywood

"Win at all costs."

"If you can get away with it, it must be okay."

I'm sure there are many who will rant, rail, and fume at my even intimating that Hollywood may be somewhat like this. But, have you ever heard the phrase, "The lady doth protest too much, methinks" from *Hamlet*?

I have seen first-hand so much stuff go down in Hollywood and been on the receiving end of so many acts of evil, great and small, that all I can say is tread carefully, if you choose to tread there at all.

The words that many industry types use sound the same as standard English, but their definitions couldn't be more disparate. In essence, though the "dialect" sounds much like what one hears on the evening news, "Hollywood" speaks a different language.

A small example of this "foreign language" could be found in the definition of the word "friend." The *American Heritage Dictionary* defines the word "friend" thus: *friend: n. A person whom one knows, likes and trusts.* A Hollywood definition of the word "friend" would read more like this: *friend: n. A person with whom one keeps in moderate contact so that in the event one can profit from the destruction of that person, that person is readily accessible.*

Harsh? When you've seen what I have, that's treating the truth with a nice candy coating.

Granted, not *everyone* in the Hollywood scene is like this. But many people are. (*The Player*, by Robert Altman, painted a pretty accurate emotional picture of how things run.) Tread carefully, and always keep your eyes open and your mind sharp.

I have done what I have done in my books so that *you* can avoid those kinds of situations. Many other filmmakers have made wonderful careers for themselves without getting involved in "the scene." If you feel the *pull* to enter into this maelstrom, keep your eyes open at all times, and be aware that the ones who think themselves immune to something are always the ones most susceptible to it.

Agents

An agent's job is to know as many people in their respective industry as possible, as closely as possible. It's a job of being everyone's "friend." The better your agent, the more "trusted" their opinions. So, when a good agent calls up his "friend" at Twentieth Century Fox and says that he has someone that the "friend" *has* to meet with, the "friend" pencils in a time and date, and before you know it, you're pulling up to the Fox lot, getting the little sticker for your car, and seeing first hand the back-lot street sets you've seen in movies.

But *getting* an agent can be a tricky thing. You've heard the phrase, "It's who you know." This is the case with Hollywood agents. Usually, the only way to land an agent is to have one of their friends introduce you.

Remember, though, not all agents are *good agents*. Before you go dancing in the streets when an agent agrees to take you on, find out other artists' opinions of how the agent has worked for them — contacts (if possible) and artists rep'd by them, past and current. However, by the same token, having an agent is better than no agent at all. It can be a great help to have someone else *also* chipping in doing the legwork of landing distribution.

Entertainment Lawyer

My impression of *entertainment law* is that you take corporate law, and really, really, really turn up the intensity of it. Entertainment law seems to be a world unto itself.

NOTE

> While negotiating an industry-related contract, I've actually had one slimeball on the other side of the table tell me, "...well if [a particular paragraph] isn't enforceable by law, just leave it in!"

I've been told that one of the most important persons that you can have in your corner is an entertainment lawyer. Like contracts that cleverly word in ways for you to sign away your rights to sue for someone stealing your ideas, your intellectual property, I have never seen more attempts of bold-faced evilness than when

working with other companies while running my studios in LA. Having a *good, ethical, intelligent*, and *well-read/well-versed* entertainment lawyer not only saves you from being preyed upon in that arena, but he can also save you the frustration of the so many times and so many ways that people try to take advantage of one another there.

But, like an agent, entertainment lawyers (the *good* ones, usually) require an introduction from a mutual "friend." They also usually require a *retainer* of some sort, which could be anywhere from a few thousand dollars to a few hundred thousand for x amount of time. So, usually you can expect to get a *good* entertainment lawyer *after* you've started being "successful," which I suppose makes one appreciate them all the more ... or something.

Distributors

Distributors can also be challenging to get on your side. Your best asset in landing one is through an agent. However, representatives of distribution companies do frequent film festivals, and it is common for people to land distribution deals after a particularly good showing at a fest.

In less than five minutes searching (using Google), I was able to come up with what appeared to be an almost complete contact list of U.S. distributors, including television syndication companies and cable networks. So *finding* them isn't hard…

But when you figure that these people have *at least* 20 new "packets" from filmmakers arriving every week, they can pick and choose.

NOTE

From my own experience of receiving stacks of demo reels, when you have the job of running a studio, that stack of tapes in your in box gets an "eenie-meenie-miney-this-one-looks-nice" kind of treatment. You do eventually get to them all, but because there can be so many, it's often only the ones that really, really, really fit exactly with the thought you have in your head at that time that catch your eye.

The trick to getting the full attention of someone in distribution seems to be to have an agent or friend place your packet of materials directly in their hand and leave them feeling that inside is something they *really* will enjoy, make them scads of money, etc.

Academy Awards

An award granted by the Academy of Motion Picture Arts and Sciences is entirely plausible for *any* filmmaker, even for the makers of short films. The Academy has a very specific set of rules that must be followed in order for a film to be *eligible for consideration/nomination*.

This year's current rules are posted on the Academy's web site: http://www.oscars.org/.

In previous years, these rules have included such things as short films are to be no longer than 40 minutes in length and they must be submitted on either 16mm, 35mm, or 70mm film stock. In order for a short film to be considered, within two years of the film's completion date, it must either have been publicly exhibited for paid admission in a commercial motion picture theatre in Los Angeles County for a run of at least three consecutive days (with no fewer than two screenings a day —student films cannot qualify in this manner) or have won a *best in category* award at one of the "Academy recognized" competitive film festivals. *If* the short film is to be exhibited on television and/or the Internet, it must have fulfilled either of these two qualifying requirements *before* being exhibited on television and/or the Internet. (Material paraphrased from the 75th Annual Academy Awards Rules for Distinguished Achievements During 2002.)

In addition to the current year's rules, the Academy's web site also lists the nearly 50 film festivals they recognize for qualification of short films, time-table requirements, and histories about the Oscars.

Paint by Numbers

Thankfully, if top on your list of dreams is simply to see the films that you've always wanted to see (and becoming the next Hayao Miyazaki, Walt Disney, or John Lassiter is second or third on your list of things to do "before breakfast"), things *will usually fall into place*. Making your first film seems to be the rite of passage that allows you to have others believe in you as being a filmmaker.

When you have that "badge" that says, "Hi, I'm a filmmaker" (kind of like the ethereal "artistic license"), it is much easier to get people to help you continue your dream. With an actual film in your hand and a product people can see, hear, and touch, that "realness" can make you the money you need to create your next "physical" product. Doing things this way, once you've covered the time you have invested in your previous film and *saved* enough to pay for your next, *you are always operating in the "black!"*

As taught by Julia Cameron in *The Artist's Way*, do what you love; the money and the time to live the life you dream will then come naturally.

So:

1. Make *your* film, and make it the best you know how. Make it the film that you have been waiting all your life to see.

2. Gain "emotional momentum" through local screenings.

3. Send your film to as many film festivals as you can, and attend as many as you can swing financially, becoming a part of the community and becoming known to them as someone who has *truthfully* dreamed aloud.

Film festivals have the greatest likelihood of getting your film to the future stages of distribution, both to home video and possibly even to mainstream cinema. It is the way that holds the greatest possibility for you to continue your dream, and find yourself among other dreamers who also have the strength to *do*.

"There will always be an audience for every type of film."
— David Strauss, *Without a Box*

Chapter 22

Postpartum

"To foresee a victory which the ordinary man can foresee is not the acme of skill."

— Sun Tzu, *The Art of War*

Every work of art, be it a painting, sketch, song, or film, must eventually stand on its own and go out into the world. It's a very emotional time. I sit and stare at the finished work, one part of my mind marveling that this cool thing was actually accomplished by me (I know me, and I'm not as "groovy" as everyone thinks), another part reliving great victories, and another part sad because the piece will no longer need my touch. I'll no longer know the moments of time lost within its spaces.

The days and weeks after its *life* has grown so vibrant that it no longer needs my support to sustain itself is very much like the experiences I've heard of *postpartum* from dear female friends. It is the same blend of happy-sad, full-empty, the "whew it's done," the "I already miss it…" It all seems to be very similar.

Treat yourself right during this time of separation. If you're doing Cameron's *The Artist's Way* exercises, take yourself *on two or three* "artist's dates" that week. Revel in and respect the beauty that you have created, and *replenish* yourself with the wonderment of what is to come next!

How do I feel about Kaze being done? In some ways, it's pretty rough. I *miss* being in those moments, *living* those animations along with the characters. I miss crying for hours as I animated Kaze in the glade. I miss the amazement of watching scenes take on a life of their own, moving my hands at the animation controls like automatic writing. I miss wishing so much for Kaze to do something I knew he would do, but letting myself believe that he could go either way until that scene had played itself out through the completion of its animation.

Kaze is a part of me, a very large part of me. Now, the experiences *shared* through working on this film I think may take years and years to understand fully. I sincerely hope that I'll be given the opportunity to make the other stories already drafted, both the episodics that extend forward from *Ghost Warrior* and the two feature films that enclose the story.

In my cabin/studio/retreat while working on the film, *Ghost Warrior* became more real to me in many ways than the world of people cutting each other off in traffic and the current state of world, national, and local political affairs. Now all that is "the real world" is coming back to me, as a foot "wakes up" after having been sat upon for some time.

In the end, I came through with what I said could be done. One man, two consumer-end PCs, and six months of production, yielding a 22-minute film that can stand on its own with the animation that inspired me so many years ago. Many people who know "the system" know just how much this flies in the face of convention. Many people were curious to see if this could actually be done.

> "You're only saying that because no one ever has."
> — the "Dread-Pirate" Wesley, *The Princess Bride*

I sincerely hope that now that it *has* been proven people can see beyond any shadow of doubt that they too can learn all that they need to in order to do this themselves. Or, small teams of dedicated dreamers who flesh out the production's needs can make works like this commonplace. It is my *job* as an *explorer* to make myself obsolete. I hope to someday soon watch *hundreds* of other animated films, spanning all the ranges of dreams and desires, all made because they were the films that their creators had wished to see more than anything else in the world.

"Postmortem"

Filmmaking, like water (like war), has no constants. That's why this book has been written in such an open-ended way. I have showed you key points of my own process, shown you where to find the answers that you might need, and left the rest *open*. There is no way to cover every contingency; one must sense what the situation needs and *adapt*.

Even at the end of this, my fourth short film (my second completely CGI short film), I'm already hard at work, thinking over ways to solve situations better next time. *Postmortem* is a *vital* part of the production process, where you go back over all that you've done, studying your notes, rehashing solutions, and making notes for how things can be handled better *the next time*.

- Knowing that story is the single, most important driving force within a film, how can the story be made even better?
- How can it be *told* better?
- How do you feel about your character's *designs*, movements, voices, and lines of dialogue?

- How do you feel about the environments? Are there ways in which they could have been improved upon without expending extra render cycles?
- What changes to the IK, skinning, and animation controls will you make next time?
- What changes to the directory structure will you make?
- How can the pipeline be improved upon?
- What do you know now about creating your own music that will shape your decisions next time?
- What have you learned about balancing the audio levels of voice, sound effects, and music that will help you in the future?

This is just the beginning of the list of questions that you should be turning over in your mind after the completion of a film. These are questions to which you need input from *all* those who helped work on your film (from all ranks within the production hierarchies). I'd even go so far as to suggest calling your voice talent or anyone who has moved on from your film, asking *them* about how they would make the process of working with *you* better.

Your job now is to take all that was learned from the experience and shape the next project so that it can be an even stronger expression of the visions that you have within your mind/heart/soul.

The Future

What happens now in CGI filmmaking is largely dependent on you. If people out there, the dedicated dreamers for whom problem solving is play (you know who you are) begin to live their dreams "out loud," I imagine we will all see some amazing changes in filmmaking over the course of the next years. I know you have the stories and you have shown that you have the intelligence. The choice solely falls upon you to put these together to create your own visions that you have always wished to see.

Me? My own plans not only include future filmmaking and other kinds of exploration, but also doing what I can to make your trek easier than I found mine. My long-term goal is to create my last studio, one that focuses on the abilities and ideals expressed within my works. I see it as a place where people can come to learn to do all that they have dreamed to do in CGI filmmaking, redefining and pushing the boundaries of both art *and* science.

Because CGI filmmaking that follows the paths outlined within this book doesn't take hordes of people to create a film, I see this studio as an environment where many films are worked on at the same time, overseen by their own visionaries — stories crafted and handled with the honor that the studio I envision stands for.

I also see this studio as a distribution channel for other CGI filmmakers throughout the world, so they can bypass "the game" of Hollywood and simply focus on being filmmakers. So someone who reads the works, dreams the dreams, and does the job can know that his work will indeed find the audiences who want to see exactly what he has produced.

It may seem lofty, but it is no more so than one man on his own in a small cabin on the very edge of the Alaskan wilderness thinking that he can produce a 22-minute short film in six months, all by himself, using only two consumer-grade PCs.

All dreams are already real. You just have to find your way to where they are.

"I learned that if one advances confidently in the direction of his dreams, and endeavors to live the life which he has imagined, he will meet with a success unexpected in common hours... "

— Henry David Thoreau

Index

Turn Your DVD Player Into A Powerful Learning Tool

the essential

Character Modeling & Animation Series

featuring Todd Grimes

This complete series offers over thirteen hours of material on a 5 DVD set. This series offers an "artist study" of the process of character animation. Observe how each element is created in detail, as it happens providing a thorough presentation of essential concepts and techniques. Watch through the eyes of the artist as he molds each object from the conceptual drawings to completed animation. Step-by-step, you are guided through the thought process and techniques to capture the essence of the character, all while learning the tools and insights of LightWave 3D.

Head Modeling - Body Modeling - Model Rigging - Facial Animation - Body Animation

---

UNDERSTANDING HYPERVOXELS
EXPLOSIVE EFFECTS WITH HYPERVOXELS

Add powerful explosive and liquid volumetric effects to your LightWave 3D animations with HyperVoxels. Learn panel by panel, setup procedures, lighting techniques, time saving rendering tips. Create stunning explosive effects. Liquid streams, Smoke trails, compound explosions, meteor showers and more.

TEXTURING CONCEPTS
TEXTURING DETAILS

Texture and animation artist Christian Bradley demonstrates the techniques for creating tiling textures to use on 3D models, video games or anywhere you need custom high quality textures. Learn the tips and tricks for creating seamless tiles, detailed panels, lighting & shadow effects and more.

HARDCORE LIGHTWAVE LOGOS

Discover professional tips & techniques for creating high quality text & logo animation in LightWave. Learn how to properly model text objects for maximum rendering quality. Convert 2D logo artwork into 3D models. Application techniques for adding bevels & extrusions for depth & dimension.

1-800-377-1039   www.desktopimages.com

Desktop Images 2603 W. Magnolia Blvd. Burbank, CA 91505, 818-841-8980 fax 818-841-8023 email - sales@desktopimages.com

VideoSyncrasies
The Motion Graphics Problem Solver

Clearly defined system-independent concepts that are essential to anyone working with motion graphics and digital video! Alpha Channels, Frame Rates, Field Rendering, Film to Video Transfer, Masking & Rotoscoping, Pixel Aspect Ratios and more! Plus new Widescreen & Luminance sections. Trish & Chris Meyer provide a wide variety of valuable concepts and insight that will save you time, money, frustration and give you happier clients. For beginner through advanced level video editors, compositors and 3D animators alike. Discover why VideoSyncrasies is "The Money" DVD!

- Alpha Channels
- Frame Rates
- Field Rendering
- Film to Video Transfer
- Masking & Rotoscoping
- Pixel Aspect Ratio
- WideScreen & Luminance

 Over 4 hours of instruction on one dual layer DVD9. Extensive menu indexing for easy review. Plus all new sections on Anamorphic Widescreen and Luminance Interpretation.

Professional Photoshop Digital Retouch Series

Tone, Exposure & Color Correction

Evaluate Image Tonality
Adjust Image Tone & Contrast
Improve Highlights & Shadows
Restore Faded Photographs
Color Correction Techniques
Exposure Compensation & Correction
Color & Lighting Enhancement

Image Restoration & Repair

Eliminate Dust and Mold
Repair Scratches & Cracks
Perspective Correction
Wire Removal
Silvering Removal
Exposure Damage
Discoloration and Stains
Color Conversion
Sharpening Techniques

Portrait Retouching

Facial & Body Toning
Accentuating the Eyes
Concealing Blemishes
Remove Red Eye
Background Retouching
Wrinkle Reduction
Glamour Techniques

1-800-377-1039   www.desktopimages.com

Desktop Images 2603 W. Magnolia Blvd. Burbank, CA 91505, 818-841-8980 fax 818-841-8023 email - sales@desktopimages.com

KEYFRAME
MAGAZINE

Keyframe Magazine has been published since January 1997, and has had a very strong readership with users of NewTek's LightWave 3D, Video Toaster, and other 2D/3D digital tools. These readers are using animation and visual effects media in their daily lives for photography, architecture, advertising, web sites, medicine, training, games and feature films. Keyframe is a magazine that provides a invaluable resource for them.

Here's your chance to have Keyframe, the industry favorite, delivered right to your door!

❏ USA 1 year (6 issues) $54

❏ USA 2 year (12 issues) $102

❏ Canada/Mexico 1 year (6 issues) $72

❏ Canada/Mexico 2 year (12 issues) $138

❏ All other countries 1 year (6 issues) $84

❏ All other countries 2 year (12 issues) $162

Name _____

Email _____

Phone _____ Fax _____

Company _____

Address _____

_____

Credit Card # _____ Exp. _____

Signature _____

Free Subscriptions!

Get your
LightWave from us
and
we'll bundle a
free subscription
with it.

Go to our Online Store at
www.dmgpublishing.com

Save $$$

by Subscribing Online!

Save up to 70% on
our Magazine Bundle Offers

Go to our Online Store at
www.dmgpublishing.com

DMG Publishing
2756 N Green Valley Pkwy # 261
Henderson, NV 89014-2120 USA
Email: info@dmgpublishing.com
Tel: 1-702-990-8656 or 1-888-778-9283
Fax: 1-702-616-9647